D1520785

NEW TREATMENT OF ALCOHOL AND DRUG ABUSE IN AKHTER AHSEN'S EIDETIC IMAGE THERAPY

Toni Nixon, Ed.D.

New Treatment of Alcohol and Drug Abuse

IN AKHTER AHSEN'S
EIDETIC IMAGE THERAPY

BRANDON HOUSE   NEW YORK

The image exercises and variations of the exercises presented in this book are from the workshops and books of Dr. Akhter Ahsen and are reprinted with his permission.

© 1997 by Toni Nixon. All Rights Reserved. No part of this book may be reproduced by any process whatsoever, without prior written permission of the copyright holder, except for brief passages included in a review.

Published by
BRANDON HOUSE, INC.
555 Riverdale Station
New York, New York 10471

For orders, write to P.O. Box 240
Bronx, New York 10471

International Standard Book Number 0-913412-39-2
Library of Congress Catalog Card Number 97-073393
Manufactured in the United States of America

Foreword

Even in this era of extensive research in clinical psychology and psychiatry, there exists an unfortunate division between the organic and the functional. Furthermore, between psychotherapy and medication, philosophy still remains an outsider. Sadly, these systems have not looked into the roots of human experience as it really exists in a sensual imagistic context. Over the years of working with those suffering from various human ailments, it became clear to me that most positive and enduring effects were procured by bringing home the message from personal experience through the images which tell it all.

The goal of treatment should not be adjusting to a disability when permanent psychological changes can be secured through a profound and long-lasting relationship with life and its high feeling inside the person. After this type of exposure, the course of various types of neuroses and the need for alcohol or drugs are demystified. This might spark a traditionally trained therapist to ask: How is it possible? Everyone knows how difficult the treatment of alcohol and drug abuse is, even when people are willing to undergo the necessary trouble and pain of sticking with the treatment. The answer is very simple. Only the true vision of life itself can smooth the way to cure. Alcohol and drugs are but metaphors for the true vision. The adult human being was fathered by, may I say, the child of imagination, the moment of ecstasy. The adult shall never mature unless he or she becomes a child again, carrying forward a vision. Alcohol and drugs are, therefore, only a metaphor. When a metaphor is taken for the reality, we have a problem. When we replace the metaphor with a feeling of the natural "high" itself contained in what I have called the *Expectation High*, this translates into the true vision of a positive and nurturing life. We finally have a solution.

Some of the associated solutions for the treatment of alcohol and drug abuse were discovered while I was treating patients for other problems. They evidenced no substance abuse symptoms, but I found that problems similar to the substance abuse had been present in them because the person's positive energies for life had remained stalemated. There was a parallel here with patients I had been treating who actually suffered from alcohol and drug abuse. This is what alerted me to look for such evidence in other areas, particularly where fixation had been in the forefront. Slowly the techniques evolved, and the methods were painstakingly developed over a long period of time covering more than three decades of research and application of imagery in various related areas. The techniques and methods for the treatment of alcohol and drug abuse developed out of all this and became a model approach which is being presented here using imagery and the highest potentials in the mind toward treatment of this profoundly difficult area.

I am happy to see this book by Toni Nixon on my methods of treatment of alcohol and drug abuse. Poring over vast material, she has successfully integrated the concepts and techniques pertinent to this topic from my published and unpublished papers, workshops and books. It was a difficult task to review the material and draw out a readable presentation which contains not only practical guidelines with numerous illustrative cases but also an incisive analysis of the notions involved. The book is admirably successful in doing this.

This book, indeed, has a spirit from the dedication that has been put into it. I highly recommend it to practitioners, as well as to the general reader. It will, no doubt, be found valuable not only to the specialist but to every human being with an interest in this important area.

AKHTER AHSEN

Image Institute
Yonkers, New York

Contents

Acknowledgments

I am deeply grateful to Akhter Ahsen for his inspirational mentorship and ongoing support of this project. He graciously provided the opportunity to observe his work directly and study his method personally. I wish to thank Judith Hochman, whose extensive theoretical knowledge of Dr. Ahsen's work was invaluable. I also thank Leslie Dagnall for providing and assembling materials that added significantly to this manuscript. Many thanks to Catherine Riley for technical expertise, editorial comments and hours of conversation about the material. I am also grateful to my friends for their patience, continued enthusiasm and encouragement during the duration of the project.

And finally, I dedicate this book to my mother, whose lifelong battle with alcohol and drugs led me on this path of inquiry and whose image has ultimately set me free.

Introduction

More than thirty years ago, Akhter Ahsen originated Eidetic Image Therapy, a remarkably innovative approach that was heralded as "one of the most significant developments yet to emerge in psychotherapy since Freud's psychoanalysis" by the *Glasgow Journal of Psychology,* and many other reviewers have since agreed: "The value of Ahsen's therapy is unquestionable" (*Journal of Personality Assessment*); "Eidetics is not a new wrinkle in psychotherapy. It is, in fact, a new psychotherapy" (*Somatics*); "Unmatched in the clinical literature...A methodological advance" (*American Journal of Psychiatry*). Now Ahsen has developed a new, specific application of his eidetic method which offers the same hope and promise for the successful treatment of addiction.

Ahsen's approach focuses on locating and revealing the source of emotional problems and their solutions through special imagery "blueprints." As a unique methodology for the treatment of alcohol and drug abuse, it centrally addresses expectancy factors and provides core organizing principles concerning addictions and related symptomatology. It differs from traditional methods in a number of ways, perhaps the most fundamental being Ahsen's approach to consciousness, which he views as a unity of mind and body. Dolan (1977a) addresses the importance of this in terms of its contribution to psychosomatics:

> But what does this emphasis practically mean? Practically, it may mean treatment of psychosomatic disorders. It may also mean that all character disorders originate from the disruption of the primal unity of Psyche and Soma, in which the ego tends to become a mind ego and discards the soma as a superfluous accretion of the mind. Wouldn't the eidetic for such a disorder lie way back in early infancy? Akhter Ahsen has not only discovered its importance in the etiology of psychosomatic ailments but has also devised an approach to therapy on this basis. (p. 33)

Ahsen's extensive research on the eidetic image demonstrates that the image is able to break through the obstructed operations of consciousness and, in the case of addictions, is able to release the addicted body into a gratifying, nonaddicted state. Classically, the term "eidetic" [pronounced eye-DET-ic; from the Greek *eidos* (form) and *idein* (to see)] means "to see form." As an experience, the eidetic is multisensory and lifelike and is seen in the mind much like a motion picture or film strip. It has three components – a visual Image (*I*), a Somatic response (*S*) and a Meaning (*M*) – and represents an integrated state of external and internal experience. When elicited, the eidetic image, also referred to as an *ISM*, recreates a vivid experience of developmental events and conflicts which may prevail there with dramatic clarity and detail, revealing a profound relationship between perception and personality. The key elements found in these experiences can be isolated and examined to reveal habitual patterns of behavior and the negative experience regarding reality and fantasy. As all of the elements of these events are discovered, assembled and organized, conflict areas and their underlying causes are identified and are ready to be resolved. The Eidetic Image Therapy approach based on these images provides a step-by-step method for restoring the mind's natural resources. It captures the core of imagination, thereby releasing the vast repository of positive potential hidden under the fixations and distorted perceptions found in addictions.

A second fundamental difference that sets this approach apart from traditional therapies is Ahsen's (1993a, p. 6) notion of the Expectation High. According to Ahsen, positive states of well-being and relaxation, or "high" states that are often associated with alcohol and drugs, are, in fact, natural states of biological health and well-being that provide the individual with a positive and energetic approach to life. High states are imbued with a spirit of enthusiasm, excitement and imagination, and are frequently associated with experiences in childhood. Over time, these natural states are often suppressed due to stressful life situations and the demands of everyday reality. In order to meet the demands of daily living and perform life's tasks effectively, a part of the mind begins to operate as manager, organizing all incoming information and processing it in a routine pattern. This managerial operation is referred to by Hilgard (1977) as an Executive Ego which organizes data from a person's external and internal world in the most efficient way possible. Eventually, however, routine solutions and habits take precedence over spontaneity and imagination. The person eventually becomes fixed in a habitual pattern of response and a repetitive manner of expression, while at the same time being haunted by a vague sense of loss, boredom and emptiness. In an attempt to remedy this discomfort, a person looks to outside sources, like alcohol or drugs, as a means of achieving a high. Ultimately, one's natural energy and enthusiasm are sabotaged and erroneously attributed to alcohol or drugs. Unless these false attributions are rooted out and the ability to retrieve the natural high states recovered, the person will be lost in a confused state of narcotized deadness. Even if alcohol and drugs are no longer used, a memory trace of the false high remains, reinforcing the idea that a substance is needed to achieve it.

The aim of Ahsen's eidetic method in the treatment of alcohol and drug abuse is to recover those natural Expectation High states that have been suppressed through addiction and bring them to the forefront of the mind. Interaction with these states, which existed prior to the formation of any learned behavior, provides access to the deepest levels of human expression. As the natural enthusiasm for life is reinstated, meaningful engagement in the world can become a central focus of positive activity, replacing the withdrawal and retreat of addiction. According to Ahsen:

> Alcoholism is a disturbance that embodies the intense desire to reach the high and pure note when it has been denied in the normal course of life to the individual. This intense desire and the natural chemicals in the mind that secure it I call the "Expectation High." Other drug addictions are indeed similar to alcoholism because they contain the same desire. Why one person chooses alcohol and another person chooses drugs is not relevant because the same approach can be used to cure either of them. The approach is to give up reliance on deception and replacement and to connect with the inborn capacity for a natural high—of going for the real thing. (personal communication, 1996)

How is this critical reconnection with high states achieved to effectively resolve the problems of addiction? In the first step of eidetic treatment, the symptoms are clearly assembled. In the second step, Expectation High states are disentangled from the false association with alcohol and drugs. A detailed investigation of a person's first experience with the substance is critical in determining the process through which the Expectation High became linked with it, since all subsequent expectancies are linked to this initial experience. Although in most cases the first experience with alcohol or drugs is reported to be a disappointing one, the unfulfilling memory of the experience is twisted into something positive later on. As Donovan and Marlatt (1980) point out, "How an individual expects to feel under the influence of alcohol does not always correspond to the actual affective states while intoxicated"(p. 1159). Interestingly, problem drinkers report that drinking more alcohol produces more euphoria, when in fact, drinking more alcohol produces depression (Southwick, Steele, Marlatt, & Lindell, 1981, p. 713). Only by separating out the specific details of the first experience and identifying the elements that have become associated with alcohol and drugs, can the false association be recognized and corrected.

After the Expectation High is recovered and separated from alcohol and drugs, the third step of treatment is initiated, in which the emotions of the Expectation High are enhanced and expanded into other areas of life. To accomplish this, problem areas are systematically reviewed to reveal sources of strength and, in this way, to work through areas of weakness. In the fourth step, a ten-year futuristic scenario is developed, and in the fifth step, a lasting and meaningful philosophy of life is evolved that centers around the expression of true "high" states based on the inner sources of strength. Special imagery tactics may also be used for strengthening gains during or after any of these steps.

Ahsen's Eidetic Image Therapy offers a new and remarkable approach to the treatment of alcohol and drug abuse. Through a practical step-by-step process, positive states of expression are retrieved and revitalized, providing a person with access to natural strengths and resources. Why the solutions tried in the absence of this primary strength are ultimately doomed to fail, or methods that attempt to recondition behavior are so often unsuccessful, should be obvious to the reader. This process is clearly illustrated in the comments of the following person:

> "I used alcohol and drugs to numb myself, aware that I was voluntarily sedating myself and dulling the world...after about ten drinks it was like being

erased. I spent a lot of time convincing myself I was cool, but did not have much self worth. I felt very insecure, very unwanted and humiliated, so I had to create my own little universe. It was as if I did not want anyone to see me and in some way wished that I did not exist. When I now see an image of myself, I see an image of myself when I am two years old. I am talking. I was always talking. My mother is cooking and I am talking and asking questions. I ask anything and everything...I want answers to all of my questions. I want to see everything. I want to know everything. I ask so many questions. This little child has a good mind. He is filled with curiosity. It is this 'I exist' feeling. I see everything and not just one thing. It was there in me then. But somewhere along the line I learned that this was not good. I have been trying to get it back. This must be the real self. This self is not cold and detached. This self says, 'I exist.'"

Only through recovery of this type of primary power represented in the eidetic image can a person engage in life with enthusiasm and hope. When the real self is rescued from addiction, it, indeed, says, "I exist."

This book presents an overview of Akhter Ahsen's eidetic imagery method for the treatment of alcohol and drug abuse. I have attempted to present the material as concisely as possible and use case examples to illustrate the process wherever possible to afford the reader a clear picture of its practical use. I have also provided a brief parallel overview of traditional treatment approaches and related research to provide some basis for reference and comparison. In presenting Ahsen's eidetic theory, I have limited myself to the most salient points that pertain directly to the understanding of this model, and have directly quoted from his work as much as possible. Finally, to provide a firsthand experience of his eidetic imagery theory and methods, I have drawn on Ahsen's many published and unpublished case reports and workshop materials.

Chapter 1

The Problem of Addiction

The problems posed by alcohol and drug abuse have grown more complex with each passing decade and effective treatment has become more elusive and enigmatic. In 1902, Shadwell wrote of alcoholism: "Surely some general lessons can be drawn from all this mass of material which would raise the question a little out of the chaotic confusion surrounding it and keep it from being so often the sport of theory, assumption, sentiment, passion, prejudice and self interest" (as cited in Vaillant, 1983, p. 11). Despite national attention, public and private funding, legislation and special governmental agencies that provide support for research, education, and treatment, no consistently effective solutions have been found. Vaillant (1995), in reviewing his findings of a forty-year study of alcoholism, comments, "our lack of knowledge about alcoholism is astonishing" (p. 1) and concurs with the findings of Gordis (1976), who stated nineteen years earlier: "Little or no progress has been made in the long term treatment of alcohol abuse over the past 25 years" (as cited in Vaillant, 1983, p. 10).

Current reports on the status of the problem are dismal at best. According to a 1996 report in *Science and Medicine*, "Alcohol and drug abuse cost the American economy 98.6 billon dollars in 1990, an increase of 40% over the previous 5 year period" (p. 60). Although 1.5 million people seek treatment for alcoholism every year (*Alcohol Alert Supplement*, July 1991), only 30% of the people who get treatment remain sober for one year (*Harvard Mental Health Letter*, September 1996, p. 3).

Reports on drug abuse reveal similar findings. A recent article in *Newsweek* reports that heroin consumption in the United States has probably doubled since the mid-1980s (1996, p. 56). In 1982, a report on drug abuse and alcoholism stated that at least 90% of heroin addicts were using narcotics post-treatment (Califano, 1982; as cited in Peele, 1989, p. 23), corroborating results from an earlier study at the Lexington Kentucky Public Hospital for the treatment of narcotic addicts (Brecher, 1972; as cited in Peele, 1989, p. 23).

These grim findings raise serious questions about our basic assumptions about alcohol and drug abuse and the current methods of treatment. They call for a new perspective on the problems of habit, addiction, behavior change and the operations involved in these processes. In essence, they call for a new approach to the study of mind in the area of addictions, and to the fundamental understanding of consciousness itself. It is to this issue that the present discussion is addressed.

Most traditional treatment methods approach the habitual use and abuse of alcohol and other drugs as either a medical illness or a behavior problem. When approached as an illness, alcohol or drug abuse is seen as a progressive and chronic disease of unknown cause, over which a person has no control. Although it is believed that there is no cure, the person suffering from the disease can interrupt the process by discontinuing or abstaining from using the substance. When viewed as a behavior problem, alcohol or drug abuse is believed to be a negative behavior that is learned over time and, therefore, can be modified or changed in favor of more positive behaviors.

The "Disease" of Addiction

Alcohol abuse was first promoted as a disease in 1784 by Benjamin Rush, a well-known Philadelphia physician and an avid supporter of temperance. Rush became America's leading reformer and prominent advocate of limited alcohol use. His ideas were expanded on by the Temperance Movement in the 1800s and Prohibition in the 1900s until it was believed that alcohol was so dangerous that even a taste could inevitably lead a person to alcoholism (Peele, 1989, p. 37). In 1951, the World Health Organization officially designated alcohol abuse a disease, a position which was soon accepted by The American Medical Association and the American College of Physicians (as cited in Vaillant, 1983, p. 3). Identifying drunkenness as an uncontrollable illness was seen as a major step forward from previous beliefs that it was the result of depraved and criminal behavior. However, as late as 1954, McGoldrick wrote, "Alcoholism is no more a disease than thieving or lynching. Like these, it is the product of a distortion of outlook, a way of life bred of ignorance and frustration" (as cited in Vaillant, 1983, p. 3).

According to *Merck* (1992), alcohol abuse implies continued or excessive consumption of alcohol despite impaired social functioning or other negative consequences. Dependence or addiction additionally includes physical toxicity, damage to tissues, and a dangerous withdrawal syndrome (p. 1551). The National Council of Alcoholism states that "A person with alcoholism cannot consistently predict at any given drinking occasion the duration of the episode or the quantity that will be consumed" (as cited in Vaillant, 1983, p. 44). Symptoms commonly associated with alcohol abuse are frequent intoxication, work absenteeism, marriage problems, arrests for drunk driving, physical injuries related to drinking, and hospitalization for alcohol related problems.

One of the most significant studies dealing with the disease notion of alcohol abuse was conducted by Vaillant (1983, 1995). Vaillant studied three different groups of men over a forty-year period to determine if there was, in fact, a progressive disease process occurring with chronic alcohol use. From his findings, he concluded that "no single set of traits invariably defines alcoholism...Alcoholism can simultaneously reflect both a conditioned habit and a disease: and the disease of alcoholism can be as well defined by a sociological model as by a medical model" (p. 308). In reviewing the effectiveness of various treatments, he reports, "Thus far, there is no compelling evidence that any specific brief clinical intervention permanently alters the course of the disorder"(p. 126). Further, he states: "Many long term studies of the course of alcoholism concur that treatment has little if any lasting effect"(p. 147). Interestingly, Vaillant found that some of the most important aspects of recovery are hope, absolution and new sources of self-esteem: "Alcoholics feel defeated, helpless and without ability to change. If their lives are to change, they need hope as much as relief of symptoms" (p. 287).

Recent research suggests that there may be different forms or types of alcohol abuse. Some types may be more influenced by heredity, while others may be more influenced by environment; some types may have a progressive course, while others may not; and some people may recover on their own, while others may need help. Lewis reports, "As new research begins to explain the variety of reactions to and consequences of drinking, we can work to fashion treatment approaches that are tailor-made for the variety of needs. One size does not fit all" (DATA, 1991, p. 10).

It has been suggested that a distinct definition of drug abuse is neither possible nor desirable due to the differing effects of various drugs. *Merck* (1992) states that drug abuse is "Definable only in terms of societal disapproval and involves different types of behavior: (1) experimental and recreational use of drugs, which usually carries the hazard of illegal behavior; (2) unwarranted use of psychoactive drugs to relieve problems or symptoms; (3) use of drugs at first for the above reasons but development later of dependence and continuation at least partially to prevent the discomfort of withdrawal...Addiction refers to a style of living that involves drug dependence, generally both physical and psychological but mainly connotes continuing compulsive use and overwhelming involvement with a drug" (p. 1549).

The Diagnostic and Statistical Manual of Mental Disorder (1994) provides a comprehensive and useful definition of addiction that is applicable to the present discussion which includes all substances. "Substance related disorders are disorders related to the taking of a drug of abuse (including alcohol) to the side effects of a medication and to toxin exposure. The term substance can refer to a drug of abuse, a medication, or a toxin....There is a pattern of repeated self administration that usually results in tolerance, withdrawal and compulsive drug taking behavior. A diagnosis of substance dependence can be applied to every class of substances and are similar across the various categories of substance,...neither tolerance nor withdrawal is necessary or sufficient for a diagnosis of substance dependence" (p. 175). The primary issue in diagnosis is the person's failure to discontinue the substance despite the difficulty it is causing.

Addiction as a "Behavior Problem"

When alcohol and drug abuse is approached as a negative pattern of behavior, it is believed to be learned and reinforced through a combination of several factors, such as the effect the substance is expected to have when it is taken, the setting or situation in which the behavior takes place, and the habits of family and friends. Behavior psychologists place major emphasis on the importance of assessing or describing the problem behavior and all of its related characteristics in order to design a treatment program that will modify or change the unwanted behavior. It has been suggested that different assessment methods should be used according to the extent and pattern of alcohol use. Donovan and Marlatt (1980) report that, although there are many different types of behavior treatments available, there appears to be "no core organizing principle" that brings together and integrates them into a unified model (p.1156).

Much of the behavior research on addiction has focused on the role that expectancy factors play in the formation of habit and habitual behavior. Expectancy factors are reported to have tremendous impact on a person's experience when using alcohol or other drugs and are seen as a critical element in the development of addictive behavior. More importantly, it has been repeatedly found that the mere anticipation of experiencing a "high" is enough to produce it even when there is no alcohol or drug present (Brown, Goldman, Inn, & Anderson, 1980; Conners, Maisto, & Watson, 1988; Donovan, & Marlatt, 1980; Sher, 1985; Hull, & Bond, 1986; LaBerg, 1986). One researcher found that the expectancy of achieving a high existed prior to any experience with either alcohol or drugs, causing him to question "how did these expectancies become associated with alcohol in the first place?" (Christiansen, Goldman, & Inn, 1982, p. 344).

Chapter 2

Traditional Theories
and Methods of Treatment

Statistically, 75% of all American adults drink alcoholic bever-
ages and it is estimated that one out of ten of these drinkers will
experience some problem with alcohol during his or her lifetime
(*Merck*, 1992, p. 1551). Alcohol is reported to contribute to more
than 100,000 deaths annually, making it the third leading cause
of preventable death in the United States. It is also considered a
significant factor in the most common causes of death among
men between the ages of twenty and forty (accidents, homicide,
suicide and cirrhosis of the liver). In 1992, 13.8 million people
ages eighteen and older, or more than 7% of the population, were
reported to have problems with alcohol (Noble, 1996, p. 60).
According to Vaillant (1983), alcohol negatively impacts one in

every three American families (p. 1) and costs the United States economy more than 50 billion dollars annually (Vaillant, 1995, p. 389).

The Medical Model: Disease and Addiction

Medically, the problem of alcohol and drug addiction has been defined as a "chronic illness of undetermined etiology with an insidious onset showing recognizable symptoms and signs proportionate to its severity" (Merck, 1992, p. 1551). An "alcoholic" is a person who is extremely dependent on or addicted to alcohol. Dependence is marked by physical dependence, a dangerous withdrawal syndrome and the degree of social impairment that occurs as a result of chronic alcohol consumption. Other factors considered important in diagnosing the illness are the patterns and behaviors associated with drinking, the frequency and severity of the symptoms, and the age at which they occur. The earlier in life these behaviors occur, the more crippling the disorder is believed to be. Though the cause of alcoholism is unknown, it has been suggested that certain characteristics are seen more frequently among alcoholics, including schizoid qualities, depression, hostile and self-destructive behavior and disturbed parental relationships (Merck, 1992, p. 1552).

In a hallmark forty-year longitudinal study, Vaillant (1983) studied alcohol use among three diversified groups of men in order to determine if there is a natural evolution of a disease process inherent in alcohol addiction, and if so, at what point it occurs and what kinds of interventions halt the process. He followed two groups of men consisting of 204 upper middle class college sophomores and 456 inner city high school juniors from 1940-1980. Extensive data about their lives, including drinking behavior, were compared to results yielded by a third group, a clinic sample of 100 alcohol-dependent men and women who had been followed for eight years following clinic admission for detoxification. In support of this approach, Vaillant (1983, p. 307) cited Freud:

> So long as we trace the development from the final outcome backwards, the chain of events appear continuous and we feel that we have gained an insight which is completely satisfactory or even exhaustive. But if we proceed in the reverse way, if we start from the premises informed from the analysis, and try to follow them up to the final result, then we no longer get the impression of an inevitable sequence of events.

To date, Vaillant's extensive investigation with its diversity of groups and the period of time over which they were followed has not been matched anywhere in the literature.

Although Vaillant (1983) approaches alcohol dependency as a "disease" process and uses a medical model to diagnose and track its progression, he also acknowledges the broader sociological implications of the problem. He suggests that no single definition of alcohol abuse and addiction can really capture all of the variations seen among subjects; the problem can reflect both a habit and a disease which can be as well defined by a sociological model as by a medical model. As he states:

> There is no so called disease in which both etiology and cure are so profoundly dependent on social, economic and cultural variables. By narrowly defining alcohol abuse as a disease, the medical model fails to account for the myriad of variables and complexities involved in the process (p. 15). In short, in our attempts to understand and study alcoholism, it behooves us to employ the models of the social scientist and of the learning theorist (p. 20). Medicine and sociology have much to teach each other....Effective treatment will always gain much from undoing the simplistic thinking of the medical model. (p. 43)

Treatment, Recovery, Absolution and Hope

Vaillant's (1983) prognosis for successful recovery is contingent on a number of surprising factors, namely hope, absolution and new sources of self-esteem. He says: "If their lives are to change, they [alcoholics] need hope as much as relief of their symptoms...if we can but combine the best placebo effects of acupuncture, Lourdes or Christian Science with the best attitude change inherent in the evangelical conversion experience, we may be on our way to an effective alcoholism program" (pp. 287-288). Effective treatment needs to provide a person with a substitute dependency, external reminders about the dangers of drinking (i.e., antibuse), social support, enhanced self-esteem and a source of inspiration and hope, according to Vaillant. He underscores the role of natural healing forces and the individual's own ability to heal him/herself to insure recovery. He states that traditional treatments often interfere with these natural healing processes: "Alcoholics recover not because we treat them but because they heal themselves...if treatment as we currently understand it does not seem more effective than the natural healing processes, then we need to understand those natural process better than we do" (pp. 315-316).

Vaillant reports that his findings dispel many of the "illusions" inherent in traditional treatment assumptions about alcohol addiction, for example, that early intensive treatment is usually effective, and he underscores this at many points:

> Thus far there is no compelling evidence that any specific brief clinical intervention permanently alters the course of the disorder. (p 126)

> Many long term studies of the course of alcoholism concur that treatment has little if any lasting effect. (p. 147)

> Neither the efforts of dedicated clinicians nor the individual's own will power appear to be able to cure an alcoholic's conditioned habit at a given time.

This should not be a cause of despair but should spur the clinician to redirect therapeutic attention toward the individual's own power of resistance. (Vaillant, 1983, p. 315)

Vaillant also comments that treatment programs such as Alcoholics Anonymous (AA) provide the support, inspiration, and hope that may help in the recovery process.

According to many treatment professionals, self-help programs like AA are the most effective methods of treating addictions. According to Harris (1983): "AA treatment centers and alcohol counselling are the only known successful methods of arresting the compulsion to drink or take drugs. Alcoholism was totally untreatable and fatal until 1935, when AA was founded" (as cited in Peele, 1989, p. 55).

Alcoholics Anonymous views alcohol abuse as a medical disease and advocates a conversion experience as the foundation of recovery. People who suffer from the disease must acknowledge and accept that they are powerless over alcohol and must adjust their lives accordingly with the help of God. Though not a religious organization, many of AA's basic tenets are drawn from an early evangelical Christian movement, which emphasized the process of self-survey, public confession, restitution and service to others (Ogborne & Glaser, 1985, p. 183). AA members are asked to take twelve steps in the process of their recovery:

1. We admit we were powerless over alcohol — that our lives had become unmanageable.
2. Came to believe that a Power greater than ourselves could restore us to sanity.
3. Made a decision to turn our will and our lives over to the care of God as we understood Him.
4. Made a searching and fearless moral inventory of ourselves.
5. Admitted to God, to ourselves, and to another human being, the exact nature of our wrongs.
6. Were entirely ready to have God remove all these defects of character.
7. Humbly asked Him to remove our shortcomings.

8. Made a list of all persons we had harmed, and became willing to make amends to them all.
9. Made direct amends to such people wherever possible, except when to do so would injure them or others.
10. Continued to take personal inventory and when we were wrong promptly admitted it.
11. Sought through prayer and meditation to improve our conscious contact with God as we understood Him, praying only for knowledge of His will for us and the power to carry that out.
12. Having had a spiritual awakening as a result of these steps, we tried to carry this message to alcoholics, and to practice these principles in all our affairs. (as cited in Vaillant, 1983, pp. 197-198)

Over the past several years, the AA model has grown in popularity and has been applied to the treatment of a variety of problem behaviors from compulsive gambling, compulsive shopping, and compulsive eating, to the treatment of people who are dependent on dependent people.

While AA has been heralded as the most effective treatment of choice for addictions, the scientific community often takes issue with the lack of data to support their claims of successful treatment. Tournier (1979) voices such a concern: "Since the founding in 1935, Alcoholics Anonymous has come to dominate alcoholism both as ideology and as method...I propose that its continued domination of the field...has fettered innovation...(and) is limited in its application to the universe of alcoholics" (p. 231). Similarly, Hore (1991) suggests that the disease concept of AA's model does not allow for the diversity and complexity of the phenomenon of alcohol addiction. Findings reported by Baekeland, Lundwall, and Kissen (1975) suggest that the general applicability of AA as a treatment method is more limited than has been supposed in the past. Available data do not support AA's claims of much higher success rates than clinic treatment. Interestingly, a report from Alcoholics Anonymous supports these findings, stating that "70% of the people who attend Alcoholics Anonymous drop out after 10 meetings, 50% drop out after 3 meetings" (as cited in *The Harvard Mental Health Letter*, September 1996, p. 3).

Peele (1989) challenged the disease concept of alcohol abuse from a different perspective, stating that disease proponents, in fact, have created a new generation of diseases by defining addiction as a disease. He commented:

> I believe that we are creating problems for ourselves, many related to addiction, and that more and more Americans feel themselves in the throes of one or several compulsions...deciding one is addicted is a complicated process, entailing that one see oneself as being out of control of one's habits. And Americans do seem to feel that they are more out of control of their lives than they have felt in the past. This loss of control, despite all claims about the discovery of new biological causes of menstrual discomfort and genetic sources of alcoholism, depression, anxiety and other conditions, is principally a social and psychological phenomenon. (p. 233)

The Behavioral Model: Expectancy Factors and Addiction

Behavioral research has placed major emphasis on the role that anticipated consequences or expectancy factors play in the development of drinking behavior. Expectancy, according to Rotter (1966), is the probability held by the individual that a particular reinforcement will occur as a function of a specific behavior. Maisto, Conners, and Sachs (1981) point out: "Drinking is a goal directed behavior: the higher the subjective probability that the alcohol will serve a desired function, the more likely drinking will occur" (as cited in Southwick, Steele, Marlatt, & Lindell, 1981, p. 714).

LaBerg (1986) reported that the pharmacological and psychological effects of alcohol strongly suggest that expectancies play a significant part in consumption and social behavior. He studied thirty subjects in four experimental conditions with each subject participating in all four conditions. Subjects were administered either a priming dose of alcohol or a placebo and were instructed that the priming dose contained alcohol in two conditions and a soft drink in the other two conditions. Subjects received alcohol in a disguised form to determine the effect of instruction on expectancy. The results indicated that the instruction was more influential than the actual presence of alcohol. In other words, the expectancy of receiving alcohol was more important than the actual pharmacological effect of alcohol.

Southwick et al. (1981) examined the effect of expectancies on the behavioral effects of alcohol and reported that heavier drinkers expect greater positive effects from drinking (p. 713). Brown, Goldman, Inn, and Anderson (1980) developed a questionnaire to identify and categorize alcohol expectancies among light and heavy drinkers. They found that low doses of alcohol appear to produce behavior that is largely dependent on expectancy while in heavy doses, expectancy stimulates pharmacological effects: "Even if alcohol itself is pharmacologically incapable of producing a particular behavior effect, once a particular effect is causally attributed to alcohol, people may drink to achieve such an effect based on their beliefs" (p. 425).

Marlatt and Rohsenow (1980) found that the positive effects which subjects expected to have in terms of mood and behavior altered with continued drinking and became much less positive. The pleasurable effects associated with the initial phase of drinking had the greatest influence on shaping expectations about alcohol's ability to reduce tension. Further, the presence of alcohol cues were more highly related to both alcohol acquisition and craving than was the actual presence of alcohol.

More recent research has reported that the tension reduction theories of alcohol use have been overly broad and that "individual characteristics must be considered to account for any stress related effects that occur from alcohol use and abuse" (Cooper et al., 1992, p. 139). In an earlier report, Cooper, Russell and Frone (1990) stated that "there appears to be only limited support for a social learning model of alcohol abuse" (p. 260). Young and Oei (1993) have recently added that: "Although research into alcohol expectancies is reasonably well established, there is scant empirical evidence to directly relate such expectancies to the treatment of problem drinking...treatments based on more superordinate cognitive sets, such as the personal philosophy that drinkers hold regarding the nature of their problem...may ultimately be appropriate. Some theorists in their vigour for promoting social learning-based treatments have neglected or undermined other therapeutic approaches" (p. 353).

Interestingly, Keehn (1970) reported that problem drinkers do not consider alcohol to be a particularly powerful reinforcer, preferring instead occupational success, loving intimacy and pleasure from nature as a primary means of deriving pleasure rather than a secondary means, that is, alcohol. Goldman, Brown, Christiansen, and Smith (1991) commented that "No biological researcher has yet demonstrated that any factor automatically 'commandeers' drinking activity, and psychosocial researchers continue to search for controlling mechanisms that connect early experiences and dispositions with later drinking patterns. It is recommended that alcohol expectancy research remain open to inputs from expectancy theories already developed in several psychological domains" (p. 137).

Perhaps the most pertinent findings to the present discussion are those of Christiansen, Goldman, and Inn (1982) and Miller, Smith, and Goldman (1990). In a study investigating alcohol expectancies among adolescents, Christiansen, Goldman and Inn developed and administered alcohol expectancy questionnaire to 1580 adolescents who were between twelve and nineteen years old. They found that "relatively well developed expectancies exist prior to alcohol use, but pharmacological experience of alcohol crystallized existing expectancies" (p. 336). The authors concluded that expectancies are present before actual experience with alcohol and that the "precondition for positive reinforcement exists in adolescents the very first time they drink" (p. 343). They also noted that identifying a cognitively mediated mechanism which has the capacity for determining behavior effects of alcohol at a time in life prior to actual experience with alcohol "threatens the researcher with an infinite regress paradox. If pharmacological mechanisms are not necessary for the manifestation of behavioral effects, then how did the expectancies become associated with alcohol in the first place?" (p. 344).

Miller, Smith and Goldman (1990) administered a variation of Christiansen, Goldman and Inn's (1982) Alcohol Expectancy Questionnaire to 114 children in grades 1 through 5. They found that

> (1) there was an overall trend of increasingly positive expectancies with age; and (2) strikingly, the bulk of the increase was observed in the third and fourth grades. In light of this close relationship between measured alcohol related expectancies and actual drinking behavior in adults and adolescents as young as 12 years of age, some etiological role for expectancies cannot be discounted. Either expectancies are closely related to other variables that have a direct causal power in the development of alcohol use or expectancies themselves may be inferred to play a causal role. Identification of the origin of the alcohol expectancies might help in untangling this etiologic knot. To date our work has indicated that an experience with drinking is not by itself the source of alcohol expectancies. (p. 343)

Much of the behavioral research regarding the role that expectancy factors play in the development of addictions raises more questions and cause for speculation rather than provides conclusions, as illustrated by the infinite regress paradox voiced by Christiansen, Goldman, and Inn (1982). Marlatt and Rohsenow (1980), in a review of the findings of expectancy effects, point out that "Perhaps the most important implication of the research...is that the primary reinforcement for drug use, the subject's experience of intoxication or the 'high' state, may be more rooted in the user's cognition than in the pharmacological properties of the drug itself" (p. 195). They suggest that Weil's (1972) comments may be a fitting summation regarding the issue:

> Pharmacologists sometimes use active placebos in contrast to inactive placebos like sugar pills, in drug testing; for example, nicotinic acid, which causes warmth and flushing, has been compared with hallucinogens in some laboratory experiments. But pharmacologists do not understand that all psychoactive drugs are really active placebos, since the psychic effects arise from consciousness, elicited by set and setting in response to physiological cues. Thus for most marijuana users, the occasion of smoking a joint becomes an opportunity or excuse for experiencing a mode of consciousness that is available to everyone all of the time, even though many people do not how to get high without using a drug. Not surprisingly, regular marijuana users often find themselves becoming high spontaneously...the user who correctly interprets the significance of his spontaneous high takes the first step away from dependence on the drug to achieve the desired state of consciousness and the first step toward freer use of his own nervous system. All drugs that seem to give highs behave this way, all are active placebos. But the less physiological noise, the easier it is for the user to understand the true nature of drugs and their highly indirect relationship to states of consciousness." (as cited in Marlatt & Rohsenow, 1980, p. 195)

Addiction and Behavior

Behavior psychologists have traditionally searched for methods to alter negative and socially undesirable behaviors in favor of more desirable ones. In the laboratory, the study of behavior has primarily focused on the physiological events that motivate and determine behavior and the processes required to change it. Theoretically, behaviorism, according to Nathan (1978a), is "...designed from its inception to be open to empirical investigation, which will ultimately permit assessment of its validity, its accuracy, by means of scientific study. More than anything, the word (behavioral) used in this context means a respect for data and evidence above inference, hypothesis or speculation" (p. 3). More recently, behavior psychologists have incorporated social learning theory into their theoretical framework, creating what they call a cognitive behavior paradigm. As Oei and Baldwin (1994) point out: "Cognitive behavioral approaches to alcohol have focused increasingly on the role of specific cognitions about the expected consequences of alcohol consumption. These cognitions have been hypothesized as playing a vital role in the development of drinking styles, and therefore, as having potential usefulness in prevention and treatment....the structure and role of the construct have not been clearly explicated in theoretical terms to date" (p. 525).

According to social learning theory, alcohol abuse is a method of coping with the everyday demands of life when a person lacks the skill or self-confidence to exercise control over tasks. Research has focused primarily on "establishing the independent links among particular aspects of theory and indices of alcohol use and abuse....The probability of alcohol use is further increased to the extent that an individual maintains strong and positive expectancies of alcohol's effects such that his or her options to achieve valued outcomes are limited to alcohol use" (Evans, & Dunn, 1995, p. 186).

When viewed as a behavior, habitual and excessive use of alcohol and other drugs is seen as a learned behavior through the mechanisms of imitation and modelling. Social reinforcers such as other people's approval (a positive reinforcer), or disapproval (a negative reinforcer), will tend to either increase or decrease the probability that the behavior will recur, according to White, Bates, and Johnson (1991). They report that "drinking behaviors and effects appear to be determined by complex interactions among alcohol, the person who drinks it and the environment" (p. 178). Nathan (1978a) reports that "alcoholics have learned that drinking alcohol reduces the unpleasant emotions of learned stress and learned anxiety" (p. 4).

Donovan and Marlatt (1980) reviewed the behavioral research on alcohol dependence and addiction from Pavlov's aversive conditioning approach in 1929 to Hull's learning theory in which drinking is seen as reinforcing because of its tension reducing properties. They reported:

> Within the behavioral perspective alcohol use and misuse are seen as socially acquired through a variety of processes including vicarious learning, peer and parent modelling, social reinforcement and the anticipated effect of alcohol as a tension reducing agent. The emphasis in behavioral assessment is placed on describing the topography of drinking behavior, the situational, cognitive and affective parameters that serve as discriminative stimuli to cue drinking; behavioral and cognitive consequences that have shaped and currently maintain the problem behavior and the therapeutic manipulations of the antecedent consequent and mediating cognitive variables necessary to modify the drinking patterns.
>
> "....There is a general lag in the development of fully integrated theoretical models that attempt to account for the etiology of alcoholism. A similar lag exists in the area of assessment of drinking...there appears to be no core organizing principle to integrate the functional interrelationship among the widely varied behavioral techniques that are currently available." (p. 1155)

Treatment Techniques

According to Wilson (1978), the goal of behavior treatment is to modify behaviors that are associated with alcohol and the person's response to them: "Competent behavioral assessment involves two major facets: first, identification of all the variables that maintain such a complex disorder as alcoholism; and second, selection of the appropriate technique that will most effectively and efficiently result in the desired behavior change" (p. 110). Over the past twenty-five years, behavior psychologists have used various techniques that attempt to recondition or modify alcohol and drug abuse behavior.

Aversive conditioning procedures pair a negative habit (drinking or drug use) with an aversive event such as electric shock, a nauseating chemical or a negative image. While initially this method was seen as representing, "the optimal behavioral treatment method for alcoholism" (Eysenck, & Beech, 1971; as cited in Wilson, 1978, p. 96), it has provoked ethical controversy, specifically those techniques using electric shock techniques. Nathan (1978b) reports: "No data exist which indicate that any of the aversion conditioning methods (including electrical, chemical or covert aversion) has the capacity alone to effect change in excessive drinking on even a short term basis." However, he continues, "Although still tentative, findings relating to the efficacy of chemical aversion indicated that this behavioral treatment approach may well show promise" (p. 88). Equally contradictory are the findings of Bandura (1969), who reported that when chemical aversion conditioning was included in follow-up sessions with alcoholics, 86% had a probability of maintaining abstinence for up to one year. Of these results, however, Bandura stated: "By the time alcoholics appear for aversion therapy they have been recipients of considerable wise counsel and impassioned appeals by significant people in their lives, repeated admonitions, rewards and a variety of remedies to no avail. Treatment outcomes are frequently attributed to common social influences as though these were encountered for the first time in the treatment situation" (as cited in Wilson, 1978, p. 99).

Lazarus (1965) proposed a broad spectrum behavioral approach to alcoholism treatment that includes systematic desensitization (suppressing the response to alcohol stimuli), aversive conditioning, medical treatment for physical problems, tests to identify specific antecedents of anxiety, assertiveness training, hypnosis and behavioral rehearsal (as cited in Nathan, 1978b, p. 82). In 1990, The National Institute on Alcohol, Alcohol Abuse and Alcoholism reported that continued attention was being given to research which compared the efficacy of behavioral oriented therapies utilizing a community reinforcement approach (CRA) with more individual models. The CRA approach encourages the problem drinker to develop social support networks in areas which may contribute to drinking problems in order to aid in the recovery process, for example, in the workplace.

Annis and Davis (1988, p. 89) examined the value of teaching problem drinkers skill building techniques using a cognitive behavioral approach. Individuals who tended to drink in response to stress were taught stress management techniques while people who drank in response to peers were taught assertiveness training. They found that for those individuals who could identify high risk drinking situations, drinking decreased. However, the authors noted that many problem drinkers could not identify these situations; hence, prevention strategies were difficult to target.

Approaching behavior change from a more sociological perspective, Peele (1989) advocates social change as the only viable method of treatment:

> The only way to actually affect our addiction rate is to bring about social change. While such change may be difficult, anything that fails to deal with real

sources of the problem is wasted effort. The few therapies that are effective succeed because they work to change real social forces in people's environments. These forces include work opportunities, family and community supports, and the moral and values atmosphere (and rewards and punishments) in people's lives. (p. 260)

Chapter 3

Eidetic Image Therapy

Eidetic Image Therapy, originated by Akhter Ahsen, offers a new method for the treatment of alcohol and drug abuse and their related symptomatologies based on the individual's innate potential of hope and the natural dynamism toward a high expression. Through a precise series of imagery exercises, these states can be retrieved to return events in the mind to a high point in the inner experience. Ahsen's views on perception differ significantly from traditional psychotherapeutic methods, as Dolan (1977a) succinctly summarized:

> Early reviewers had noted the new creative thrust of Ahsen's work and its synthesizing character. For them, the orientation of his work had revealed a fuller meaning of perception; how it is registered, stored, and reproduced, and in the complex yet understandable ramifications of systems in the areas of conflict

and resolution. These scientific ideas embodied a breakthrough in psychotherapy diametrically opposed to the currently accepted principles in psychology which described perception as merely a one-dimensional, impotent mental event subject to conscious thought and manipulation. By revealing new vital aspects of perception in self kinetic forms, Ahsen brought to clinical light hitherto unrecognized aspects of human development and mental functioning and moved the perception theory in the direction of long overdue synthesis" (p. 24)...Ahsen's exceptional conception for the psyche gives the therapeutic process a transparency, determinism, freedom and potency which is not available in any other known psychological model." (p. 35)

In Eidetic Image Therapy, emotional conflicts and their natural solutions are seen as key elements of a bipolar event, separated from wholeness through a variety of developmental fixations and distorted perceptions. The eidetic image recreates a vivid experience of developmental events and conflicts in detail, revealing the multileveled relationships between perception and personality. It is able to effectively isolate the negative structures found in perception and to reveal the habitual patterns of response and the experience regarding reality and fantasy. Dolan (1977a) elaborates on the possibilities from various perspectives:

> The unification of conflictual elements in the experience and generation of entirely new purposeful experience are the main creative aspects of the eidetic image; and precisely these attributes differentiate the eidetic from all other psychical phenomena. The main thrust of the eidetic experience is not toward breakdown but enactment, unification and resolution, which generate repetitive behavior in the original elements causing them to recur again and again for the individual's consideration. This repetitive tendency toward unification, Ahsen links with purposeful bio-

logical behavior. He distinguishes death-oriented repetition from life-oriented repetition, the former being
a symptom-based, non-resolutory fixation, the latter a
repetition which progresses Life. (p. 21)

Man is considered both determined and free, determined in the vicissitudes of development but free in
internal perception potential. Ahsen stresses that experiences and traumata, along with original potentials are
stored mechanistically by the central nervous system in
the form of vivid visual pictures, namely the eidetics.
He bases his method on the capacity in the eidetics to
effect ready recall through instantaneous playback of
any type of experience in the psyche. The method
allows the individual a command on his consciousness
and enables him to manipulate mental events in such a
manner that he can evoke, study and resolve a problematic experience at will. (p. 16)

The approach offered through Ahsen's work should
strengthen hope in those who have been discouraged
by emergence of a negative emphasis in most traditional systems of mental change. The analysis
approach presented here generates change by using
a precision tool which identifies experience in a clear
yet personal manner. By providing a personal view
of the mental content in the most lucid manner, this
new method allows freedom of choice, self direction
and self change to take place in the spirit of self testi-
mony. (p. 40)

The Eidetic Experience

The eidetic is an internal image which is spearheaded by a
light cue in consciousness. In a sense, this inner visual experience can be seen as mirroring the primary importance of light
in the outside as well as the inside world. Insufficient light due
to the gaseous materials that surrounded the planet resulted in
a slow emergence of life through the process of oxidation, or
chemosynthesis. As light became more abundant, the phenom-

ena of life rapidly escalated through the process of photosynthesis, and the earth was soon covered with green vegetation. As animals evolved, they became dependent on the visual ability to identify and locate food sources. Though smell and sound played an important role, light proved the best vehicle for providing cues to locate food and the eye reigned supreme as the optimal cue provider in the field

Likewise, in comparison to other sensory experiences, the visual experience functions as a far better medium for space-time conceptions. The visual image is extremely well suited for identical reproduction of events and is highly efficient for the formulation and storage of experience by virtue of its ability to retrieve and symbolize events. It represents the interplay of light values and chromatic variations and, in essence, comprises the sum total of life.

In humans, the visual process is much more complex and more developed than in animals because of the human mind's vast extra-sensitive memory ability. Recall of experience through the visual image engages not only events in the outside world but also in one's internal world. Thus, there are visual images which derive from external objects, others which recall past experiences, and still others which are purely imaginary and symbolic.

According to Ahsen, the eidetic is encoded with three basic elements: the visual image of the event, the body's response to the event, and the meaning that is associated with it. The eidetic image is, therefore, a three-part unit succinctly coded as an "ISM" (Image, Somatic response, and Meaning). The ISM contains a record of the events from personal history, the structure of which influences perception, behavior and the development of personality. Activation of an eidetic image through a specific step-by-step method reveals a lucid record of an event as it was originally experienced with all of these basic elements intact.

The eidetic begins as a living precept, essentially an active remembrance, that is stored in the mind for later recall. In very stressful situations, or if an emotionally disturbing event is not resolved, the ISM structure tends to break down into its separate parts, eluding the rational mind and causing the individual to experience a vague sense of encounter that is not understood. The negative ISM is preserved in a fragmented state, never moving to a natural resolution of the conflict nor reuniting with its other structural components which are floating around. By uncovering each of these events and actively reuniting all the elements—the image, the body response and the meaning—the person feels a sense of resolution and is able to understand and overcome the problems posed in the original experience.

The eidetic image differs from other types of mental images in its clear, repeatable, consistent quality. Penfield (1952) referred to these types of images as "experiential responses" or "strips of time" having a high fidelity quality. Interest in these unique mental processes has a long history in the field of philosophy and psychology, from the early writings of the Greeks to the contemporary neurological investigation of the holographic qualities of neurons (Pribram, 1971).

The eidetic emerges as distinctly different from ordinary memory. Ahsen (1984a) elaborates this important distinction in terms of what he calls the problematic Memory Complex as follows:

> By definition a memory image is a complex which only serves recall. If the image does not totally duplicate an original detail it cannot be categorized as real: it is a misrecall or a creation. Where a memory image ceases to be a memory image, a different type of imagery has, in fact, begun to operate, namely, the eidetic imagery. Most of the time a memory image is a very incomplete version of the original event in the sense that the registering of the original event took place under a special circumstance in which the detail was handled with selective emphasis or was even frankly misinterpreted because of prevailing ego needs. When such a memory image is replayed

the original eidetic component still attached to the selected recall process is reactivated. However, as the Memory Complex resists the emergence of this original component, the dynamics at this juncture appear to be most intriguing. One asks the question: If memory is merely doing its legitimate archaeological work of recall, why does it resist realignment with the original total experience? Unless memory is, in fact, acting as a Memory Complex, that is, inhibition against total and true recall, this excessive fixation cannot be explained. It is precisely this over fixation which explains the growth of a Memory Complex as a disturbing nucleus out of the memory faculty. Considering this, the desirability of rescuing the original experience from the clutches of the Memory Complex cannot be overemphasized. (p. 59)

In a comprehensive examination of Ahsen's Image Psychology, Hochman (1994) focused especially on parents and primordiality in Ahsen's theory of personality development and therapeutic change. She notes the interplay between historical and non-historical consciousness in this regard as follows:

The eidetics are thus "sources of action" in Ahsen's Image Psychology and the parents who "have a supreme importance in the life of the child" form the basic ground for the emergence of these images. The infant comes into the world with a "nebulous, undifferentiated monoconsciousness" which is primordially integrated in its own right but does not centralize around any particular nucleus. The infant lives in an egoless state of primevality with minimum historical organization. The mother, as the person who first handles and looks after the child, becomes a dynamic nucleus around which inner and outer become integrated. Personal identity begins to emerge in the child though at first it is dependent on the mother, who has almost a mythic portrait...As time goes on, the child's personal identity develops and the psychic space between the child and the mother likewise develops. The mother's image bifurcates into the nourishing mother and the character mother, the one who has historical problems, manifested in her denying and inhibiting aspects. As this happens, the child becomes more aware of the father, who now begins to establish his own nucleus in the child's consciousness. At first he appears as a benevolent outsider. Later he becomes known as a powerful, loving and protective figure who introduces the child to the world outside the house. At this point the parents become contending psychical figures since the previously powerful mother is now facing a diminution by an emergent powerful father. The father's image also becomes bifurcated, one side protective and the other side manifesting his aggressive tendencies. As the child develops, he or she develops an initial view of which parent is responsible for what in the real world; at the same time, however, at first the child instinctively sides with the mother, who formed the basis of his or her first security. Ultimately, the parents become somewhat adjusted and reconciled figures at both the historical and the non-historical levels of consciousness. (pp. 17-18)

The eidetic images of parents obviously exert enormous control over the mind. The individual's identity and the experience of feeling whole or divided develops out of the sane or disturbed parental figures. The eidetic image reflects psychical dynamics in the comparative brilliance values and interactive effects when the parents are seen standing side by side in the psychical visual space in front. This spatial image, unconnected with any real historical scene, demonstrates the power of the parental image to influence mind and body responses in the child. The goals of Eidetic Image Therapy in this respect are recounted by Hochman (1994):

...to work toward solution, elementally, the image is repeatedly projected and the eidetic is lived as a current event. The stages toward solution are Progression, or the unfolding of the theme; Emanation, where the person's own image reactivity develops out of a previous passive or weak or negative self-image and gradually changes into an active self image containing positive overt expression and feelings of release; Catharsis, in which the eidetic creates a powerful impact on the mind, leading to a feeling that one has fully lived and overcome the emotion involved; Interaction with image objects toward expression, which may involve introduction of a new situation or element into the projection to generate a response or reaction; Insight, or a completely new experiential outlook based on the meanings and feelings within the eidetic structure. (p. 84)

Basic Qualities of the Eidetic

Ahsen's approach, as described above, represents a new psychology of consciousness which differs markedly from other systems in its fundamental assertion that consciousness has a psychosomatic quality in the very act of perception which is represented in the eidetic image. For Ahsen, perception is a composite phenomenon entailing visual elements, physiological response and meaning. The visual dimension serves as a core manifestation of the whole state and provides access to meaningful experiences, thereby enabling an individual's original strength and dynamism to be fully utilized. In addition, Ahsen has found that certain psychic dynamics function the way in which imagery works, according to its natural structures. Those that are particularly important for effective treatment of alcohol and drug abuse are briefly described below. These should be kept in mind while the eidetic work is being conducted for most successful results. (The interested reader is especially referred to Ahsen's 1965, 1968, 1972 and 1977a books for more detailed discussions of these and other principles for eidetic work.)

Seriality
Eidetic images, according to Ahsen, are stored serially in the mind in a unique fashion. For each experience, the mind chooses a single element out of the situation and organizes the rest of the event around it. When another similar event is experienced, the first event links with the second and a new relationship with the event is created. Access to the first event is no longer directly possible. However, the first event can be recalled when the second has been activated and any residual conflict associated with it has been resolved. This means that the first event has not been forgotten but rather arranged behind the second one sequentially. It will emerge only when it is approached through subsequent experiences.

Bipolarity
Any psychical involvement is a repeatable, bipolar structure which has an expressive, oscillating quality. For any given event, it will manifest one of two opposite expressive possibilities. An ISM will be assigned with either a negative or a positive value to each possibility, resulting in two ISM's. Each event is, therefore, finally assigned either a positive quality or a negative one. A positive event is one that is experienced as enhancing well-being, whereas a negative event diminishes well-being. Relegating the experience in this bipolar fashion provides a reference and direction for later recall and use of the event. When there is a fixation on the negative end of the pole, it leads to a repetition of the original negative side of the event. Repeated negative experiences and unresolved conflicts lead a person to a habitually negative experience of life with the positive aspects all but forgotten. However, the eidetic image retains the original positive potential that existed when the original experience occurred, and it can be brought to light to reinstate a more positive orientation toward life.
Operationally, bipolar configuration is like opposing pairs of

muscles in which one pair does not inhibit the opposite pair; it merely expresses its own potential in the form of a tension, which means that it mechanically involves relinquishing the opposite possibility. This operation does not involve active inhibition by interference, as suggested by the behaviorists' notion of reciprocal inhibition; rather, it is more in keeping with the conception of mental field as described by Ahsen (1965) and Hilgard (1973, 1977). Both of these authors have demonstrated that at any given moment there are countless activities going on within a person's sensory field such as heartbeat, breathing, perceptions, feelings from internal organs, and input through the external organs. They have pointed out that these activities are occurring simultaneously at all times though a person is only selectively aware of them at any one time. These partially integrated patterns or loose dessociational or neo-dissociational fields exist in a flexible and changeable hierarchy that is regulated by what is called the Executive Ego which selects, rejects and integrates all incoming experience. Both Ahsen and Hilgard emphasize that this loose viewing of the current mental and sensory field can provide basic material for developing combinations of experience which may be useful to the organism.

According to Ahsen, the initial function of the ego is the utilization and expression of the organism's potential. However, this function is gradually corrupted through a combination of incessant demands from external reality and the individual's internal environment. As the Executive Ego emerges and engages in a relationship with the environment, its intentionality imparts a touch of its own identity to every involvement and, out of this, ego-like states are born. If these states are not integrated properly, they can be subject to repetition and recurrence. The Executive Ego must be, therefore, provided with a power that will enhance its role and organize information toward healthful, dynamic expression. This power is available in the eidetic.

Intentionality

In his notion of intentionality, Thomas Aquinas asserted that the self, in the act of perceiving objects, stretches forth and draws them into itself. The object is said to exist after this intentionally in the mind and in this way it is always related to real objects. Brentano extended this concept to include all consciousness, real or imaginary, referring to an indwelling of objects in consciousness. He believed that to know the content of consciousness is to know the object itself. This, in turn, led Husserl to attribute a certain quality to consciousness which he termed "eidetic essence."

For Ahsen, the eidetic essence or trace of the object is left behind in the form of an image, which once carried a moment of strong intentionality. One of the most important aspects of this notion is that the term is fundamentally futuristic. As the intellect extends into the object, it is, at that moment, interacting with it, rather than just memorizing it. The intention of the interaction is to know the object, a process which is in essence goal-oriented and futuristic. There is a striking difference between this process and ordinary memory. The function of ordinary memory is to serve recall, but the function of intentionality is to know the object by interacting with it in the mind. According to Hebb, (1968) "the object is actively explored through the motor process involved in the act of seeing" (as cited in Ahsen, 1984a, p. 53). Perception becomes an act that includes some kind of action being taken on that which is perceived. Ahsen (1984a) states in this regard:

> What is the process of seeing an object? Is it mere passive receiving of sense impressions, rational critical examination, or active beholding? In experiencing an object, the sense impression as well as the intention are recognized, but in the middle falls the all important element of indeterminate, free and unpredictable interaction through the person in which the impres-

sion and intention are thrown into a synthesis. The final emergence of objects is thus not carried out in a mechanical way as Gestalt theory suggests, but through a dramatic mode. It is not mechanical rule of pattern formation but critical dramatic action which hammers out the final shape of the object. The classical psychological theory not only mistakenly made sensory impression and memory independent but also committed a serious error in making even the imagination function separate, diluted and autonomous, in brief, undramatic. Husserl used the term thin-autonomy to describe the imaginative function's possible and all the more tragic alienation and indifference from the concrete aspects and concerns of a real "life-world." The dangers of a diluted autonomous imagination are no doubt obvious and well known. Heidegger pointed out that solitude of imagination represents a deficient mode of living and being human. (p. 54)

Biolatency

According to Ahsen, the organism is genetically endowed at birth with positive life impressions encoded at a primary cellular level in the form of arrested pictures. Even when life activity has been traumatized and mutilated, these strong encoded pictures which preserve the original life process remain whole and complete and can be rejuvenated.

The eidetic image is a dynamic entity which contains all of the elements of an earlier experience waiting to be discovered and deciphered. Through dialogue and interaction with the image, more and more information is revealed which, in turn, provides access to solutions of longstanding problems and gives rise to a feeling of expectancy and futurism. Past fixations are released through the active engagement with the image; thus, the past provides a destiny with a futuristic emphasis. The eidetic image provides access to the vast potential of consciousness afresh, as if nothing had been lost.

Chapter 4

The Expectation High

According to Ahsen (1993a), the innate dynamism and resilience of the individual is nowhere more clearly demonstrated that in the states of expectancy and futurism found in the Expectation High. To him this is a powerful state that connects to both inner and outer stimuli. The state may be conscious or preconscious, clearly formed or amorphous, but always ready to be brought forward in an eidetic image. This holistic image contains a state of anticipation with an orientation toward something beyond habituation. It provides a variety of elements which are oriented toward expression and remains covertly operational all of the time. Ahsen (1979) differentiates this state from ordinary imagery: "In an ordinary imagery state, as in the rational process, a person may search in a panic for a solution, but no solution may come through. On the other hand, this energized imagery is characterized by a definite alertness and an inherent capacity for solutions channelled from the deepest potentials of the organism. During high consciousness imagery states, the individual feels vital and confident; and his imagery experiences give him the feeling of being in command of the situation" (p. 23). High states of consciousness like those found in the Expectation High are, in essence, the nucleus of biological wholeness, highly energetic and dynamically linked to early states of development when the child freely participated in the world with enthusiasm and hope.

Imagery, Expectancy and Neural Connection

Early imagery research on expectancy dates back to the experimental work of Mowrer (1938), Curtis (1937), Upton (1929), Wever (1930), and Schlosberg (1934), among others.

In 1938, Mowrer found that conditioned responses could be suddenly established and equally as suddenly abolished in human beings by controlling the subject's state of expectancy or preparatory set. During specific mental operations, longstanding mental structures could be broken down and reestablished in seconds. In the experiments a different structure appeared as it was replaced by a new expectancy state involving more relevant or valid imagery. Apparent conditioned responses respond in a resilient way, quite opposite to the process of conditioning proposed by classical behavior psychologists. Mowrer (1977), commenting on a conversation with behaviorist Clark Hull, reported, "Clark Hull once told me that he did not find my notions about expectancy at all useful and saw no future for this line of inquiry" (p. 314).

Illustrating the above-mentioned process in imagery is a fascinating case report by Ahsen (1968) utilizing the Age Projection Test (APT), an imagery test aimed at revealing self-images at various age levels and their mental structures in the treatment of somatic complaints. (For further elucidation of the Age

Projection Test, see Ahsen, 1988a; Dolan 1997). Briefly, a subject saw himself wearing a particular shirt at a certain age level, which, in fact, belonged to another age level eight years earlier. While concentrating on this mental image, he realized that this shirt belonged to an age level when he felt very secure. He reported that recall of this positive image represented his desire to withdraw from a painful event in favor of a more positive one (p. 275). The spontaneous appearance of the older shirt in connection with the more recent memory image, though previously out of his awareness, provided a more positive mental state. This process, in which subjects are shown to act on information that reached them when they were not aware of it, illustrates what Morton Prince (1906) referred to as co-consciousness in which attention operates from far beyond the bounds of realistic perception.

The term "co-consciousness," first proposed by Janet in 1889, Prince in 1906 and later refined by Hilgard (1973), refers to mental states that exist within an individual's consciousness but outside the limits of immediate awareness, as illustrated in the case of the shirt. This state not only exists between the various levels of the mind and the experiences retained there, but is an implicit strategy between one level and another, a condition fundamentally cooperative and "biolatent" in nature. Though various states of consciousness may be out of awareness, they are linked together through this process, which has a wholistic knowledge of the total organism. Consciousness is organic in this sense, having a special operational consciousness of its own. The notion of co-consciousness, together with the notions of biolatency and intentionality, represent the core of Ahsen's eidetic theory, which asserts that consciousness has an active, dynamic quality that moves intentionally toward biological health and well-being. The eidetic image serves to activate these dynamic processes that have been suppressed through developmental fixations and emotional obstructions.

To further illustrate this point, Ahsen (1977a) reports a patient who came to psychotherapy with a complaint of sleepwalking. The patient recounted an event from childhood in which a train on which he was travelling became subject to a robbery. As the robbers approached his car, he became terrified, got up suddenly, jumped from the train and ran into the fields. As he ran to safety, he was still half asleep. When the Age Projection Test was administered, the man saw himself in a state of dread, one year prior to the robbery. When he was instructed to stand before his parental images, have a temper tantrum and throw his shirt before them (a step of the APT instructions), he saw his mother pick up the shirt and place it in a box where he saw a pistol. He reported that he had never possessed a pistol nor ever imagined possessing one prior to this point. When he was handed the pistol in the image, the dread he was experiencing suddenly disappeared. He reported a very positive state as a result of the image and his sleepwalking symptoms were relieved. Through a spontaneous mental operation, the pre-existing negative mental structure was obliterated in favor of a more healthy one without training (p. 92).

Curtis (1937) had found that when administering a shock to condition a response of foot flexion in a pig, the shock itself was eventually a signal for relief. The expectancy of the shock brought about the relief which was simultaneously present in the shock. Curtis' results in this area remain confirmed and recent research in pharmacology reports related findings. During the learning of a task, neurons which are not necessarily used in learning the task may become active and fire anyway, producing images beside those that concern the task directly (Gero, 1985). This process, as in the example of the foot flexion, works paradoxically; it focuses consciousness, forcing it to become narrow, while at the same time, consciousness continues to be activated.

There are two types of neural processes related to expectancy and habituation. In expectancy, processing of information seems to diminish with repetition. In performance, enhanced efficiency of output seems to occur with repetition. Behavior becomes reflexive once habituation occurs, thereby diminishing expectancy via the processing of input. The more expectancy becomes habit, the less contact there is with input, that is, there is less contact with actual experience once habituation occurs. As task efficiency increases, the less input necessary.

Sokolov's (1960) findings report a similar effect. An individual will respond to stimuli with either an orienting reaction or habituation. For example, orienting to the beep of a horn involves characteristic electrical activity in the brain and certain physiological characteristics, such as increase of blood flow to the head and less to the fingertips. Habituation occurs when these reactions diminish after frequent repetition of the beep. Sokolov found that although it appeared that the person had habituated to the beep, if the stimulus was changed slightly, for instance, if the beep became softer, all of the initial orienting reactions would recur. This finding suggests that the person who is habituated may be matching the current experience against a stored representation of prior experiences.

Because behavior is derived from the nervous system, its organization and neurological functioning depend on the semipermanent constructions that develop through the input and output of stimuli by which the brain maintains communication with the environment. Pribram (1971) describes the operation of the neural structure and its functions as a hologram:

> The neural hologram deals with the facts of disruptions of the input systems...Memory mechanisms other than those that fit the holographic analogy must play a role...even in imaging and certainly in recognition...the holographic hypothesis does not upset classical neurophysiological conceptions; it

enriches them by a shift in emphasis from axonal
nerve impulses to the slow potential microstructure that develops in post synaptic, dendritic networks. At the same time, the holographic hypothesis enriches psychology by providing a plausible
mechanism for understanding phenomenal experience. This permits consideration of components
of psychological functions which become lumped
together in a restricted behavioristic framework.
Pattern recognition is a complex process in which
feature analysis and the formation of central representation of input are steps. Given the neuronal
hologram, these steps lead to image construction.
(pp. 165-166)

According to Pribram (1971, p. 15), there are two classes of
neural codes: those involving discrete nerve impulse and those
that produce a steady state or slow potentials. Nerve impulses
are propagated while slow potentials wax and wane locally in
the brain tissue and are sensitive to a variety of influences such
as the local chemical environment, which is not strictly neuronal. Nerve impulses arriving at the synaptic junction interact
with the environment to produce new images by virtue of
spontaneous neuronal activity and previous experience, for
example, variation in the tonality of the beeps. From this point
of interaction, new patterns of departure are initiated.

Many neurophysiologists now believe that neural activity
is the result of the sum of excitation of many neurons. The
fact that neurons lead in a variety of directions and can
synapse with dendrites, cell bodies and axons allows greater
efficiency at the level of expectancy. The divergent conduc-
tion of impulses at the junctional microstructure serves to
enrich the associative cortex and the energetic functioning of
the organism. These interactions are important to the organization of behavior, and indicate that they are not permanently fixed but can be altered to attain different states depending

on the electrochemical environment. These findings suggest that habituation is dependent on interactions among several levels. Experiments replicating Sherrington's (1906) direction reveal that interneurons connecting input and output neurons involved in reflex change are critical in habituation, not the input and output neurons themselves. The evidence indicates that, at times, the process in habituation seems to depend on mechanisms other than synaptic changes. At other times, depletion or augmentation of the transmitter substance is involved.

It has been demonstrated in the literature that alcohol and drugs interrupt the action of neurotransmitter substances in the brain. Dopamine and serotonin, both of which are of central importance during affective states such as mood, personality and motivation are especially affected. Research has shown that dopamine uptake is inhibited at the junctional microstructure by alcohol intake, causing the functions that naturally occur to be usurped by the external substance. The intake of the substance prevents naturally occurring neurological operations from taking place, replacing them with an artificial process, and the individual loses the ability to access dopamine-mediated processes. In the case of serotonin, there is an increased affinity for serotonin uptake with alcohol intake; thus, the functions of relaxation and restfulness that occur as a result of serotonin transmission are likewise usurped and allocated to the drug. Crack cocaine is a dramatic illustration of this process. Crack is a one-time addicting drug that releases such an intense state of euphoria in approximately thirty seconds that the organism's own ability is totally surpassed, hooking the person on the instantaneous pleasure and suppressing the body's natural capabilities. In the case of nicotine, production of dopamine is also inhibited at the junctional microstructure. As the person begins to associate the act of smoking with the experience of pleasure, the anticipation of the enjoyment becomes the cue that releases dopamine. The expectation of pleasure and the act of smoking become entangled so that the two become inseparable. Giving up smoking means giving up the anticipated pleasure which the cue that releases dopamine provides. If other areas of pleasure that stimulate dopamine release have not been developed, the person will be unable to give up the habit successfully. This process applies to all substances.

According to Ahsen (1978) research on the junctional behavior of the brain only provides the first picture of the operations involved in the process and he states:

> Neurological researchers admit the profound importance of the junctional behavior of the brain, i.e. the play of orientations and the importance of balance and meaning in the interconnections. But the popular representation of neurological research has so far offered only a skeleton picture of the neural juncture, essentially devoid of its complex emotive nature which comprises psychical balance. In the face of complex emotional history and concepts, this balance becomes progressively corrupted. As chaos develops due to inappropriate symbols that prevail there derived from inappropriate experience, it plays havoc with the organism. If the natural psychical balance is not reinstated, the organism becomes progressively more self-restrictive and self-hindering, damaging its natural neurological condition.
>
> The neurological research which emphasizes the central importance of junctional behavior implicitly acknowledges the important clinical questions: How does emotional pathology create a morbid junctional condition which perpetuates malfunction of the natural neurological gift? A person who has suffered a trauma or is emotionally confused is obviously also neurologically disturbed. The neural juncture, therefore, must be repaired not in a simple way as if by sewing together the nerves, but in a complex way through reinstatement of the appropriate emotions of life. A disruptive emotional condition which creates

serious neurological consequences is healed not by conditioning, almost a surgical process of joining (surgery is advisable if there is physical damage) nor by a chemically corrective process (which is also acceptable as a temporary measure). It requires, in the final analysis, a permanent restructuring of the juncture through the instrument of mentation. Authentic access to the original potential must be achieved with complete clarity to reinstate proper experiential neurological functioning. If someone says, "There is nothing wrong with your nerves, it is only ideas which are bothering you," the statement is paradoxical because, due to the influence of pathological ideas, the nerves do 'suffer' and such suffering over a long period of time does become physical suffering. We need this total approach to abolish the artificial boundaries caused by simplistic thinking. The images must be equated with neurological conditions, and the method of how to abolish pathological images in order to restore the organism to a perfect neurological condition must be found. (pp. 16-17)

The Expectation High and the Executive Ego

Life in its healthy state is made up of a series of self-realizing events that represent effective experiences for fruitful living. Conditioning represents only a temporary movement toward a forced behavior, and away from natural expression. States of expectancy and anticipation such as those expressed in the Expectation High represent a full and heightened inner state of activation which, in turn, dynamically directs the organism toward engagement with the experience. When one pattern of activity is no longer useful, new ones arise. In its true state the organism is energetic, alert, and engaged, actively moving toward success. In this state there is optimism and positive anticipation toward the future. Even when thwarted, the intrinsic dynamism toward life remains intact.

In its experiential form, the Expectation High is in perfect balance with the operation of the Executive Ego. As the pressing demands of organizing information from the external and internal environments bombard the ego structure, a habituated pattern of selection and response arises which becomes fixed and repetitive, inhibiting natural and spontaneous expression. As a result, the input processing becomes limited to efficiency in task performance and the organism becomes habituated to a specific mode of operation until it finally becomes attached to memories and habitual solutions to routine problems. The Expectation High is isolated and suppressed while habits and mechanistic solutions become predominant.

In its role as an organizer and manager of incoming information, the Executive Ego categorizes all events according to specific positive or negative criteria. Positive images are releasing and rich with potential while negative images exert a limiting influence and dominate consciousness in a unipolar way, as seen in obsessive thought, phobias and addictions. As the Executive Ego goes through critical states of involvement with experiences, it generates, separates and then centralizes the events around the two opposing nuclei. The Executive Ego can never fixate on both poles simultaneously; it accepts one and rejects the other, the negative choice resulting in an imbalanced state containing a single strong negative image, suggesting a unipolar configuration.

The effect of the Executive Ego's attempt to organize the barrage of incoming information efficiently can be seen in the process of recalling a particular memory event. For instance, an individual who has recently gone through an experience will initially recall the experience in totality – the visual cues or image (I), the physical and emotional reactions (S), and the overall meaning and significance (M) – as if it were being lived through all over again. However, as time passes, the person will begin to recall the experience with fewer details, relying on those cues that will quickly call up the event for reference according to the category the Executive Ego has assigned to it. As more time passes, the habitual process of recall becomes more rigid and routine and all other components of the experience drop out completely. Eventually, the person will recall only the visual memory and will not refer to the other relevant somatic and meaning patterns which once originated with it. As a result of efficiently reducing the experience to chromatic values, other key elements of the event are suppressed. The associated somatic response becomes separated from the ISM eidetic image unity and haunts the person in its detached state as an organic disturbance. While the main objective of the Executive Ego was to insure an impersonal and unemotional recollection of the event for more efficient functioning, it has relegated the person to a desomatized life.

Autosuggestion
    Because the Executive Ego develops a highly efficient and mechanical view of reality and mixes it with autosuggestion (i.e., more drinking is more positive), it compels the person to cooperate with its limited point of view. However, a person is still drawn to states of desire and anticipation which embody the Expectation High while never truly being able to achieve it, integrate it and act on it. Repeatedly exposed to the habitual routine of the Executive Ego with its limited expression, the individual slowly feels drained and exhausted. The Executive Ego, in this final form, is a highly efficient organizational robot which relies on a network of easily accessible experiences and the power of autosuggestion to indirectly exploit the energies of the Expectation High. At this point, the constraints of superficial reason and autosuggestion appear to work hand in hand, sabotaging the organism's true intention, the expression of a true high state of being. Alcohol and drugs become identified as a means to this end, and through the process of autosuggestion the organism convinces itself of the truth in its pursuit, no mat-

ter how contrary the actual experience may be. As Donovan
and Marlatt (1980) state:

> How an individual expects to feel under the influence
> of alcohol does not always correspond to actual affec-
> tive states while intoxicated. Subsequent drinking is
> built on more autosuggestion and its failure to pro-
> duce the desired effect. A person will continually
> repeat the process in the hope that the true state will be
> achieved. There is a progressive mixture of failure and
> autosuggestion and more alcohol or drug use over
> time endlessly repeating the cycle of failure. (p. 1159)

The notion of autosuggestion is important. At certain times,
an eidetic image or ISM may become embedded in the mind in
a manner that it resides outside awareness until it begins to
exert power. When reality testing has been diminished in some
way (e.g., through stress or fatigue) or is overshadowed by
strong emotions (such as those associated with addiction), the
Executive Ego can repeatedly and negatively reinforce itself
independent of outside reality (i.e., drinking more alcohol produces more euphoria). There is a progressive decrease of sensitivity to a variety of stimuli and information. At this point the
body response appears to detach from the real experience and
procure a life of its own.

To illustrate this point, Ahsen (1989a) recounts the following
anecdote in which various aspects of the mind were found to be
in a very clear and conflicted interlock typical of autosuggestion. It appears that in autosuggestion there may be a condition
in which the Executive Ego has become divided into two roles,
that of the suggester and that of the suggestee.

A Case of Autosuggestion

"I was attending a conference and had just come
down from my room in the hotel to have breakfast
with a woman I knew who was also participating in
the conference. She had asked for a brief discussion

of something over breakfast in the cafe. When I came down to join her, I said that I would pay for my own bill, although she had offered to pay for me. I was somewhat in a hurry, and halfway through the breakfast I asked for my bill from the waiter. Meanwhile, I suddenly remembered that I had something of urgency to attend to in my room. At this thought, I quickly left the breakfast half finished and said that I would be back immediately and finish the breakfast. After five minutes, I returned from my room and resumed eating breakfast. At the end of breakfast, I said to my breakfast companion, 'Where is the bill? The waiter is late with the bill.' She replied, 'Oh, don't worry about that. I paid the bill.' I suddenly felt very embarrassed. I vaguely suspected that I had been too busy with my thoughts and did not notice the waiter who came to the table while I was eating and the bill was paid by my companion. I questioned myself, 'Why the hell didn't I notice the waiter?' I did not connect in my mind that the waiter had come during my absence and the bill was paid while I was away in my room attending the urgent business. Due to pressure and hurry, the separate time segments, of my absence from the table, and the waiter coming and the bill being paid during my absence, did not interconnect in my mind. Instead, the sudden information that the bill had been paid threw into high gear my feeling of embarrassment that I was too damned engrossed in my own thoughts while eating breakfast, not noticing at all the waiter, who stood near my elbow with the bill. In fact, I began to see images of the waiter which were very strong and seemed like a recall of what really took place while I was eating breakfast. I even actually saw images of the waiter coming, presenting my bill, the breakfast companion paying it, and these images ran before me like a movie. These images appeared near the periphery of the visual field while I was narrowly focused on the breakfast plate and my thoughts. The images were so strong that they gave me a feeling of recall of a real event which did take place. The images were so authentic that each time I saw them I experienced a feeling of shock. Finally, I came out of my sense of embarrassment and said to my breakfast companion, 'Why did you pay my bill? You know that I was supposed to pay it. We had agreed to that.' She said, 'Don't bother please, it was not much. The bill came when you went upstairs to your room. It was a very small bill.' I suddenly heaved a sigh of relief, finding that the payment didn't take place while I was present. However, the image of the waiter standing there with the bill continued to remain very active in my mind. My other sense of having seen the event actually take place was so strong that it was impossible to get rid of the image. The image had somehow positioned itself in such a vantage point in my consciousness, that I was finding it impossible to push it back. I could not say, 'Eh, this was only my imagination.' Every time the image recurred, it came back with the same feeling of being completely real.

"After this brief episode, I left the breakfast table knowing the full story about this waiter in my head. I was now in the conference hall, but in my head I was still struggling with this as-if memory, trying to reduce it to what it really was; a piece of my own imagination. I was finding it very difficult, and a couple of times even a thought came to my mind, was the woman being courteous to me and was she not telling me the true story, that I really sat there while the waiter was being paid by her in my own presence? I knew, to be sure, according to the time logic, that this was not true, and that the bill had been paid during my absence. However, these images were so strong that they had built their own separate reality with the whole convincing rationale of being true. I could clearly see that my ability to imagine lucidly had in some way gotten out of hand at the time when there was some possibility of my memory playing a trick on me. I knew that during one moment in the complex sequence of events, the reality testing had gotten a bit confused, failing to recall correctly on my behalf my real absence and so forth and connecting that with the bill being paid by the gracious lady. The brief moment when all these forces got a temporary opportunity, a kind of reprieve from the reality testing mechanism, they were all let loose in their original ferocity.

"In this way, the function of imagination revealed to me what it was really capable of doing, if and when it could get hold of the Executive Ego. During the rest of the conference I continued to struggle with the image. It was very fascinating for me to see how the powerful autosuggested image tended to pop into my mind every time with the same feeling of reality.

"Even after passage of a complete month since the incident took place, I could still see the waiter with the same original intensity. Surprisingly, however, to the original scenario was added another feature that also had been secretly added from nowhere. I was now seeing the waiter with a smirk on his face, as if he was saying to me. 'Are you still busy re-inventing parts of that story to avoid your embarrassment?' Over this period the waiter had developed a strange independence in my mind, like a character in a novel, although I knew that it was just an image in my head. What amused me most was how my imagination was now impishly poised to claim even more independence if I gave it a chance. The image was not being suggested to me by myself, it was now suggesting itself to me. Originally, it came as a result of the conversation, which was erroneously interpreted by me to mean that the waiter came when I was eating, although no words were said to that effect. The imagery had not been suggested to me by myself, but I had put myself into some kind of empty state of

mind or trance to receive it, being a product of a perfectly normal piece of real occurrences which could
be easily misinterpreted in the way that I did. The
feeling of embarrassment on my part had been also
perfectly expected. The image, as a whole, therefore,
could be categorized as a product of autosuggestion
because I basically did it to myself, and since it had
no basis in reality, it was an autosuggestion. Yet as I
have shown above, this was a very normal occur-
rence in every way, so to speak." (pp. 66-68)

As illustrated in the above example, the power of autosuggestion, when coupled with the persuasive force of the
Executive Ego and fueled by the intensity of a strong emotion,
can take on a life of its own, producing its own creation independent of external reality. Peele (1989) made a similar observation: "One of the key dynamics in the alcoholism or addiction
cycle is the repeated failure of the alcoholic or addict to gain
exactly the state that he or she seeks, while still persisting in the
addicted behavior. For example, alcoholics report that they
anticipate alcohol to be calming, yet when they drink, they
become increasingly agitated and depressed. The process
whereby people desperately pursue some feeling that becomes
more elusive the harder they pursue it is a common one, and
appears among compulsive gamblers, shoppers, over-eaters,
love addicts and the like. It is this cycle of desperate search, temporary or inadequate satisfaction, and renewed desperation
that most characterizes addiction" (p. 151). There is a repeated
attempt over time to recapture a state that was not actually present in the experience but rather a product of autosuggestion,
containing an idea that more drinking produces more euphoria.

Operations of the Executive Ego

The Expectation High is a special state of ego functioning in
which the person wants to express the elation and expansion
of the Self, a positive condition which has been covered up by

developmental constraints. Against this the Executive Ego uses only a mechanistic view of reality and mixes it with suggestion and compels the organism to cooperate with its limited point of view (Ahsen 1988b, p. 36). Despite the Executive Ego's attempt to limit expression, the person is still drawn to desire and anticipation. This struggle is illustrated in the following report from Ahsen (1988b) in which the subject is reflecting on the impact of the Executive Ego's constraints on the expression of the Expectation High.

JL, Male, Age 45

"To initiate behavior of my own, there is an anxiety there. Although I am doing what I wanted to do, I have been doing what others wanted me to do.

"I see that to initiate behavior of my own I have to start from the Expectation High. Another word for that state for me is the manic condition. In the manic state I will do what I want to do. Before this state hits you, you feel that you are carrying a ton of bricks. In the Expectation High, the bricks are lifted from my chest. I had always felt that at birth I got a life sentence and I did not know it. Perhaps a struggle against this kind of feeling is played out by everyone in my life. But that is what I feel the main feeling of my own life is all about; a struggle between these two main mood swings and you do not know where you actually belong.

"At this point I began to think in terms of movies, which I usually do. In the French film, *A Day in the Country*, a free spirited young woman who cannot pull her life together experiences flashbacks to her childhood in which her mother admonishes her, 'You want too much, you want too much, too much.' This reminds me that my mother too, expressed similar feelings. She would say of famous or successful people – 'What do they want out of life, anyway...They want too much!' And she would say to me – 'Get wise to yourself, you want too much,' in a tone simi-

lar to the mother in the movie – a tone of admonish-
ment and put-down. For in her mind, 'to want' itself
was somehow wrong. My mother did not want success for her children. What she wanted, on the other
hand, was that her children would stay close to God
and the Sacraments. To her, success was at odds with
this and with being good. Oh, there was nothing
wrong with hard work, but with success, in her
words, – 'Well, the grace of God before it.' In her
vocabulary the word, 'poor' was a synonym for
goodness, kindness, and virtue – an endearing com-
pliment – thus, poor George, poor Mike, poor Anne,
etc. Success – acting on high expectations – preclud-
ed being good and mediocrity became a virtue. I find
depression lurking here. Now, there is obviously
some truth in this concept, since success can be a trap
and an obstacle to some ethical behavior. But there is
also some stupidity in this notion. The idea goes
unchallenged because it is framed in religious trap-
pings. Some people use God to validate their preju-
dices and to put them above examination. Who can
argue with God! Or maybe it's all nothing more than
the mundane proclivity, passed down generation
upon generation – that irresistible urge to burst the
bubble – to put down anyone with high expectations.

"And yet my mother admired ambition in others,
particularly if it was middle class or excessively
practical. I can still hear her remarking that, 'So-
and-so is ambitious. You have to give them credit
for that; they're ambitious, smart and successful.'
As if these were unique special gifts – to tally out of
the ordinary – and when she talked this way she
wasn't talking about Thomas Edison or Donald
Trump. She was talking about ordinary people. I
can also hear my mother admonishing me. 'You're
not going to go out of your mind if you don't get
anywhere as an artist. You're not going to lose your
mind are you?'

"These comments were not addressed to any

grandiosity on my part. These were addressed to my simple desire to be an artist and my expression of it. She was suspicious of the natural tendency in me toward the Expectation High.

"I believe her attitudes with respect to success, actually with respect to failure, were more grounded in the separation between Expectation High and Executive Ego than in any religious view of the ethical limitation of success. And when I add this to my father's neutrality, his inability to express interest or encouragement, I begin to see the origin of my secretiveness concerning my desire and my feelings of 'What's the use?' I felt obliged to keep my desires hidden if only to preserve them. In such attitudes, theirs and mine, I believe the separation began in me. For somehow, 'wanting' is itself unseemly and shameful – and denied – well, that is just good manners. Case in point. I can remember as a child visiting family friends and when asked if I'd like a piece of cake, I recall responding resolutely, "No, no, thank you," even though I was dying for it – anticipating the gooey icing. But I would say, 'no' and 'no' again and again until my mother interceded and I'd agree to have a piece of cake. As I got older I realized that some people consider refusal in children a measure of good behavior. But not, I believe, that such denial (even in its more subtle forms such as rationalizations, negative projections, sour grapes, reminding oneself, 'Why should I bother, for the experience will only pass away anyhow – I'll get over it,' or protracted procrastination – putting action off till the desire fades) are based on the separation of the Executive Ego and Expectation High. At a young age I began to practice self-denial. (I think this is a particularly religious disease.) I am reminded here of the conventional maxim – diabetics are starving in the midst of plenty. In my mind's eye, I see both an image of that gooey Cushman layer cake and an image of my brother who was diabetic.

"Depression seems an obvious result of the separation of the Executive Ego and Expectation High,
but what of the effect of this separation in the body
rather than the psyche? What of the physical ramifications? Blood sugars and a pancreas that works
erratically. They too, seem to be the result of the separation between desire and execution. Perhaps, due
to the image of my brother, I compulsively feel that
diabetes is a symptom of this separation. I am also
reminded of how I sabotage myself, my own expectations – particularly when I begin to entertain exe-
cuting them. Perhaps this is why I feel that I often
was not able to enjoy myself. At the threshold of
action, at the possibility of execution, I become anxious. Thus, I engage my expectations only mentally
as fantasies; I do this to avoid anxiety. But, I would
not call such fantasies sublimations. For in sublima-
tion, desire is acted upon, albeit, in a modified and/
or soundly acceptable manner; whereas, in ego fantasies the issue is precisely the inability to act, the
refusal to act. For me personally, this has a lot to do
with a major depression that has stolen a large por-
tion of my life and which continues to limit my getting and going somewhere with my life. Thus, I still
feel doomed, fated, even though I am no longer
deeply depressed. I have called this separation the
wall – a barrier between myself and action. I have
also registered the complaint, that for me, even to
desire involves anxiety and a feeling of impending
loss. I become uncomfortable (like I want to get out
of my skin) at the point where I seriously entertain
acting upon my deeper expectations. There is a hur-
dle here, and I usually have to just jump over it –
even in small matters – to get on with my life. I do
not believe that this anxiety is just disguised excitement, as it sometimes is for shy people. In me this
anxiety has dread and nausea in it. For me, to desire
in reality rather than in fantasy involves discomfort.
Consequently, I do not always act upon my expec-

tations. The words of the song, 'Georgie Girl' – 'You're always window shopping but never stopping to buy' – says it all, not only with respect to my purchasing but also with respect to the things which I contemplate doing. I think about them over and over, but in the end I give up on them. I pass them by. I practice self-denial not as a religious ideal or discipline. I practice it compulsively, even like a pact with death.

"Consequently, failure, or more accurately, a sense of threat of failure (in actuality, it is not authentic failure, since I would have to act in order to fail) poisons my ability to act upon my expectations. I fail before I begin by failing to begin. I procrastinate not only over what is painful and unpleasant – I procrastinate over what is pleasurable and good. For me procrastination is not just a tactic of waiting, or patience – it is a way of avoidance, a way of stalling until one no longer desires. I have often expressed this lack of desire by quoting the Scripture, 'If the salt of the earth loses its flavor, with what shall it be salted?' This I have stated as a particularly central issue in my life. What happens when desire is lost? Through procrastination I lost my desire to act and my Executive Ego became neutralized; that is, it became separate from action and engaged consequently only in fantasy, which in the end only testified to my inability to act and further feelings of self-contempt. Thus, I felt invalidated, like some sort of anomaly or invalid.

"I believe that the separation of the Expectation High from the Executive Ego originates because society and parents perpetuate it. They install it in children as an internal mechanism of control. This installment is both willful and unwillful, non-conscious and conscious. It prevents people from acting. It puts them into a state, a sort of limbo between desire and enactment. It is a state of anxious waiting and of reoccurring hope and hopelessness. And so

people waste their lives and begin to detest themselves. They cannot take the initiative and thus idle
and waste away. I see this in other members of my
family. I believe that it may also be the hidden
specter behind teenage suicides – for in the case of
those who come into the prime of their lives physically and mentally, the pressures that accompany this
state and the inability to act must be so explosive that
an individual would almost have to self-destruct –
particularly, if secondary relief systems were wanting.
I am thinking of Mellencamp's song, 'Jack and Diane'
– 'Life goes on, long after the thrill of living is gone,'
or Neil Young, 'It's better to burn than rust away.'

"A life lived in this separation is like a life sentence
where real death is liberation. This is why convicts
have understood the psychological and metaphysical
ramifications inherent in Becket's *Waiting for Godot*
and academics have not. To paraphrase Becket, the
doctor with forceps, the grave digger with the spade,
are one and the same. This separation is the disease
of our time – T.S. Eliot's 'whimper rather than a bang'
and Heidegger's view that our time is too late for
man, too early for the gods and so we must wait. For
me wanting, waiting and wishing are all tied together. Wanting turns to waiting — turns to wishing and
ultimately to despair and then to the beginning of the
whole cycle again.

"The separation of the Expectation High from the
Executive Ego also leads to the separation of mind
from body. One needs the body to engage in reality
but one only needs the mind to engage in fantasy.
Thus, as one becomes removed from the execution of
expectation, one no longer needs the body. When
wish fulfillment replaces actions, the body becomes
superfluous. I believe that this is why I was left back
in school and was always such a klutz. I was not in
my body, I was in my mind. Thus, I was not attentive
to what was happening all around me. This is why I
was a terrible athlete. I was not in my body. I did not

strike the high note. I did not uncover the Expectation High." (pp. 38-42)

Dynamic Natural States in the Expectation High

The case history of the dog Reiner, one of Ahsen's clinical allegories, provides an interesting lesson concerning the Expectation High. As Ahsen (1979a) writes: "a dog does not lose hope in life but humans do. In contrast to the animal, a person goes one step beyond, into a condition of self-imposed fixation on negativism and hopelessness" (p. 18). Ahsen proposes that Nature keeps reality awareness spontaneously available to the dog, but human beings go beyond this and interpret the cause of depression in an overly negative and fixated manner. This adds memory and its prejudiced leanings to the situation and turns it into a symbolic trauma. When a person broods over a transitory trauma, the result can be isolation from one's true nature, attachment to memory mechanisms and new levels of interpretation that even justify the memory fixation. The person, however, unlike the dog, is without natural grace but can learn freedom from fixation through scientific investigation. Through the scientific process, the person can find new hope as he or she replays and investigates important pieces of inner reality. As Ahsen states, imagery releases life in its original form with dynamism and happiness, along with the Expectation High.

The case history of Reiner is reproduced below from Ahsen (1979), graphically illustrating these important aspects.

Case History: Reiner

Reiner is a nice, well-behaved dog, young in years and capable of vital energetic behavior. Not a very long time back, only three years ago, for a period of two years, he was regularly taken out for a 15-minute walk every day, at 6:30 pm, by the father of the family, Mr. Tompkins. When Mr. Tompkins would be away at his job, Reiner always spent his time lying around in the basement. However, with clock-like regularity, at approximately 6:00 pm, the time of Mr. Tompkins' return, Reiner would always come upstairs and pace the floor. Then he would sit near the door, at times looking around, especially toward Mr. Tompkins if he was home, in anticipation of the evening walk. Reiner would also emit excited sounds and show playful behavior in the general vicinity of Mr. Tompkins. As soon as Mr. Tompkins would say the words "walk" or "leash," Reiner would respond by jumping up and down then running to the basement, where his leash was kept. After the leash was procured, he would slip excitedly into the collar and then would lash out for a 15-minute walk with Mr. Tompkins.

This had been the pattern of life for two years. The third year, Mr. Tompkins had to be out of town for almost a whole year. During this time, Reiner underwent a sequence of behavior changes and adjustments totally spontaneous in nature. The behavior changes occurring during the first two years and the year following are listed in order of appearance and their significance is discussed briefly.

1. *High Event*. The first two years in the Tompkins' household was a very happy and buoyant period for Reiner. The evening walk was the high event, and it represented the essence of his life. He looked forward to it with no previous training whatever. He did not need to be taught to enjoy pleasure and freedom, it came to him effortlessly. The evening walk was truly a high event bringing release and fulfillment of his nature.

Reiner showed a willingness to learn almost anything within his capabilities, if it was presented as a condition for the walk; for example, he would wear the collar peacefully, even excitedly. He even developed spontaneously the behavior of picking up the

ball when thrown during the walk because it pleased
his master. The evening walk was very central to the
learning of these responses.

2. *High Expectation.* During the two years prior to
Mr. Tompkins' departure, Reiner showed a consistent mood of positive anticipation regarding the
evening walks. He knew that the high event was
always predictable, that it occurred without any significant break in the regularity. He was aware of this
predictable reality at various levels, and he offered
postures toward it in the form of a totally internal
process, probably imagistic in nature, as Mowrer has
suggested.

Reiner's primary behavior at the time of the
evening walk reflected heightened buoyancy at
many levels. It directly derived its character from
his internal imagery experience involving the high
event and was reflected in intense pleasurable
behavior which was both reality related and fantasy based. To whatever was directly or indirectly
connected with the high event, Reiner responded
with positive expectation. The idea of the walk
prompted even an element of fore enjoyment and
reverie: in that at the utterance of the words "walk"
or "leash" he would jump up and down excitedly.
Just as poets have written that they "enjoy" the daf-
fodils in a poetic fancy, Reiner enjoyed the high
event in dog fantasy.

3. *Futurism.* Reiner appeared to have a firm belief
in the future reality of the evening walk, that from the
start of each day, events would lead up to the high
event. This was proven by his general behavior and
by the fact that his whole behavior changed when
Mr. Tompkins suddenly stopped taking him out for
the walk. He started to become sullen from the first
hours of the day and remained withdrawn and
depressed from then onward. If he had not believed
in the continued future reality of the walk and was

not clearly protesting against the unfortunate turn of
events, he would not have responded with morose-
ness from the beginning of the day. He was truly
futuristic in his attitudes.

Reiner, however, did not give in to depression
immediately after Mr. Tompkins' departure. He continued to hope for some time and this hope was mir-
rored in some positive activity. By his look, he would
implore Mr. Tompkins' daughter and son to take him
out for the evening walk and he would try to follow
them out the door. Reiner really knew what he wanted. He even tried to coax them into responding affir-
matively by his efforts to please them such as by wag-
ging his tail. Finally, after continued rejection, he
showed separation from them characterized by clear
signs of anger, irritation and sullenness.

Reiner was quite aware of the reality of events and
adjusted accordingly. When the daughter took him
out for a walk, he was very pleased and friendly with
her and there was a marked change in his behavior
by the next morning after the first outing. But when
she finally stopped taking him out, he again became
sullen. However, he was not as indifferent toward
her as he was toward the son, who never took him
out and from whom he became completely detached.

4. *Reality Replay.* In place of the walk in the
evening, Reiner now began to sit in the living room
before a huge picture window which looked into the
woods. There he watched leaves and birds and sometimes acted in a hallucinatory way, as if he were outside. But his excitement and buoyancy revealed that
he was still aware of reality; he seemed to know that
he was inside the house, and not outside. He knew
exactly what he was missing and why and had not
been confused into a total acceptance of the new conditions. In short, he had not yet been conditioned into
an acceptance of a new hopeless interpretation of life,
that once life goes away it never returns and whatever loss has filled in the horrible vacuum, it must be

embraced with total resignation. In fact, such a total conditioning could never occur in him, due to the fact that he was a whole being, having an unconditional gift of life within.

In the last stages, Reiner became ultimately depressed and was guided by the final pre-attentive scanning signal, called here the "Sokolov Signal" (this signal did not appear in full detail like a vivid conscious picture but as a brief scanning signal containing a picture of the reality which he had lost. All other expectations were arranged behind this signal, which was non-conscious and all but invisible at the surface, but it was vigorously operative under the surface, as suggested in Sokolov's experiment in which the signal for relief was simultaneously present in the shock). Reiner was with and without hope at the same time, looking for the return of reality. On the surface he was withdrawn and slept most of the time in a state of depression, but under the surface he was still watching the flow of events. This permanent negative posture of depression toward a permanent negative environment concealed a state of high expectation. In this light his depression could not be called a meaningless phenomenon but a highly meaningful Sokolov Signal, a watching without watching.

The Expectation High in Reiner revealed some fundamental levels of behavior and imagery processes connected with states of expectancy and anticipation. His behavior, from the explicit expectation of the walk to the implicit expectation during rejection and dog depression, contained many cogent structures. These structures originated entirely from a great spontaneous source, the Expectation High, which has little to do with his training or learning. Reiner's elated and buoyant behavior manifest during the walk spread over only a 15-minute period; however, the Expectation High behavior extended beyond that, over the 30 minutes prior to the walk and even into the next morning, as the analysis under futurism showed. If closely examined, all of these behaviors such as his anticipation, fore-enjoyment, reverie, even reinforced behavior and his behavior during the actual walk were completely unlearned, originating spontaneously from his personal nature. Reiner's behavior even gave evidence of discerning intelligence, he cleverly courted the second best, the daughter, rather than the son, when he couldn't have the best, the father. Although reality replacement briefly occurred while sitting before the window, he remained aware of reality, aware that he had been forced into a negative condition of existence. Yet his capacity for reality replay in his mind was always ready in case the reality signal changed and circumstances gave his evening walk back to him. Reiner, in the middle of these many structures, in fact, acted like a strategist and a poet. In himself he was hopeful about the future. In the deepest depression, he was still very much alive; he would sit, wait and see. He was attentive and yet not attentive, oriented toward reality yet aware that it was kind of an illusion. (pp. 17-19)

The innate dynamism and resilience of the individual is nowhere more dramatically illustrated than in the states of expectancy and futurism found in the Expectation High. In it resides the core of biological health and well-being. In essence, it represents the sum total of life. Through the demands and disappointments of life, high states are often suppressed by the pressures of everyday reality. Alcohol and drug abuse represent the desperate search and the repeated failure to recover these states through artificial means. Ahsen's eidetic method rescues the Expectation High from alcohol and other drugs and brings it to the forefront of the mind, reinstating hope and the innate enthusiasm for life.

Chapter 5

Methodology:
Core Procedures

The goal of Ahsen's Eidetic Image Therapy in the treatment of alcohol and drug abuse is to retrieve the natural states of positive expectation and expression that promote fulfilling engagement in reality. By linking these states to their proper mental structures, healthful neurological and biological functioning can be restored. Positive states like those found in the Expectation High represent an individual's most basic positive life potential and exist long before any learned behavior.

In Step 1 of treatment, the symptoms are carefully assembled. In Step 2 the Expectation High is untangled from its faulty connection with alcohol and drugs. This is achieved through a detailed investigation of the person's involvement with the substance, both in terms of the present life situation and his or her history with it. As all aspects of the person's experience are closely examined, the power and magic of the drug are demystified. The Expectation High is drawn out and the experience of the natural high is enhanced to correct distorted projections and free the experience from further contamination. In Step 3, the developmental history is reviewed to identify areas of conflict and sources of weakness that may suppress the full expression of the Expectation High. Step 4 involves a realistic appraisal of the current lifestyle and a projection of future realities if the addiction is not fully understood and addressed. Step 5, the final phase of treatment, involves the evolution of a positive philosophy of life and a meaningful lifestyle that is dedicated to productive engagement in the world rather than withdrawal into addiction.

Treatment Methodology

STEP 1

Initial Symptom Report

The Initial Symptom Report provided by the patient upon entering therapy provides a comprehensive picture of complaints. Within the Initial Symptom Report are embedded features such as the current emotional state along with its ISM dynamics and variations. Viewing the Initial Symptom Report from this perspective is preparatory to a deep understanding of the eidetic material revealed during the treatment, as the following examples illustrate.

a. The person may initially describe the problem in terms of present feelings and emotions, without reflection or disclosure of history. The problem may be reported somatically (S only) with no content, meaning (M) or image (I).

Example. The person may say, "I am feeling terrible. I don't know what is wrong with me."

b. The person may intellectually report the problem or be in a Meaning (*M*) mode. In this case, the person will analyze or report about the problem. There is a dissociation from the emotional experience and no somatic component in the report.

Example. "I think what bothers me most of the time is an issue with procrastination; it seems to affect my work on various projects."

c. The person may describe the problem by recalling or reflecting on events of the past. In this case, there are dissociated segments of images which the person may superficially hold to in an attempt to justify the current problem. The problem is described in terms of fragmented images (*I* aspect only).

Example. The person may say, "I remember my sister used to pick on me all the time and my parents always took her side. I never had any real support, which is why I started to drink."

The Initial Symptom Report will also reveal an individual's emotional orientation toward the problem through reference to time, as follows.

a. The person may be nostalgically oriented toward the past and blame people in the past for the present condition. If the person lives only in the past, there is no experience of the present, its realities or opportunities, and no reference to the future.

b. The person may be oriented toward the present and be constantly immersed in the discomfort and emotional pain of the problem. If there is no connection with the past, there is no understanding of why and how the present came into being, nor is there hope because there is no sense of the future.

c. The person may only be oriented toward the future and have no reference to either the past or the present. If there is no reference to either past or present, there is no sense of reality and experience to draw upon, thus the past cannot provide knowledge nor can the present provide opportunities for the future.

RT, Male, Age 36

Initial Symptom Report

"The major reason I came to this city is that I was drinking too much alcohol. I was getting more depressed. I wasn't working and had a difficult time finding work. I had stopped going to the gym. I was in a relationship for two years which wasn't very good to begin with and it just got worse as time went on. I was having difficulty in school, finishing my thesis, my relationship was getting worse and I was just watching my whole life get worse. It was like watching a movie and seeing all the areas but I couldn't figure out how to fix any of the problems. I saw no solutions. I stopped drinking and all the problems were still there and I still don't see any solution. The problems are not as bad now that I am sober, but they are still there and they always bother me. I don't have any relief from this relationship. It is not healthy. It is like alcohol. I like alcohol and it is not good for me. I like Joanne but she is not good for me. I think the one thing I miss is the drive. I used to be able to go to work and go twelve to fifteen hours a day, and I just don't have that anymore. That scares me. I need to finish my thesis. I miss teaching. I don't have the drive to get started, I don't know what it is, whether it is initiative or something else. When it gets like that I lose my focus on what is important and then I don't have the drive or the initiative to move forward and I can't figure out the solution on my own. It is very confusing. I don't experience any inner focus or vision. I am always preoccupied with my relationship or school. I am just distracted all of the time. It is worse during the day and lately I have liked the nights much better because they are quieter and more peaceful."

STEP 2

First Substance Use Experience (FISUE)

The next step in the treatment process is to gather information about the person's first experience with alcohol or drugs as a way of beginning to decipher the underlying expectancies that became associated with the experience. The person's first experience with the substance represents a critical event because it was at this very point that the Expectation High was activated. Subsequent alcohol and drug use is built on a distortion of the memory of the original experience as one in which the "high" was actually believed to have been achieved. Interestingly, when subjects are asked to compare their expectations to their first experience, they consistently reported that their expectations were not met and they did not, in fact, experience the high they had hoped for. Only after a few tries did they experience the high.

Peele (1989) reports that the first-time opiate user often reports unpleasant feelings of fear and anxiety or dysphoria as compared to the euphoria that is attributed to the drug. Within the first experience, therefore, lies the undiscovered core of the Expectation High and the mechanism which enabled alcohol and drugs to usurp its expression and power. In Eidetic Image Therapy the Expectation High is drawn out of the first substance use experience and concentrated on, first through recall and then through imagery. Through the process of concentration and enhancement, the person begins to identify the various aspects of the experience and the positive states connected with the Expectation High which have been lost, as follows.

Identifying the Expectation High

1. *Recall the first experience with alcohol or the drug. (The details of the event are recorded in the person's own words. This maintains a sense of internal consistency and preserves the links of the event.)*
2. *Concentrate on and enhance the first substance use experience so that various aspects become clear.*
3. *Bring the specific elements to light so that you can decipher the underlying expectations. (The information will be segmented into*

specific components, both positive and negative, to break the event
down into its discrete elements and thereby demystify it.)
4. *Repeatedly explore the specific segments in the event.*
5. *Concentrate on those elements which have greatest meaning and*
validity to remove any confusion.

The following case examples illustrate this process.

MM, Male, Age 22
First Use of Marijuana

"The first time I used drugs, I thought that it
makes things more interesting, a little different. It creates a little adventure. It was fun, it was a little exciting. It was pretty innocent. I did not experience a
high the first time but the second time. I can recapture the high. I don't know whether I want to. When
I am asked to recapture it, I don't want to. It is totally finished, the drug business. I want to leave it. On
the second request to experience it, I feel a little sorry.
Maybe there is a little guilt there or something. I
know it is all over now. If I went back to relive my
life, I would probably do the same thing over. I made
a lot of trouble for myself and for everybody around
me. If it was up to me, I would still do the same thing.

"I don't experience any temptation to go back to
it. I experience the memory as distasteful; it makes
me sick. The memory is not without an edge, though.
If it was edgeless, I would not worry about remem-
bering it. Trying to forget it is like having a bad taste
in my mouth. When I think about it, there is still a
connection left. I never thought about it, but I recognize it now."

Gathering the information in this way brings the first experience into focus. In this case it is evident that although there is an
effort to forget the memory and the entire experience, there is a
residue and a somatic response, "It makes me sick...a bad taste
in my mouth," which still retains some kind of power in the
individual's mind.

PK, Male, Age 57

"I was twenty when I had my first drink and that was something sweet like cider. I did not like beer. I would drink the odd beer, but I really did not enjoy it. I was probably experimenting. I can remember trying stout and I had a half glass of it and became dizzy and went into the bathroom and threw up. Around that time, I think I was experimenting, and that experimenting convinced me that I did not like stout but apple cider. I liked it and did drink sherry at home but only after my father's death. I was twenty when he died. I am not sure that I ever drank before his death. I never drank hard liquor until I was twenty-four and that was gin and tonic. When I left home I thought it was high time I introduce myself to gin and tonic and I found that I liked the taste. I would not drink very much in those days. I was a social drinker. I drank sherry at home. It was confined to having a glass of sherry before Sunday dinner, after my father died. I think if I were to get to the core, I probably felt free after my father's death to have a glass of sherry in the house.

"The first time I had a drink, I remember I had finished playing a rugby game and the team went into the bar. I felt – well, everyone else was having a drink so I would have a drink. At this point going to a bar was new to me. I chose what I perceived to be a fairly mild sweet drink. This is after high school, when I was in the university. It was fall, the fall after my father's death. I remember before the moment I had the drink, I was sort of apprehensive about what this thing was going to do to me. I think I felt more apprehension than any expectation of pleasure. I went into the club house and the club house had a bar. I had just joined this club so I did not know these people and many of them were older than I was. It was a strange environment for me. Someone asked me if I would like a drink. I thought cider would be socially acceptable. It was mostly consumed by women, which is why I thought it was safe, but it was also a thirst quencher, so I thought it would not be unusual for a man to have a glass of cider after physical exertion, so I thought it was a good choice. There was a social expectation. I had left high school and thought that it was high time that I had a drink and joined the adults. Part of the culture was that there was no drinking in high school so that the graduates coming out of high school really did not drink on the sly. There is some unease in the situation for me. In effect I was saying to myself, 'It is time you had a drink, you are living in an adult world.' What was mingled with it was a feeling of apprehension, but I was going for it anyway. The other people were doing it, including my brother, and it seemed okay for them, so why not? And there was also the feeling that I was able to make the decision. The high experience includes these things, taking risks, being an adult, making decisions.

"In recent years my drinking has taken on a pattern. I used to drink socially and gradually the number of drinks increased and it occurred to me that I needed the drinks, particularly I needed the sixth or seventh drink. I never drink during the rest of the day and never drink after dinner. But I figured out that there is almost a purpose to this. I have a fairly strong feeling of depression. I go through the day with a sense of anxiety and when I arrive home I feel like I have completed the day's work and I have earned a release from the feelings of depression and the lack of self-worth. The alcohol does that for me. What I am trying to do with alcohol is to cover up the depression and make myself feel better. I often throw up after I drink and it sort of interferes with the feeling, but the drinking is the only time I get out of the depression."

EW, Female, Age 43

"I remember going to a party with my high school boyfriend. I think it was a party after his junior prom. I was a year younger than he was. It is a very clear image for me. I remember walking across the front lawn of the house where the party was going on, and something inside of me seemed to just click, and I decided 'to hell with it.' I was just going to go for it. There was a sense of abandon, of freedom in the decision. I did not care what the consequences were, there was some kind of freedom in it. Up until that point there was a feeling of holding things together. I think I was about fifteen at the time. My home life was very depressing, everyone was always sick or dying. My father had left when I was very young, and I did not see him. My mother was alcoholic. We lived in the basement of my grandfather's apartment. It was very grim. My family was working class poor people whose philosophy of life was 'You're born, you work and you die.' Despite my mother's alcoholism, she always worked. It was all very grim and depressing. There was no freedom in it at all. I remember the feeling of just going for it no matter what the consequences. I remember the alcohol made me very sick, but I can still recall the feeling of freedom in just going for it.

"I think, over the years, my drinking has been really connected to this initial experience. I do it for abandon, for enjoyment, pleasure. Just to hang out and forget about everything. But as in the first experience, it has always made me feel terrible and made me feel even more depressed, which is probably why it never really swept me away completely.

"With drugs, I just wanted to be anesthetized, numbed to my life. Again the theme was abandon, pleasure and, most importantly, relief from the grimness. I preferred drugs that would stop feelings, like tranquilizers or barbiturates, never anything that heightened sensation. Just things that offered relief and the ability to get away from it."

DM, Male, Age 23

"It is like a required part of the fun, part of the ritual. I don't lose control when I drink. I don't get high.

I get drunk but I don't lose control. I will pass out before I will change. I am me personified, magnified, but not offensively. When I get a buzz on, it dulls the periphery. It helps you just enjoy the moment more. It is more pleasant; it makes things more pleasant. It is like wearing sunglasses; it dulls things. It is fun, like a game. It makes things easier so that you don't think about things. It makes it easier to pick up girls. The first time, I was an infant, my father used to put brandy on my gums to put me to sleep. I guess I was geared from the beginning. I was in the seventh grade and we used to keep beer. Nobody drinks beer in my house, we had some for my grandfather. It was summer and we were playing hockey in the basement and it was real hot. We were thirsty and we did not feel like going upstairs so I chugged two sixteen-ounce beers and I was pretty drunk but I was sweating a lot. I don't remember getting sloppy; we just got silly and got real tired. Up until grade nine, I was still a good kid. I did everything that I was supposed to do. But I was a little mischievous. Sometimes I did things that I was not supposed to do. Up until this point, it was just little things. This was a big break from that. I was surprised at my parents' reaction to it. They were so concerned.

"There is a difference between the buzz high and being blasted. With the buzz high, you still feel very much alive, just relaxed. At that point the inhibitions are gone but not dulled to the world. Whatever number of drinks it takes to get to that point, it does not retard my natural state. When I see a person, I see the outline of the person and everything inside the outline is natural and there are these fuzzy things buzzing around their heads, like all of the problems that have not been resolved yet. After about five drinks the black fuzzy things get erased; after six drinks the border around the person starts to be erased and gray because the outside air is getting in the inside and polluting it. It is like being erased.

"I am losing interest in the bar scene, but I do not completely feel like growing up right now. It is nice to hold onto something that you found that you like as long as possible."

SR, Female, Age 40

"Grade nine, there was pleasure in doing what I was not supposed to be doing. It got my father's attention. I always felt that I was on the outside of the group and I had to do something unique for attention. I was like a rebel. My way of having fun was always flirting with danger. I felt freer to be myself with people, with men. I felt uninhibited when I was drinking. I wanted to continue the feeling of floating away from reality. The desire was to float away from reality. The reality was that I did not think that I was good enough the way I was and with the help of alcohol or drugs, I could find the key and unlock the magic that was there. I could not get it without the help of alcohol. I am always comparing myself with others, always feeling I never measure up, always feeling desperate, lonely, hopeless and helpless, always turning to drugs and alcohol to ease the pain and always putting on false pretenses. I would find a partner to associate with who would temporarily make me feel okay about everything, but the feeling would never last and I would never feel good enough. The periods of elation would never last. In high school, I see myself as very rebellious, very angry at my family situation, very left out, associating with the wrong kind of people. My sister had just drowned in the swimming pool and no one had any time to pay attention to me. It was just horrible and I went out to drown my miseries. I would say in that year my drinking really intensified.

"The first time I tried smoking pot, I was in the tenth or eleventh grade. I did not like it, I felt out of control, paranoid, but if I could get drunk enough, then smoke pot, I would like it. I would elevate the craziness. The first time I was with a bunch of guys, and I felt that anything I said would not come out right. Pot had the reverse effect that alcohol had on me. It made me feel more shy, more inadequate, more afraid to participate. I remember that I kept trying to do it because it was the in thing to do, because everyone was doing it. I felt very uncomfortable until I would get alcohol and get really drunk. There are tremendous feelings of insecurity of not measuring up and not being cool enough, wanting to impress the guy that I was with by getting stoned with him. The feelings are of not being good enough. I also remember experiences of crystal methadrine six months later with the same boyfriend, and that seemed like a good experience. I liked the way that it made me feel. I became very talkative. I was funny. I felt like I had a personality, that I was acceptable. The feeling with speed was fun, it was depression with alcohol, there was the feeling of sadness. There were other experiences, a couple with hallucinogenics. I loved how insane and wild one could get with colors and visual effects, but it was more of an individual experience, where I felt no one was paying attention to me and I couldn't control it. Then there were downs. I enjoyed doing them because I felt in control. I felt very sensual. I felt as if I could get other people's approval, especially men. There is a positive feeling with that. I also did a lot of cocaine for a while, at that time. A lot of alcohol, a lot of cocaine and a lot of downs. Then I was so numb most of the time that I wasn't aware of feeling uncomfortable, shy or inadequate."

After the FISUE is recalled, each event is experienced in images in detail, including any values, beliefs, and associated memories. It is replayed in the mind and the positive states are deepened. This focus and concentration enable the original Expectation High to develop clearly in the person's experience. The following imagery exercise illustrates the process of concentration and segmentation. By segmenting the experience into discrete elements, each aspect, both positive and negative, can be fully explored to remove any distortion or inaccurate association with the drug. The aim of this technique is to draw out the Expectation High in its pure essence and demystify the power of the substance.

Segmenting Elements of the Expectation High

1. *See yourself when you took the first drink (drug).*
2. *Just before that moment you were expecting something from it.*
3. *See that you were expecting something, and there was a feeling to it.*
4. *Experience the moment right now.*
5. *The drink did not give you that; you were feeling that before the drink.*
6. *This is the Expectation High. Experience the Expectation High now without the drink and let it become intense, have a peak.*
7. *This is your real self; this is how you should feel in your inner self all of the time. Do not cover it up with alcohol.*

EW, Female, Age 43

"I see myself going to the party, and the feeling of just going for it. There is a feeling of mania, of breaking out of my inhibition, my depression moving toward freedom. When I concentrate on it, there is tremendous energy in it. It is as if I break free of all that grimness, there are no limits. I feel indomitable. When I feel that now, I feel like my body is very powerful, I have a lot of strength, I can see everything at once, yet I can focus clearly. It is as if all of my power has been mobilized. When I feel the Expectation High, I feel there is a primal energy in my body, it focuses my mind and body in the direction of activity. I usually feel depressed and burdened. This feeling makes me feel like I have boundless energy. I feel directed and clear, that there are no limits as to what I can accomplish. With drinking it clouds the issues, de-energizes me. With this feeling there is a very powerful feeling as if I have unlimited resources."

After the Expectation High in the FISUE is identified, segmented and concentrated on so that any confusion regarding its true source is removed, it is repeated several times to enhance and deepen the experience. Any difficulties that may diminish the experience are surfaced and addressed at this time. The process is repeated until the Expectation High is extended into other areas of consciousness.

Extending and Enhancing Experience
of the Expectation High

1. *See yourself a moment before you took the first drink (drug).*
2. *At that moment you were expecting a great feeling.*
3. *See that you are expecting that great feeling.*
4. *Experience the moment right now.*
5. *The drink did not give you that; you were feeling that before the drink.*
6. *This is the Expectation High. Experience the Expectation High now without the drink and let it become intense, have a peak.*
7. *This is your real self; this is how you should feel in your inner self all of the time.*
8. *Allow this experience to extend into other areas of your life.*
9. *See yourself in different situations experiencing this high state.*
10. *Let the experience become intense.*

The images which emerge at this level are always revealing, as the following cases show.

SR, Female, Age 40

"When I see the image of the Expectation High, I now have an image of running through a field of flowers. I am free and smelling nature and totally fulfilled. I feel very moved by it. I look very youthful. I look like a young girl. I see myself enjoying everything around me, I am not desperate, not impatient. Now I feel that I am good. I just had an image of somebody opening my soul and saying, 'It is okay, let it out. Trust yourself.' I feel moved. I have an image of a hand on my head; it is like God's hand or some very powerful person putting his hand on my head saying, 'It is all right, it is all right.' It is a blessing. It is like I have been blessed. It is a godly image. I feel very moved, very peaceful. I feel like I can see this godly image incorporated within myself. It feels comfortable. This feels like my real self."

CB, Male, Age 19

"I remember the first time I drank alcohol, I was a mess. I drank so much I could not walk, barely speak, laughing at everything. Laughing was the biggest thing, I was so relaxed. It was a thrill. My parents were going out and there was so much excitement that they were going out. I also sensed a little bit of nerves. I was doing it behind their backs. That is part of the high. I do not like the nervous thing. It is a combination of plunging into the unknown, doing something that my parents do not know about, something that they would not want me to do. In plunging into the unknown there is excitement and curiosity. I do not understand the nervousness. There is a feeling of a thrill.

"When I feel the curiosity there is still the nervous thing. It is still confusing me. The Expectation High is getting overpowered by the nervousness. My mind is wandering. I can actually feel the nervous thing. It is an obstructed feeling. Right now it is making it hard for me to recall the Expectation High. This is what happens when I get up to do something in my life. When I go back to the feeling of curiosity, I can feel it but it is not as strong as it was before. What is running this energy is that I am doing this behind my parents' back. I can get the Expectation High and feel it.

"When I feel curious and see a girl, it is more positive than with the alcohol. I am curious about her. I am curious and I want to find out what it is all about. Then I think of curiosity, of being a little pest. I see the effectiveness of being a pest. He gets things done. He does not have a barrier. He has curiosity, no holds. I hate getting nervous, the little pest does not get nervous. He has the outlet at his immediate disposal.

"There is a feeling of sexuality in the curiosity. It is

a good feeling. The curiosity has eroticism in it. When I look at the girl, there is this whole other person and what makes it more interesting is the sexual part. She is different and that makes it more interesting. I can see how it works and can grasp it, but still being the way I am it would not come naturally, not like the little pest who has it at his immediate disposal. I can bring it back but it is hard. I feel closer to it now. I did not feel that this existed before. I repressed it before. It is not that I did not know it existed but what holds me back? How do I let it flow?"

   This process is repeated several times to enhance the qualities of the Expectation High and draw out any difficulties that diminish the experience.

   "I see my parents getting ready to go out. I feel excitement that they will not be home. I am excited that I will have more freedom to do what I want. I am thinking about having a good time without any restrictions. I see myself partying with my friends. They are coming in the house. I am able to stay up late. I am about ten or eleven years old. There was a thrill that they were going out. Sometimes I used to go out and set off fireworks. I wanted to use the car, take it out. I would have been interested in having girls over too. It is a nice picture. Me and my friends sit around having a good time. Parents are out, I can do anything I want. I play with girls — do anything I want. I am definitely the center of attention. I am the host; that gives me a high too. I am interested in mostly entertaining people with my brain. I am telling stories to make them laugh and being quick with wit and sarcasm. I am quick-witted. Now I see an image of getting a girlfriend, selecting people that I want to meet and having a band.

   "Now I see myself doing things. I am hang gliding. I see myself circle around my apartment and then around the city, then whipping around in the universe. The stars were going all over the place. I feel the energy and there is also a release, a rebirth. I feel the excitement in the image. I am going to a tropical island. I like it there, it feels like a beach in Greece. I like it there, the history and the myths. It is a place where you have a direct line to God. I am on some kind of quest, I am giving orders. There is another image that is even stronger. I am on a horse and I am with the Huns. I am leading these people into new frontiers. The images are not empty. They are full of surprises."

Through this process of exploring various reported segments, the hidden Expectation High and the positive states associated with it are drawn out and experienced fully. Any false or distorted beliefs and memories are separated and removed from the experience. As this state is explored and developed further, the person begins to clearly decipher the underlying components of the high event and can begin to reinstate the proper orientation toward life.

STEP 3

History with the Parents

The next step is to examine more extensively early developmental states and the emotional history with the parents to uncover areas of obstruction that limit or prevent high emotional expression. Dolan (1977a) describes Ahsen's concept of parents "as foundation images playing a central role as psychical instigators in the development, not only during childhood but also in later life. All pleasure or conflict originates from pleasure or conflict with or between the parents, and the individual receives only the end result of this healthy or disruptive mode of biological functioning. According to Ahsen, the parental images function at the very core of the mind stuff....Thus, the images of the parents appearing in the eidetics in most cases offer clues to the developmental problems being linked with them and needless to mention here that such images differ in quality from ordinary images of the parents" (p. 22). Ahsen (1984a) states in this regard:

> Numerous imagery systems crisscross various levels in the psyche and each system represents a hierarchy of natural pictures for illumination of consciousness. Each hierarchy is approachable through its own special cue-picture and special sequences of consciousness. All hierarchies are however, centrally tied to a universal experience of parents' images. Why? Since the beginning of time, parental figures have been associated with procreation, early support and development of consciousness. The analytic dive into early dramatics of these structures should be conducted through exposing the individual to a sufficiently deep experience of eidetic images of personal parents selected from past history. It is known that much of the neurotic inflexibility stems from fixation on negative experiences from childhood. Since most parents fall short of ideally relating to children, the mind selectively concentrates on the negative memories connected with them. Through systematic enactment of primary image situations involving such scenes as parents in the house, parents' interactions with each other and with children and parents' positive and negative behaviors and body images in a variety of biological relationships, the individual can come to grips with a new awareness of his primary consciousness. Later on when the same images are progressed towards more interaction, it enables the mind to view emotional issues from a more creative angle. (p. 62)

Through administration of a series of image scenarios which depict the parents in a variety of important situations, the emotional climate of developmental history is revealed. The Eidetic Parents Test was devised by Ahsen to especially reveal the relationship with the parents at various levels of the mind from infancy to adulthood. Within the eidetic structures resides important information regarding the relationship with the parents which provides significant material regarding the evolution of the addiction. When a parent has an undiagnosed alcohol or drug problem, it will be revealed through the test.

The Eidetic Parents Test images follow with a brief explanation regarding the meaning and significance of each image scene (see also Appendix B for stepwise EPT instructions; for extensive analysis and explanation of EPT images, see Ahsen's *Eidetic Parents Test and Analysis*, 1972). The person is asked to let the image form in the mind as the instruction is being read and to allow any thoughts, feeling or memories to develop. The description is then recorded in the person's own words.

Eidetic Parents Test

EP1. IMAGE: HOUSE
Picture your parents in the house where you lived most of the time with them, the house which gives you the feeling of a home. Where do you see them? What are they doing? How do you feel when you see the images? Are there any memories connected with this picture?

The house is a key image that reveals immense information about the relationship with the parents and siblings and the atmosphere in the home. The home should create feelings of security and warmth in the child. As the subject concentrates on these figures, the feelings attached to them become clear and early childhood memories are evoked. The aim is to search these memories and relate them to therapy.

EP2. IMAGE: LEFT-RIGHT POSITION OF PARENTS
Now, set aside this picture of the house and see your parents standing directly in front of you. Tell me, as you look at them, who is standing on your left and who is standing on your right? Now, try to switch their positions. Do you experience any difficulty or discomfort when you do this?

Try to switch their positions again. Do you again feel any difficulty? Do you feel that these images are independent of your control?

The position of the parents as they stand in front of the subject always appears fixed. Inability to switch their position without some difficulty suggests that these images are strongly localized in the mind and that their spatial relationship has a specific neurological representation. Most commonly, the father appears on the left and the mother on the right (FM). Their appearance in an inverted position (MF), or in any position other than father left-mother right (FM), should be explored. The aim is to restore the FM position by bringing forth those memories that support this position.

EP3. IMAGE: PARENTS SEPARATED OR UNITED
As you see your parents standing in front of you, do they appear separated or united as a couple? Describe the character of the space each occupies. Do the spaces differ in temperature and illumination?

In this image context the parental unity or disunity becomes visible as the spaces occupied by the parents reflect their feelings of togetherness or conflict. The personality of each parent infuses into the image space the parent occupies. The goal in therapy is to restore the feeling of unity and pleasure between parents; this helps create similar positive feelings instead of empty feelings.

EP4. IMAGE: ACTIVE-PASSIVE PARENTS
As you see them standing in front of you, which parent seems to be more active and aggressive in the picture. Is he/she extremely active, very active, or just active? How is the other parent in comparison? Is he/she extremely passive, very passive, or just passive?

The parents standing in front of the subject communicate a feeling of intensity and energy. How the parents interact with each other, actively or passively, determines the amount and character of energy the child will project into the world and

whether he or she will be active, domineering, weak or ineffective. Normally the parents should appear active, capable of
give-and-take and helpfully involved with each other. Therapy
aims at releasing these energies from the source to provide a
sense of stability and strength where feelings of weakness and
instability prevail.

EP5. IMAGE: RUNNING FASTER
Now set aside this image and picture your parents run-
ning in an open countryside. Are they both running? Who
seems to be running faster? Is he/she running extremely
fast, very fast, or just fast? How is the other parent run-
ning: extremely slow, very slow or just slow?

The act of running in a forward motion describes the parents'
mode of energy release and signifies their ability to actualize
their inner energy in an outward movement. The goal is to provide to the person a similar feeling of forward and outward
movement rather than being stuck.

EP6. IMAGE: PATTERN OF RUNNING
Continue watching your parents running in the open
countryside. Now pay attention to the way in which they
run. Describe how each parent is running, the style and
pattern of his running. What seems to be the purpose of
their running? Why are they running?

Parents running in a open countryside surfaces information
about their goal-mindedness and describes the nature of their
physical activity in pursuit of their goals. The patterns of these
movements, if positive, appear pleasing to the child and impart
feelings of health and reality. The aim in the therapy is to provide a sense of goal to the person rather than let the events drag
down the person.

EP7. IMAGE: FREEDOM OF LIMBS
As you see your parents running, do their limbs appear
stiff or relaxed? Whose limbs appear more stiff and whose
limbs appear more relaxed?

The enjoyment or inhibition in the movements reveals the presence or absence of unity between the parents' mind and body feelings and also whether a parent is generally relaxed and whole in everyday life. The natural feeling of being relaxed in the body can be procured through the images rather than seeking relaxation through a drink or drug.

EP8. IMAGE: BRILLIANCE OF PARENTS' EYES
Now set aside this picture and see your parents standing directly in front of you again. Look at their eyes (do not recollect their real eyes). Whose eyes are more brilliant? Are they extremely brilliant, very brilliant, or just brilliant? How do the other parent's eyes appear?

The picture is expected to surface the nature of each parent's relationship with the subject and whether it is based on love or rejection. The goal of therapy is to establish a good eye contact with the parents; this helps remove feelings of guilt.

EP9. IMAGE: OBJECT ORIENTATION
Now set aside this image and look at me. As I look at objects, my eyes focus on one object and then another. Now, I am staring into space and my eyes focus on nothing. Now see your parents' eyes in the image again. Whose eyes focus on objects more easily? Are the eyes extremely object-oriented, very object-oriented, or just object-oriented? How are the other parent's eyes?

The inability to focus on an external object means denial of reality. This image is expected to reveal whether a parent is objective and reality-oriented. The therapy should aim at creating a fair and reliable sense of reality and objectivity in the person who is currently living an unrealistic life.

EP10. IMAGE: STORY IN THE EYES
Continue concentrating on your parents' eyes in the picture. Do they give you any feeling or tell you any story?

The eyes are an organ of silent communication and convey a story about the parent's life, describing whether the parent views the events of his or her life in a happy or complaining manner. The story of the person's own life should be studied in the light of the two stories from the parents. This should provide ideas for improvement.

> *EP11. IMAGE: LOUDNESS OF PARENTS' VOICES*
> *Now set aside this picture and see that you are hearing your parents' voices. Whose voice sounds louder to you? Is it extremely loud, very loud, or just loud? How does the other parent's voice sound to you?*

The voice communicates internal thoughts to the child. Ideas which have reached a conceptual clarity are expressed in words and the emotions are expressed in the voice tones, pitch and volume. The aim of therapy is to open up all these channels of sensations and communication in the person.

> *EP12. IMAGE: MEANINGFULNESS OF VOICES*
> *Now hear your parents' voices again. Do the voices seem meaningful, or are they merely patterns of sound in the air? Whose voice carries more meaning? Is it extremely meaningful, very meaningful, or just meaningful? How does the other parent's voice sound to you?*

A good voice is not merely logical but capable of a positive orientation which is helpfully related to the world. This picture is expected to reveal proper communication. The therapy should be directed at helping the person to relate to the world by creating a new and sustaining meaning in life.

> *EP13. IMAGE: STORY IN THE VOICES*
> *Continue listening to your parents' voices. Do they give you any feeling or tell you any story?*

The voice is an organ of communication and tells a story of how the parents view the events in their lives. This image is expected to surface the usual life story of a parent and the subject's reactions to it. A critical understanding of the world can be created in the person by reviewing the stories and what they lead to.

EP14. IMAGE: HEARING BY PARENTS' EARS
Now see yourself talking to both your parents. Who seems
to hear you better or has good ears for you? Does he/she
hear you extremely well, very well, or just well? Describe
how the other parent hears you.

Through hearing properly, the parents establish a healthy relationship with the child and generate feelings of security in him or her. Through the attentive ears of the parents, the child learns to relate to the world and develops confidence in the ability to communicate with others. The therapy should aim to create an attentive ear in the person while ideas about the issues are introduced and their appropriateness discussed.

EP15. IMAGE: UNDERSTANDING BY EARS
As you talk to your parents in the image, do they seem to
understand you? Who seems to understand you better? Does
he/she understand you extremely well, very well, or just
well? Describe how much the other parent understands you.

If one hears but does not understand what has been said, one is not properly communicating with the other person. The parents' ability to pay attention to and understand what has been said creates confidence in the child and serves as a bridge to reality. The ability to hear and understand should be regenerated in the person.

EP16. IMAGE: PARENTS SNIFFING
Now set aside this image and look at me. I am sniffing the
air here in this room, and you can tell by my facial expres-
sion whether I like the air or not. Now see your parents
sniffing the air in the house in the same way. Do they
appear to like or dislike the house atmosphere?

This picture is expected to reveal the parents' relationship with the house in the context of family living and whether they approve or disapprove of the house atmosphere. The issues that exist in the person at the same level should be brought forth and a congenial relationship with the house should be developed.

EP17. IMAGE: WARMTH OF PARENTS' BODIES
Now see your parents standing directly in front of you
again. Do you get a feeling of personal warmth from their
bodies? Whose body gives you a better feeling of personal
warmth? What kind of feeling does the other parent's
body give?

This picture is expected to reveal whether the parents are able to express love in a tender and personal way. How is the love life of the person? Does it have warmth in it? Are people around the person warm and responsive?

EP18. IMAGE: BODY ACCEPTANCE
Now look at your parents' skin and concentrate on it for
a while. Does it seem to accept you or reject you? Describe
how you feel when you look at their skin.

The care given by the parents is reflected in the feelings which their skin generates when they come into contact with the body of the child. The picture is expected to reveal whether the parents are accepting or rejecting toward the subject. Some fulfillment should be created through the help of images.

EP19. IMAGE: HEALTH OF SKIN
Continue looking at your parents' skin. Does it appear
healthy or unhealthy? Whose skin appears healthier?

The parents' intimate physical contact while holding the child conveys their internal feelings for the child through the skin. This picture is expected to surface the nature of internal feelings in the parents and whether conflict exists in them. The conflict should be removed by using positive images.

EP20. IMAGE: ARMS GIVING
Now picture your parents giving you something. Which
parent extends the hand more completely for giving?
Show me how your mother extends her arms when she
gives? How does your father extend his arms when he
gives?

The parents' hands represent an intermediary function between the parent and the child. They engage in activities centering around the feelings and expressions of love. This picture is expected to surface any resistance in giving in the parent. A positive imagery experience should be developed involving holding, touching, doing some activity with parents.

EP21. IMAGE: ARMS RECEIVING
Now picture yourself taking something from your parents.
To whom do you extend your arms completely?

The act of extending the hands to receive from the parents describes the child's confidence in approaching them. Repeated use of giving and receiving in the images opens the person up socially to ideas of give-and-take and change of attitudes.

EP22. IMAGE: STRENGTH OF GRASP
Now see that your parents are holding something in their
hands. Tell me which parent grasps more firmly. How is
the grasp of the other parent?

When the parents are able to hold things with proper strength, it describes their healthy relationship with objects and imparts feelings of confidence and reality to the child. Does the person hold onto ideas too rigidly? Some relaxation can help.

EP23. IMAGE: SWALLOWING FOOD
Now see your parents eating. Do they swallow easily?
Who swallows with more ease?

The ease with which the parents swallow food symbolically extends to their other activities, revealing the ease with which their life processes function in general. This picture is expected to surface the parents' relationship with food, economics and people. The relationship with food should be improved and enjoyment of food in the absence of alcohol or drugs should be developed.

EP24. IMAGE: DRINKING FLUID
Now see your parents drinking fluid. Who drinks faster?

Drinking fluids bring out how the parents related to intake and is expected to surface parental alcoholism and related issues. The information should be developed.

EP25. IMAGE: JAW PRESSURE
Now see your parents chewing something. Describe how they chew. Do they chew with pressure? Who chews with more pressure?

The function of chewing expresses an emotional relationship with incorporated food. The pressure exerted by the jaws may be appropriate in strength to the breakdown of food, or it may appear as an isolated aggressive function. This picture is expected to reveal the nature of the pressure. This pressure should be related to the alcohol or the drug problem.

EP26. IMAGE: PARENTS' BRAINS
Now look at me. Imagine that my upper skull has been surgically removed and that you can see my brain. You can touch my visible brain with your finger and feel the temperature there. Now picture your parents in a similar way. Touch their brains alternately with your finger. You will similarly get a feeling of temperature there. Describe the temperature of each parent's brain. Is it cold, warm, or hot?

A parent's thought processes are reflected in the thermal images of the brain, the normal temperature representing normal activity and abnormal temperature representing abnormal activity. This picture is expected to surface the nature of mental activity in the parents. The person's own reaction and its relation to alcohol and drug abuse should be explored.

EP27. IMAGE: BRAIN EFFICIENCY
Look at your parents' exposed brains again. Imagine them as thinking machines and describe how they look. How do you feel about their efficiency as thinking machines? Whose brain looks more efficient?

This picture is expected to reveal whether the character of thinking in each parent is efficient or inefficient, healthy or morbid. Is the person's own brain efficient in the area of examining the consequences of alcohol and drug abuse?

EP28. IMAGE: PARENTS' HEARTBEATS
Now see your parents' complete images standing in front of you again. Imagine that a window has been carved in each chest and that you can see their hearts beating there. See the hearts beating, and describe how each parent's heart beats. Is there any sign of anxiety in the heartbeats?

The image of the beating heart in the parent's chest symbolizes the presence of love. This picture is expected to reveal whether the parents are tender in their expression of love. What is the role of the person's own heart in alcohol and drug abuse?

EP29. IMAGE: PARENTS' INTESTINES
Now look at your parents' intestines. Do they appear healthy or unhealthy? Whose intestines appear healthier?

The intestines absorb food into the body and perform the cleansing function. When parents are healthy their intestines appear strong, smooth and without blemish. This picture is expected to reveal the parents' economic anxiety or a problem in expressiveness with regard to other people. How does the person relate this to the current problem of alcohol and drug abuse?

EP30. IMAGE: PARENTS' GENITALS
Now see your parents' genitals. Touch the genitals of each parent and describe the feelings of temperature there. Describe how each parent reacts to the touch and any feelings you have while seeing this image. Are there any memories associated with this image?

The genitals of the parents are the procreative organs and represent a feelingful relationship with life and its functions. When the genitals are touched in the image, the disposition of the parent is surfaced regarding feelings of acceptance and benevolence as well as the child's attitude toward the sexual organs and their function. How does the information in this area relate to the current alcohol and drug abuse?

The following examples illustrate the quality of material that can be evoked by various image scenarios presented in the Eidetic Parents Test. In the first example, the material reveals considerable information about important emotional themes and provides extensive therapeutic potential. In the second, there is a sparseness of information and very limited information about the development of emotional life, but the information can be developed through the eidetic. According to Ahsen (1972): "A good eidetic response is always pictorial in nature and emotive and carries sufficient detail for fruitful investigation....When a patient gives insufficient response as a regular pattern, it implies that he is not open to his emotional life" (p. 159).

CC, Female, Age 36

EP1. IMAGE: HOUSE
"I see a beautiful old, big, rambling house. My parents are always on vacation together and I was always there alone. My parents were always romantically involved with each other and the kids were always secondary. I was really by myself. I see myself roaming around looking for somebody. I see myself alone looking out the window, dreaming introspectively."

EL, Female, Age 21

EP4. IMAGE: ACTIVE-PASSIVE PARENTS
"My father is more active, very active. He is moving his arms around furiously and he looks uptight. My mother is very passive; she is just watching my dad."

The following examples illustrate the potential dynamism of the eidetic image to move toward a more positive feeling. As the images are explored, the mind may tend to fixate on negative events which have obstructed expression. At these points of conflict, the positive qualities of the psyche are enacted to move the conflict toward a state of resolution.

BG, Male, Age 45

EP1. IMAGE: HOUSE

"When I look at my mother I see her playing the piano, doing her music. When I see her doing that, she is happy and creative. I remember wanting her to do more of that.

"When I see the image, I am five, about as tall as the dachshund. We are in the music room. There is a sofa and oriental rugs, things that are soft and warm and fuzzy, a lot of colors, dark red, yellows, and the dog is there. My mother is free to play. I hoped she would find more sheet music and she would keep playing. It is a real positive image.

"As I keep looking at the image, I see that the piano keys are ivory white. I lose myself in the piano keys and feel empowered and set free by her."

The eidetic image progressively moves toward a more positive feeling of expression the more it is explored. States of expectancy and enjoyment are revealed as well as areas of conflict and difficulty. As the process is repeated, healthful states like those represented in the Expectation High are drawn out, concentrated on and deeply developed. Areas of conflict are reenacted through the image scenario toward a resolution.

In Steps 2 and 3 of the eidetic therapeutic process, the Expectation High was identified and separated from its false association with alcohol and drugs, segmented, enhanced, extended to other events and properly linked to other high states of consciousness revealed through exploration of the parental figures and other developmental events. The original early positive high states were retrieved and experienced independent of alcohol or other chemicals. In Step 4, the person's current involvement with alcohol and drugs is realistically explored. In order to develop a successful lifestyle, the qualities of the Expectation High must be applied to all areas of life in an active and dynamic way. Only through fruitful and meaningful engagement in reality will the need for the substance be eliminated. The person who abuses alcohol and other drugs is usually not in touch with his or her present circumstances and lacks understanding of the current experience. Ahsen's method systematically addresses the issues of denial and detachment from reality in the next phase of treatment.

STEP 4

Ten-Year Scenario

According to Steele and Josephs (1990), people caught in the habitual use of alcohol and drugs are unable to decipher their current situation realistically and are suffering from what they call "alcohol myopia," a state of shortsightedness in which superficially understood, immediate aspects of experience have a disproportionate influence on behavior and emotion, a state in which we can see the tree, albeit more dimly, but miss the forest altogether (p. 923). Often, people report that they feel they will be able to stop their addiction some time before things get out of hand. There is usually a fantasy operating with features of escape, a shutting off of emotions and a lack of awareness of the reality of the current situation. According to medical disease proponents, the "denial" of the problem is a critical component of the disease process that prevents the person from seeing the problem for what it is, its ramifications, and taking appropriate action to obtain treatment. The realities of the present become so vague and driven by autosuggestion (more drinking causes more euphoria) that a realistic appraisal of the current situation and the implications for the future are completely obscured.

The Ten-Year Scenario imagery procedure was devised by Ahsen to enable the person to perceive more clearly the reality of present circumstances and, based on this, the direction of future events. According to Ahsen (1989a): "the role of futurism is to overcome the dissipation let loose in the imaginal mind. It is clear that unless the mind is touched by the future, the abilities in the mind do not orientate themselves toward a solution. In some way the mind should be made to connect with its futuristic side in the precise area where a failing appears to manifest itself and is defended by obsessive thinking or imaginal dissipation"(p. 52). In addiction, disconnection with future possibilities enables the syndrome to remain operative. As the negative futuristic scenarios are systematically developed with the image of the compulsion toward more and more addiction, the vision of the future becomes a clear, present reality. The frames of these image scenarios are projected over a ten-year period, each year being evolved slowly and in detail to insure that a meaningful and realistic picture is evoked. The vision of future events is operating within the current mind, either as vague or vivid images involving negative or false positive anticipation. This interconnects feelings of hope with uneasiness, guilt or a sense of foreboding within the context of realism. Each picture needs to be brought to the surface and explored to elucidate the way a variety of areas of life (i.e., relationships, job, health), will be eventually affected. The more these images are explored and developed, the more the underlying emotions (i.e., anger, anxiety and numbness as well as hope) will arise. As the details of the scenarios unfold, the desire to escape through the addiction can be understood and the fears that attend it clarified.

Ten-Year Scenario Instructions

1. *See your current problem in realistic detail. Begin describing your present life situation and the related emotional states (i.e., career, family, relationship, health).*

2. *See each year and progress the images through the ten years, with each year's detail leading to the next year.*

3. *Pay close attention to each year and to the emotional and physical aspects of each imaged situation. Are any fantasies operating underneath the situation? Is it being made light of or cut short in some way? (For example, does the person say, "I see that if I continue drinking I will lose my job and live on the street, my ulcer will really get bad, it could kill me," or does the person report, "Another street person will take care of me, my wife will take me back if my ulcer gets bad, or my ulcer really won't be affected after all.")*

4. *As the imagery scenarios unfold, are there points worthy of elaborate discussion within the material? Through interaction, more underlying emotions will be surfaced, revealing their impact on various aspects of life. (For example, a person reported, " I am sitting at my desk, making myself connect with my assignment." As this image scenario was explored further, the feeling of force hinted at in the image in order to make the connection with work became critical. When the issue of force was further brought to the center of attention and explored, a feeling of anger and irritation emerged. At this point the person said, "I am beginning to feel anger, but I do not show this emotion outwardly, I always try to suppress it. Then I just feel numb." The image scenario had spontaneously progressed from evoking the feeling of force to anger and then to numbness.)*

5. *As each emotional response is explored, try to relate to the images realistically throughout the process. Relate the emotional impact to daily life (i.e., how it has affected the job, the relationship, etc. For instance, if the person says, "I will just get other jobs, just start over again if I screw up," the person is instructed to see realistically who will hire someone who keeps losing jobs, and what kind of job that person will realistically be able to obtain in the end.)*

The Ten-Year Scenario can be self-administered or administered by a therapist. The first administration evokes basic responses which contain certain attributes and aspects that can serve as indicators for development and analysis. The following points should be noted.

Developing and Analyzing the Ten-Year Scenario

1. *Sparseness of response indicates a defensiveness or constriction in dealing with the material. The more sparse, the greater the indication of constriction.*

2. *If the sparseness continues throughout the entire ten scenarios, it indicates profound constriction in the mind. The person's mind needs to be activated and become more open to allow the development of the material in a positive direction.*

3. *When the person expresses self-pity, it indicates a poor grasp of the helpful potential available within the image scenarios.*

4. *When the person expresses irritation and anger with the process, it also represents a poor grasp of the helpful potential.*

5. *When the material evolves over the ten-year scenario and has specific distinctions and details, it can be utilized as a foundation for further development of consciousness.*

6. *When there is feeling of hope in the material, it indicates a positive orientation and a good prognosis. These positive aspects should be the focus of concentration.*

7. *When there is no positive feeling or hopefulness throughout the process, each scenario should be explored more deeply toward a goal of discovering the positive aspects within the image. The person can be instructed to bring a feeling of hope to the scenario. The first administration will be revised over and over again by adding a positive feeling of hopefulness to each scenario.*

8. *In cases where positive states are present, the second administration measures the degree to which these have been integrated and gives direction for further work in the problem area, as sessions proceed.*

9. *When there is a lack of engagement or response to the material, the person needs to project the ability to interact and become involved with it.*

10. *A second administration of the image scenarios elucidates the person's progress in relation to the material evolved in the first test.*

In the following case, the first administration surfaced emotional elements that were further explored to reveal points of difficulty. By the second administration the Expectation High had been retrieved and enhanced to provide a more hopeful and positive orientation.

DF, Male, Age 36

First Administration of Ten-Year Scenario

1st Year. "In order to do the things which I do now, I have to force myself, push myself through it with brute force, just sit down and do it. At least ninety percent of it is not pleasurable so I have to use brute force. It is not that I dislike the things that I do. I just don't find pleasure in it. In this first year the brute force will do it. That is exactly where I am now."

2nd Year. "I could continue through brute force to accomplish the job at hand and bring in sufficient revenue to accommodate my needs. By the end of year two, I think that I will probably move from enjoying ten percent of what I did to probably seven percent. The predominant feeling is that I did that and completed it, although the reduction in happiness is three percent."

3rd Year. "Similar to the second year, I think the amount of happiness would be around three to four percent, which would be as far as I could go. By the end of the third year, if there had not been some significant change in some aspect of my life, then I quit and go to the woods, skip the job part."

4th Year. "If did not quit, the focus or push would not be enough for me to continue on. I would have to become numb to the situation. The fourth year would be the most difficult. I would have to become totally numb to the circumstance. By becoming that numb I have to believe that I would lose the intuitive abilities that I have now to accomplish the sales aspects of the job that I do. At that point I would begin to become angry. Rather than just being anxious, I would become angry. Numbness is the main characteristic of the fourth year."

5th Year. "It would have to be a little different, assuming the anger and the numbness. At that point my income would begin to decline, I could not perform.

Decline in income would only compound my anger. Assuming that my revenue would have declined fifty percent on an average of the previous four years. More decline is expected. I would make much less revenue because I would only be working fifty percent of the time and the other fifty percent I would probably be drunk. The drinking makes me numb so I avoid the issue of anger. I very seldom express anger outwardly. Generally speaking, my anger is directed inward. I think everyone has the right to do whatever they want to do. When I do get mad the anger is always at me for not handling the situation correctly. If you deal with an idiot in a certain way you will get the result you wish. It is true I have always felt that.

"When I get angry I become lazy, it begins to erode the drive and focus, necessary to go forward. I think it also damages my health. I think that my health may begin to decline. When I see an image of myself, I see that I am twenty-five percent weaker than I am now. It takes more effort to climb steps. I get tired out. It is hard to get up in the morning. Two things come to mind about my physical health. I would have continuous backaches and my hair would probably fall out. Most probably I would have hemorrhoids."

6th Year. "I don't know if I could function throughout the entire sixth year. In the fifth year, I would be drinking once per week and in the sixth year I would drink twice a week and I don't know how I would make any money. With my hair falling out, hemorrhoids, drunk twice per week, I have to think that I would be pretty close to crazy by then. I don't know if I can get any work done this year. I need more time and more money for drinking."

7th Year. "After the sixth year I do not know what is left. I would have to make a decision either to change or I would be in jail for being drunk or be crazy, but if that is an escape, then I think I would be out of money in the the seventh year."

8th Year. "The only thing I can say here is that at that point, I must have pushed myself so far down I would have to start all over again. I would have to start everything brand new."

9th Year. "I would take a lesser job with a new boss. When I look at the new boss, I see in his face a lack of trust. I think he is desperate. He is hiring me because he is expanding his business and he needs to hire people. He hires me because he is looking for employees. He will even hire people who will damage his business. I am doing accounting in his place. I am reliable. At that point I might be happy that I have been given a second chance but I can deteriorate here too. I don't know how long I would be happy at the job. I see a split scene. Either I get along real well with the co-workers at the inferior level or it would become really unbearable fairly quickly. In the event that the job just bored the hell out of me, I would get fired and go from lesser job to lesser job."

10th Year. "After the ninth year, getting fired again, I go from job to job, each time declining in pay. Jobs would become fewer and farther apart. I look pretty scruffy by then. I don't think I would be taking permanent jobs, just part time. I would just be in existence. Menial temporary labor."

Second Administration

After two and one-half months of treatment, the Ten-Year Scenario procedure was readministered. At this point in the treatment, the Expectation High had been retrieved and the states related to it explored and developed. The feelings of numbness was found to be related to a business deal that had not come through.

1st Year. "I am trying to work, trying to make phone calls to keep going. I have to go to the library. I can't seem to get to the deal to make it work. I will have to find something to play with or do, like go swimming or walking. I have not used brute force lately."

2nd Year. "I have been having fifty percent more enjoyment now. Things probably would get better. I would be relaxed more with more access to information. I need to recognize when things are not good. I have to move on if it doesn't work. This frustrates me."

3rd Year. "Giving up is the last thought on my mind. I never have given up on anything. I have no concerns about my survival, none."

4th Year. "I am not in the same place that I was in two months ago when I first did this. But there is still numbness and severe boredom. I have exhausted every avenue with this business deal. The numbness is mostly in my head. The anger that I feel is a result of frustration and I begin to get angry when things don't work out. I get angry at myself, put myself down. I used to drink in this state. Now I am not drinking. I get tired here. Weaker than usual, and my stomach gets ground up and churning. There is some acid in my throat, some heartburn."

5th Year. "If I stay with the feeling of anger and let it increase, this is when I would be drunk all of the time. I am going crazy running up and down the street breaking windows. I used to do that as a kid. Once I got real mad at my ex-wife and broke a cup in my hand. I see myself lying on the bed frustrated and angry, doing nothing, just lazy. The numbness, anger and not doing anything are all there. Again, I want to do something to change it, I want to escape. If I let it increase, I finally come to a realization. It snaps, that is it. There is a feeling of a clean slate, that I have a clean slate. Now I have a little bit of excitement and wonder as I begin to create new things. It is a spurt of new things. It is a situation where all things are possible, the moment after the burst, it is a whole new life, like being reborn. My whole body tingles, releasing what was holding me where I was. There is a feeling that my options outweigh my concerns. In the Expectation High, the energy is good and strong and I feel a twist inside me that is lighter and freer and it feels good. My head is no longer numb. I am smiling, I feel like I will succeed. I don't have anxiety about seeing people. It is not what they think of me as the dominant force. When I am angry, I numb myself out. I usually keep the anger within, but by keeping anger in I become numb. If the energy did not disperse, then I would be angry, lethargic and lay around. There would be a slow decline in my health."

At this point, enough material had been gathered in relation to the first administration and had indicated that the Expectation High and its positive states had been integrated to provide further positive direction for treatment.

The following example is presented to briefly illustrate a case in which there is a constriction or repression in dealing with the material. There is a sparseness of detail and a repetition of response in each scenario. There is also a lack of emotional engagement in the material as the person responds to the instruction.

DL, Male, Age 34

1st Year. "I see that I stop going to the gym and AA meetings. I drop out of everything, school does not get finished and I am drinking every day."

2nd Year. "I have no connection to anything. I have dropped out. I have cursory contact with people. There is more anxiety in this image. The predominant feeling is depression. There is no feeling of happiness."

3rd Year. "Everything is much worse. I have no contact with anything. There are days when I drink harder. I don't see anything for my career. Not if there is so much anger and isolation. I am living in my truck, then crashing with people for a week, doing odd jobs for money. I have anxiety about school."

4th Year. "Dealing drugs for money. I am taking drugs and alcohol, wasted life. I have repressed all anxiety and stay loaded most of the day. Drugs numb me, no contact with family and friends."

5th Year. "I had more money in the fourth year, now loaded most of the time. Place to live with four or five other people. Angry all of the time, explosively angry and I go off on people. It is physical, pushing and kicking."

6th Year. "Nothing is working, drugs and alcohol don't numb me. I see an image of myself going on forty; no credit, no cash, just living day to day, and loaded most of the time. I reminisce how I squandered good luck. I am standing in the house. No one is there. Anger is inward, more drugs and alcohol, coke and downs. I am ten to fifteen pounds overweight, I am bloated and red, eyes are clouded and bloodshot, liver has been affected, clouded and yellow, no pain, I have a beer belly."

7th Year. "I have this lifestyle, twenty pounds overweight, have no looks, no health, no contacts from earlier life. No way out, real hopeless, resignation and depression, drinking every day, real heavy, living day to day, hand to mouth."

8th Year. "I don't see an eighth year. I want to check out. I never get busted, I am cautious, my liver is affected, nothing is working, sell drugs to regular clientele, I am thinking of going to dry out."

9th Year. "I trashed my body, I look about sixty-five years old, I am sober, contemplating drying out, I look sixty-five, bad color, overweight, really look terrible, no money, no place to live. The house I am in reminds me of my home from the Eidetic Parents Test. I am contemplating starting from scratch."

10th Year. "I am still in Eidetic Parents Test house, sitting and pacing, trying to get angry enough to move forward. Where to go, no money, no real contact. I see in the image that no one is in the house. The house has not been lived in for years. Cobwebs, I walk around, I see my reflection in a mirror. I am trying to get angry enough or sustain the anger to get anything done. I can't stay focused on it. I see the bathroom, I look really old. My eyes are all wrinkly and baggy. There is depression and resignation. I am trying to get angry enough to get sober. Now I am not drinking. I am not pleased. Then I get drunk. I will think about getting sober tomorrow. I am thinking about the destructiveness of alcohol. Then I think about what a screw-up I became. I get drunk to anesthetize myself. I am going back and forth. It is too insurmountable. Then I wonder if I should ever bother. I did not finish what I wanted to anyway. I feel at the end. Nothing really there, not even a voice or emptiness and no somatic connection. It is just blankness, total blankness, nothing there. I am angry at myself. The self-anger creates the abuse of alcohol. I get angry in order not to feel like a victim."

STEP 5

Philosophy of Life

According to Ahsen (1993a): "Alcoholism and drug abuse represent a person's lack of a workable philosophy of life. It is not just trauma or the absence of proper reasoning that is the problem but there is an absence of a true connection with the meaning of life. The person cannot leave the compulsion unless he can find another resource within. If he cannot rely on his own self more than he relies on a substance, he is no longer himself the source of meaning which would fulfill his life. Somewhere along the line he lost contact with a fulfilling philosophy and now instead he chooses only temporary measures and looks for props that do not originate in him" (p. 25).

In the following report, the person reflects on her history of addiction as a search for a "transcendent" experience and her attempt to create a poetic philosophy of life through addiction.

TP, Female, Age 42

"When I was fifteen, I started drinking. In my teens my drug of choice became hashish. I experimented with hallucinogens, then in my late twenties got very seriously addicted to amphetamines. I drank when I did drugs, but I never really considered that alcohol was a problem, but then I never considered drugs were a problem either; they were so much a part of my life and what I did to make my life interesting. I never reflected on any negative effects they may have been having. I thought that I understood the nature of addiction and in light of my understanding never considered myself an addict. Quitting was never an issue because I never thought addiction was an issue and I never wanted to quit. Because of my friends, I never had a sense of the quantity I consumed. What seems a lot to me now, seemed like a little to me then. I quit using amphetamines when I moved to Hawaii but when I returned, my life was very ugly. I continued to use hashish very heavily despite repeated bouts of pleurisy and a serious period of depression that totally immobilized me.

"At that point I was deeply involved in a very destructive relationship with a man who was alcoholic and in light of his drinking, my own consumption did not seem considerable. It was only after the end of that relationship that my own drinking went really wild, although I always drank steadily before. At the end of that relationship I made an agreement with myself — to let myself run to the end of the summer, run as fast as I could. I think what I intended to do was implied in my choice of words. Escape. I relinquished any semblance of control and drank as much as I could whenever I could, which was all the time, virtually every day. I balanced my drunkenness with cocaine. I would snort coke or smoke crack to straighten out.

"The image I have is myself on an empty street. I am running as fast as I can, blind – my arm is flung across my eyes as I run. I was telling myself that it was okay, I was allowed to do this, that I needed to do this. The problem was, at the end of the summer I could not stop myself. Once I started running I couldn't stop. I just disconnected and told myself it was okay to have a good time. I started working out, my body was beginning to change, lose weight, put on muscle. I could feel my muscles. In a sense I was strong enough to sustain the punishment. I thought I was looking better and feeling better than I had in years. Concurrent with all of this, I was experiencing chronic bulimia that was connected to my use of hashish and marijuana. I would sit at home and smoke by myself. When I did that I would have a compulsion to act out a bulimic episode.

"But, any negative concerns about my acting out behaviors were pushed aside by my superficial appearance of health. I always put up that appearance: calm, well-controlled business person. There was a real duality in how I lived my life in terms of the external appearance and what was really going on. It got very confusing. Some of the time I would be really sick from drinking and drugs, especially when I would do a grand marnier and cocaine binge, which was often. I was in such a terrible state but could put on suitable clothing and go to work, functioning. At that time one of my concerns was keeping the surface smooth, not letting people suspect what was really going on. It was affecting my performance at work, attendance at work. I was trying to keep that together. At that point I was drinking every day at lunch and every night after work, having to take cabs home four or five nights a week because I was too drunk to get home.

"At that time, my job changed and I had a choice

to take another job or take a severance package. I decided to take the money and set myself up in business and I wouldn't have to work in a corporate environment anymore. I got myself started, but then over the course of the next summer, I went down the toilet. I had no sense of purpose, no sense of direction. I had no desire. I wanted to do things that I had no ability to do at that time. When it came to transforming that desire into fulfillment, I did not have the initiative, the get-up-and-go to do it. I was in this horrible state of inertia.

"I ended up in this pattern of waking and sleeping and drinking and drugging. I spent a lot of time out of town. I would go to a friend's place and buy a few bottles of wine and drink them, smoke hash. It was easier to drink than do anything else. I was getting myself into some dangerous and compromising situations with men when I was drunk or taking drugs. Those encounters – I would seek them, things would happen. I guess I was always expecting a grand adventure, but always ended up feeling very shaky and very isolated and violated. I don't know why that word 'violated,' comes to mind because every incident was my own creation. Nothing was satisfactory. If I was alone in the city, I would smoke up and buy the National Enquirer and binge on junk food. I had to have this totally mindless thing to read while I binged on junk food. This is how I passed my day until it was time to go out and drink. I would get to the point of drunkenness where I would see double, I would make myself throw up and then do cocaine to straighten myself out. The coke gave me the illusion of control over alcohol. I was trying to balance one off the other. It was hopeless.

"As I kept on going, as the blackouts got more frequent, as did those incidents during which I would seemingly, without provocation, go into these crying jags – I would be totally heartbroken, convinced that the world was dying and I was dying – that everything was dying. I began to have this fantasy that one time I was going to wake up out of a blackout and find myself handcuffed to a rusty metal bed frame in some sordid, shabby hotel room and I wouldn't know how I had gotten there or how I was going to get out. I began to be really afraid. I did not know how to stop the madness. I did not know how to live without it. My feelings were so intense but nothing was clear. I couldn't tell anymore who I was and what I was doing. I was floundering around in this masquerade pretending I was having fun. Who was I fooling?

"When I think of the Expectation High, the first time I used drugs I was expecting a transcendental experience, a magical transformation. I was expecting the world to come alive in a new way. My anticipation was also about sharing the experience with my beloved friend. There was the expectation of an experience of unity with her, a kindred bonding, a shared experience and a secret experience that would be private and unique to the two of us. Something that would set us apart from the world and make us special in some way.

"In the alcohol and drug experience over time I was looking for exalted expression, uninhibited freedom of expression and action. Again, that sense of special bonding with another human being, the intimacy of a profound, shared experience that was unique to just the two of us. I sought this in my relationships with women as well as men.

"If I had not stopped drinking and drugging, I would be dead. I would have killed myself by taking one risk too many, going home with one stranger too many. It could have been an accidental death if I did not kill myself first. I was also beginning to express some violence in certain situations and someone else could have killed me. I would have provoked someone to do it. I had already been hospitalized a couple of times before and realized that couldn't help me. I tried to convince myself that I loved my pain. I tried to live out Oscar Wilde's notion that while joy might ennoble the body, only grief ennobles the soul. I tried to romanticize my pain to make it worth something. To make it a transcendental experience, it did not work. Tragedy might make good poetry, but it doesn't make a good life."

In Eidetic Image Therapy, issues concerning alcohol and drug abuse are organized around a dynamic theory of consciousness and dedicated to developing a lifestyle of activation and energy connected with the real self. As the Expectation High is more deeply developed and extended into the present constricted lifestyle, the person begins to gain appreciation for the magical and poetic potential of the real self that was once falsely attributed to alcohol and drugs. In the final phase of treatment, the Expectation High is translated into daily life in a gratifying and meaningful way, thereby eliminating the need for the substance. Ahsen (1993a, p. 26) has outlined some of the guidelines for this process as follows.

Developing an Expectation High Philosophy and Lifestyle

1. *As imagery is extensively evolved through the eidetic process, the person experiences a greater appreciation for emergence of the real self.*
2. *The person comes to feel that the real self is truly magical and healing, and that the magicality inheres in the self rather than in the alcohol or drug.*
3. *Retrieval of the self has a larger context and must be brought home through the person's lifestyle. By reviewing the lifestyle and translating the Expectation High into real life scenarios that are gratifying and meaningful, the need for the drug is thereby eliminated.*
4. *In the final phase of treatment, futuristic dimensions of the lifestyle are evolved and the individual is involved in a gratifying context of fruitful activities.*
5. *Any lack in a meaningful and fulfilling context will take away strength from the larger view and from the philosophical attitude which ultimately gives the person a natural feeling of a high.*

The goal of Ahsen's methodology is to retrieve the natural states of positive expectation and expression that promote fulfilling engagement with reality. By linking these states to their proper foundation, healthful neurological and biological functioning can be restored. Positive states like those found in the Expectation High exist prior to any learned behavior and represent an individual's most basic life potential.

In the core approach presented in this chapter, the Expectation High was rescued from the false connection with alcohol and drugs, the power of the drug was demystified and the real self was revitalized. Areas of conflict and sources of weakness were systematically identified and resolved. The current lifestyle was realistically appraised and infused with the primary power found in the eidetic. This core process is applicable to all substance abuse and is the foundation of treatment. There are also specific imagery tactics that are of tremendous therapeutic value in providing additional insight into particularly difficult areas, thereby enhancing high states and activating the person's resources and strengths. The following chapter outlines several additional techniques and procedures that may be used to process information in difficult areas and to strengthen the gains made with the core method.

Chapter 6

Special Imagery Tactics

The various imagery exercises presented in this chapter can be used for gathering additional material relevant to the addiction, to aid in removing further difficulties in the treatment, and to promote self-awareness and self-change. The movement initiated through these exercises assists in elaboration of positive experiences by developing the undeveloped nourishing aspects of life and also unearths material concerning denial, resistance and defensiveness that support and maintain the addiction. When the person's conscious and nonconscious views and beliefs about the addiction are examined in light of the material unearthed in these exercises, precisely where and how defenses are maintained is clarified. Further, the manner in which the person deals with this new information indicates the degree of difficulty or ease with which recovery will proceed. Ahsen (1977a) states in this regard: "The individual obstructs the emergence of these real images by maintaining the attitude of isolation toward these pictures and superimposing on the isolation a version of life in which parents become an aspect of unreality. Once one breaks through this barrier of unreality and isolation and reaches the real images of parents, one starts experiencing the original source of pleasure and anxiety" (p. 98). And: " ....When he is able to deal with these images without distance, without fear, and without any need to defend himself from the pain associated with the situation, the self-protective barriers in the ego are lifted and the original strength and harmony of the self is experientially revealed" (p. 130).

The special imagery tactics discussed in this chapter include in-depth administration of the Eidetic Parents Test item EP24 concerning parents drinking fluid; parental filters; Expectation High parent image and filter; unvivid filters and images; antidote imagery; self-image technique; early ego states; the futuristic dot; and the eidetic heart imagery.

Eidetic Parents Test Item EP24

Now see your parents drinking fluid. Who drinks faster?

The image of the parents drinking fluid can provide important information regarding each parent's attitudes and beliefs about alcohol and the patient's reaction to them. When elaborated in depth, this image from Ahsen's Eidetic Parents Test (EP24) is a superb investigative tool that reveals information about the parent's personality, deeper problems and posture toward drinking, which is useful in treatment. Ahsen (1972) suggests that the following features should be noted.

> The ease or difficulty with which the person drinks any ordinary liquid such as water will extend to other intakes as well. The feelings connected with drinking may become connected with sensory cues related to drinking alcohol and point to parents' ten-

dency toward alcoholism if it exists. Normally the parents should drink an ordinary liquid with ease and pleasure. The fluid which the parent drinks should be noted. If the parent is drinking water, alcohol or another fluid, the parent's thoughts connected with the drink should be explored. If the parent is alcoholic, the history and the effects of alcoholism on the subject should be explored thoroughly and the subject's reactions should be brought to the surface. Severe disturbance is indicated when a parent cannot drink at all or drinks in an extremely fast and violent manner. When a parent drinks liquid with difficulty it indicates depression. Absence of drinking in the image may indicate severe depression or a repression of the drinking problem in the parent involved. Fast drinking or quick gulping so that the liquid cannot be detected indicates a tendency toward alcoholism which the parent prefers to hide. A patient reported seeing his father drinking extremely fast and this reminded him of his father's alcoholism. He said, "He was a weak and selfish person who would isolate himself in the drink. His presence in the home symbolized fear and terror." (p. 98)

In each of the following case examples, a parent's problem with alcohol was indicated in the patient's response to EP24.

TS, Female, Age 36

"My mother drinks faster, she does everything faster. She is drinking tea. He is drinking tea. He drinks calmly, slowly. When I see the image of my mother, I get a feeling of anxiety. If I concentrate on him, it calms me down."

RJ, Male, Age 44

"My mother drinks more, faster. She is drinking juice or water. He is drinking booze. He does it in gulps, my mother just pours it down."

PB, Female, Age 54

"My father drinks faster than my mother; she sips. In the image, he is drinking beer. He is relaxed and seems to be in a good mood; he is having a nice rest now. I remember one summer day when we were at the cottage, he made sarsparilla from some kind of a root; it got all effervescent. I remember that we all sat on the lawn and had ham sandwiches. He and my mother had drinks and the kids had the sarsparilla. I remember he would make his own tonic every year. It was a dark brown color; he said it was supposed to be good for him. He said it was passed down in the family."

ST, Male, Age 29

"My father drinks faster, my mother drinks slower. He is drinking beer. Seeing my father drink in the image is unpleasant. His attitude is that he has no shame. My mother is drinking coffee. It is pleasant; she has an easy attitude about it. My father's drinking attracts my attention more than my mother's because of the style of his drinking. He is tilting the bottle upright; it is practically upside down. It is really noticeable. When I continue to look at the image, I get an image of a lot of men sitting at the kitchen table. There are a lot of beer bottles and beer glasses on the table. When I see the beer in the glasses, it is very foamy, white and bubbly. It looks like acid. I feel nauseous when I look at it. My mother is also at the table with all the men. She is fighting with my father. It is an awful image."

MO, Female, Age 39

"My mother drinks faster. She is drinking a glass of water. I just saw her drinking a very tall glass of water. She is really pouring it down. My father is sipping a cup of tea. He is drinking from a tea cup, although I never saw him do that. He is sipping his tea and reading. When she drinks, she is much sloppier. She is very thirsty in the image. My father is sipping.

FT, Female, Age 42

"I see her with a pail, dumping liquid all over herself. Though I know she was alcoholic, the image really brings out a part of her that was hidden, that she was really totally out of control with it. I guess she just inundated herself with the stuff. I feel shocked when I see the image. I guess I was afraid to really admit how it was, but it rings true when I see the image. She just can't get enough fast enough. What it shows me is the degree to which she was out of control. I always thought it was more in my imagination and that maybe it wasn't really that bad or that she just wanted to do it. This shows me that she had to do it, she was really at the effect of it. It puts a different light on the problem. I don't feel so guilty or responsible when I see the image, but I also feel sadness in the reality of the situation."

EP24 Repeated

"My father comes in and helps her put the pail down. He says, 'Come on, this is foolishness. Let's go and relax and talk about what is bothering you.' She looks at him helplessly and follows his instructions. It is obvious that she was out of control, not able to take control of herself and he was able to intervene in her favor."

EP24 Repeated (see filter technique)

"Now I see her drinking at a bar, slumped over the bar, drunk, miserable. She is in her cups. It looks like a western bar. Father comes in through the swinging doors, sees her there, and says, 'Oh boy, this is no good. I wonder what got into her.' He takes her back to the room which is over the saloon, puts her in bed and puts an ice pack on her head. She wakes up and sees him and says, 'How did you get here?' He says, 'I got here late.' She says, 'What a mess. I have been so depressed, not knowing what to do or how to do things without you.' He says, 'That is all over now. We can go home again.' She smiles and they hug."

EP24 Repeated (see filter technique)
"I see her staggering down the street and holding
onto a lamp post, trying to stand up. I see him walking down the street with a cigarette in his mouth, and
a hat on. He stops next to her. She is enraged at him.
She says, 'Where were you, you bum? You are never
around when I need you.' He says, 'What can I do? I
do the best I can, but I can't be here enough to meet
your needs.' She says, 'I just want a nice home like
my mother had with nice Sunday dinners and the
good life.' He says, 'You can't have a full plate if
someone else is starving. I can't live with it.' She does
not give a damn about anyone else's problems. She
has her own needs and those of her child and they
come first, after all. She says, 'We all have the things
that will make us happy and you need to be there
too.' He helps her home and says that they will talk
about it tomorrow."

From the material yielded in this image, aspects of the personality of the alcoholic parent that had been previously out
of the patient's awareness were revealed. This information
was later used in another special tactic (see "Parental Filters
with EPT Parental Images" below). The tendency toward
problems with other substances may also be revealed in EP24,
as in the following case example where the father's tendency
toward addiction was indicated. As this theme was related to
other imagery scenarios, his personality was more clearly
revealed and connected to his addiction to heroin. This
proved to be extremely helpful in therapy.

QP, Male, Age 34

EP24. IMAGE: DRINKING FLUID
"My mother drinks faster. Her intent is to finish eating so she can get to the dishes. She is drinking tea.
My father is drinking red wine; he is drinking slowly, savoring it. His only concern is his own enjoyment."

EP26 brought the problem further into focus. The patient reported: "My father's brain is really hot, but when I touch his brain with my finger, my finger gets numb. It is like his brain causes some kind of desensitization."

From this point on, several memories were reported:

> "These images that come to me now must have always existed. I don't remember my dad ever taking his shirt off. He would always wear paisley shirts with a lot of different colors on it and he always wore sunglasses. I remember we had two bathrooms in the house where I grew up. The downstairs bathroom was my father's bathroom and it had red toilet paper in it. I thought it was funny then. I also remember he did not like to swim in public places, which now makes sense to me. In the summer he would drive the car with his gloves on and his sunglasses on. I can't see his eyes because he always had the sunglasses on. When I look at him driving, it seems like he is dozing off at the wheel. He would have to pull over sometimes. I did not think anything of it then. One time I remember we were with a friend of his and he stopped at someone's house and my father and his friend went in the house and left me and my sister in the car for a really long time; it must have been over an hour. I was ten and my sister was eight. It was summer and it was really hot in the car. I now realize that he must have been getting drugs. I did not think anything of it then, but now I think it was really irresponsible."

EP24 can provide a base for further exploration of addiction problems. The information revealed in this image can be evolved thematically and connected to other images to uncover deeper aspects of the addiction. (See also later section on "An Antidote Image" for another application of the EP24 image.) These images help expand a patient's consciousness.

Parents as Filters

Parental Filters with EPT Parental Images

> *Keep your parent (mother or father) in mind while seeing*
> *an image (from the Eidetic Parents Test).*

Ahsen's application of image "filters" is also of immense value in unearthing the underlying impact of parental behavior on a person's experience. Briefly, a filter is a thought or image which is kept in mind while an image is being seen simultaneously. A filter also may color everyday life positively or negatively, as events and people are perceived through it. In the case of alcoholism and drug abuse, when a parental filter is used, it activates certain processes that have been repressed in consciousness. When a person is instructed to see the image scenarios in the Eidetic Parents Test while keeping the parent in mind who has a problem with alcohol or drugs or keeping in mind the nonalcoholic parent, very specific information is revealed which is different in each case. This material, when compared to the responses of the initial projection of the parental images, yields illuminating information regarding the impact of a parent's influence on the patient and provides access to areas that can resolve internal conflicts.

Case Report: FT, Female, Age 42

In the following case report, the Eidetic Parents Test (EPT) had been administered at various points during the progression of treatment. The readministration of the EPT is a useful technique that provides important information regarding the progress of treatment, the resolution of specific areas of conflict and newly surfaced areas to be addressed. In the following imagery series, early traumatic events and conflict areas have been addressed in this manner. Three different administrations are provided: (1) the third administration of the 30 EPT items, including for the comparison the first administration responses on the house image (EP1), the left-right image of parents (EP2), and parents drinking fluid (EP24) to illustrate the progression of images in the conflict areas; (2) a re-administration of the EPT images with the Alcoholic Mother Filter; (3) a re-administration of EP1, EP2 and EP24 alcoholic mother images with the Positive Non-alcoholic Father Filter. Keeping the father in the mind while seeing the alcoholic mother provided the point of resolution for the repressed underlying traumatic theme regarding alcoholism.

Third Administration of Eidetic Parents Test

EP1. IMAGE: HOUSE
"I see my mother and father standing in the back yard, they are very young. There is a feeling of warmth between them. I am an infant. He is holding me. There is a great sense of being taken care of, they are concerned about me. It is a good feeling."

[First administration: "The image is empty, I feel vacant looking at it. I have this vague feeling of my mother and grandmother being in the house. There is a ghostly figure of my grandfather in the living room. I am 12 or 13, there is an overriding feeling of emptiness. It feels like summer and the wind blows the sheer curtains and it is very still. If I were to change the scene to winter, I see an image of a funeral."]

EP2. IMAGE: LEFT-RIGHT POSITION OF PARENTS
"Father on the left, Mother on the right. They can't switch easily."

[First administration. "I see my mother on the right, my father on the left. She wants to take over the whole space, she looks like a big blob. The image feels totally out of control."]

EP3. IMAGE: PARENTS SEPARATED OR UNITED
"They seem united as a couple."

EP4. IMAGE: ACTIVE-PASSIVE PARENTS
"My father is active in physical strength. He is hard working. Mother is more content to make a home. She is more docile than passive."

EP5. IMAGE: RUNNING FASTER
"I see them riding horses in the open countryside. They are riding fast, having a joyous time of it.

There is a sense of sporting competition. They appear free and masterful on the horses and they thrive on the sportsmanship of the ride. I can see them running now; she is a bit ahead. He chases her playfully."

EP6. IMAGE: PATTERN OF RUNNING
"The purpose is a day in the country, playfulness."

EP7. IMAGE: FREEDOM OF LIMBS
"Both appear relaxed. Father's limbs are strong, sure-footed, muscular. Mother's are graceful and light."

EP8. IMAGE: BRILLIANCE OF PARENTS' EYES
"Father's eyes have a far away look. He sees something beyond, something for a better life for people. It is like a call from the distance, like a rumbling call, the need to go to war with an ideal in mind. My mother's eyes are almost doe-like. They relish comfort and pleasure and a peaceable kingdom."

EP9. IMAGE: OBJECT ORIENTATION
"My mother's eyes look at objects as a source of beauty. She admires beautiful things and has a deep appreciation. My father's eyes look at people and objects as a mere obstruction in his ability to see truth and reality."

EP10. IMAGE: STORY IN THE EYES
"My mother's eyes tell me she lives in a time when things were safe and secure, when roles were clear and she was protected and destinies were predictable. My father's eyes say that there is work to be done and there can be no rest or security if there are people suffering injustice."

EP11. IMAGE: LOUDNESS OF PARENTS' VOICES
"Father's voice sounds louder. He is demanding that we have to do something about this, the situation in the world. My mother's voice is imploring to see that he can't do that much to change things. She gets frustrated by his insistence. When I see this, my chest feels tight."

EP12. IMAGE: MEANINGFULNESS OF VOICES
"Father's voice has meaning and has stubbornness in it. Her voice has meaning but directs itself to the delicacies of the world."

EP13. IMAGE: STORY IN THE VOICES
"The story in his voice is that he cannot rest without taking action. Her voice says, 'Just let well enough alone. Can't you find pleasure in a life where there are so many beautiful things to enjoy? The world will wait.'"

EP14. IMAGE: HEARING BY PARENTS' EARS
"Neither of them hear me. They are too involved in this discussion. I have too small a voice to be heard. I see myself pull on their arms and go back and forth between them. They pat me and keep talking. My mother picks me up and walks away with me in a huff. I look over her shoulder at him. He is still sitting there brooding because she is not receptive to his point."

EP15. IMAGE: UNDERSTANDING BY EARS
"I see myself run up to Father and tell him what is bothering me. I say that I don't want to go with Mother only, that we should stay together as before. He hears me and says that it is up to her, he can't do anymore but he understands that it is hard on me. I run back to her and she tells me I don't understand anything of the situation. She overrides my concern with her own analysis of the situation."

EP16. IMAGE: PARENTS SNIFFING
"They both like the atmosphere of the house. She knows when it is just right. When there is something not quite right, she will adjust it and make it right."

EP17. IMAGE: WARMTH OF PARENTS' BODIES
"There is great personal warmth from both of their bodies."

EP18. IMAGE: BODY ACCEPTANCE
"My father's skin is tanned and very healthy, soft and smooth. It smells warm and sunburned, heated

by the sun. My mother's is fairer, but also burnt from the sun, as if she has been riding outside in the sun. Both accept me."

EP19. IMAGE: HEALTH OF SKIN
"His looks healthy and strong. Hers looks strong through conditioning, though she is not innately tough-skinned. She has become tough-skinned by weathering."

EP20. IMAGE: ARMS GIVING
"My father gives me a cube. Inside the cube a little city unfolds. It pops out of the cube when it is opened. The city sprawls before me, the little replica of a city has some kind of glittering magicality. The lights of the little city twinkle and I can appreciate its beauty. Also in the cube are many tools and objects that are practical in nature. Things that you can do things with, mechanical things, things that operate other things. There is also money in the cube. The money is banded together in bunches, stacks, and there is a monopoly game, and he tells me the directions for how to play the game. I see that it is a game of dice and he instructs me in the rules of what to look for when betting and throwing the dice. He gives me a sure-fired way to win. He says, 'Always watch the dealer. He will give himself away, you just have to watch him long enough. Then when you know him and his weakness, make your move, but wait until you know the ropes.' My mother hands me a little china tea cup. She hands it over and it is shaking a bit when she hands it to me. I guess she is shaking a bit though she does not look to be. In the cup is my imagination. It spills over and there is magic there. Little animals, flowers, scents of lilacs in the cup, perfume. The cup has an endless bottom. It is a cup for dreaming. As I saw this image, I saw that at the bottom of the cup there was brandy. I could see it shimmering and I could smell it also."

(Note: The reference to shaking and the brandy is a cue of mother's alcoholism.)

EP21. IMAGE: ARMS RECEIVING
"I am taking a gun from my father. He is showing me how to shoot. He directs me to point and aim and keep steady. He is teaching me to be a crack shot. From my mother I take a dagger. It symbolizes quick-wittedness, a fast tongue and slipperiness with words. She says, 'You can slay them faster with words and wit than any other way.'"

EP22. IMAGE: STRENGTH OF GRASP
"My mother holds a small bird in her hand. She holds it freely, with reverence and appreciation for its beauty. My father holds a knife and he is carving something from wood. He is careful and intentional as he carves."

EP23. IMAGE: SWALLOWING FOOD
"Father swallows easily. He takes in food with gusto. My mother savors the food, almost in reverence. She finds it so enjoyable and can just luxuriate in the process."

EP24. IMAGE: DRINKING FLUID
"He drinks a small bottle of milk that he pours into a cobalt blue glass. He drinks it heartily and clearly enjoys it. She drinks tea out of a cup. It is a small cup and saucer, Victorian design. She sips and relishes the delicacy of the aroma and flavor. It is almost as it she is smelling flowers as she is drinking."

   [First administration: "Mother tries to gulp it down so fast it pours all over her. She is a sloppy drunk. He can hold his liquor."]

EP25. IMAGE: JAW PRESSURE
"They chew with equal pressure taking in food."

EP26. IMAGE: PARENTS' BRAINS
"Father's brain is cool, but a perfect temperature. Hers feels sunnier, warmer, lighter."

EP27. IMAGE: BRAIN EFFICIENCY
"His mind is tightly operating, efficient, compact and does a lot of work and uses energy well. Her mind is more loosely structured. She is much more fanciful and literary."

EP28. IMAGE: PARENTS' HEARTBEATS
"His heart is very strong, beats slow, bass-like and rhythmic. Hers is smaller, full, almost musical in its continual rhythmic action."

EP29. IMAGE: PARENTS' INTESTINES
"His are white, thick, sturdy, almost like they are padded for better wear and action, like when pipes are wrapped to keep in the heat and insulation. My mother's are more translucent. You can see the materials being broken down and they are quite efficient though things seem to slide through a bit more."

EP30. IMAGE: PARENTS' GENITALS
"His are warm and healthy. He is proud of them. With mother, the same thing. They are saying, 'We are all from the same family. We are all part of the same species.' It is a very natural image."

Re-Administration of EPT with Alcoholic Mother Filter

EP1. IMAGE: HOUSE
"I see Mother in the house. She is passed out in the chair in the living room. I am between twelve and fifteen years old. I hate her. She is big and disgusting and drunk. I have to get her dead weight out of the chair and down to bed. I am screaming obscenities at her. I am worried that she will remember what I am saying because she is not totally passed out. She is in her forties. Father is not present."

EP2. IMAGE: LEFT-RIGHT POSITION OF PARENTS
"She is a big green wall of boiling puke. She overshadows my father, who shrinks into a tiny image next to her overpowering one. I feel sick. I hate this. There is nothing to switch. She consumes the center of the image."

EP3. IMAGE: PARENTS SEPARATED OR UNITED
"They are not united as a couple. He is not there or only as a miniscule image."

EP4. IMAGE: ACTIVE-PASSIVE PARENTS
"She is active in her frantic state, pacing, nervous,

sick, unhappy. She is beside herself, not knowing what to do. He has become almost wooden, not at all lifelike. I have the feeling he is not alive."

EP5. IMAGE: RUNNING FASTER
"This is awful. She is running and falling down, stumbling around, going nowhere in the field. It is a horrible image. She is pathetic and tragic. I feel horrible for her. I want to help her and make her sober up and be okay. It makes me sick. He has left the image, riding away quickly."

EP6. IMAGE: PATTERN OF RUNNING
"I can't watch her run around; it is too pathetic. She is lost and drunk. She runs in circles."

EP7. IMAGE: FREEDOM OF LIMBS
"I see him running on a rise above her. He is running along in the twilight; she is running below in circles."

EP8. IMAGE: BRILLIANCE OF PARENTS' EYES
"She is anesthetized. Her eyes are half open. She is oblivious. This is painful and nauseating. She sees nothing and wants to be left alone. He is like a wooden figure again, but there is light in his eyes. A white light streaming forth indicating that he is in the wooden figure and his vision is strong."

EP9. IMAGE: OBJECT ORIENTATION
"She can't even see objects. When she does happen upon one, she seizes it and clutches it in her hand and holds it to her for dear life. Now he has the bird in his hand protectively and then lets it fly away."

EP10. IMAGE: STORY IN THE EYES
"My mother's oblivion tells me to get lost, she has enough to deal with and, please, could I handle stuff myself. She would like to help but can't get up to do anything. Just leave her alone or else I'll be in big trouble. He tells me that despite his bad condition, that he is made of wood, he still has vision."

EP11. IMAGE: LOUDNESS OF PARENTS' VOICES
"I hear her voice. It is a horrible sound, it drones on and on. I have to cover my ears so I can't hear her. She is making me crazy. I can't stand the sound of it. She says things that I don't believe or understand. She says things that are outlandish, that don't fit with reality at all. It makes me think that I am crazy, so all I do is sit on the floor and cover my ears and rock back and forth. His voice is silent. I hear it on the inside."

EP12. IMAGE: MEANINGFULNESS OF VOICES
"Mother's voice is meaningful. It says to me that I am nuts constantly. My father's voice is a sensation in my heart. It is like a distant call."

EP13. IMAGE: STORY IN THE VOICES
"Her voice says, 'It is your attitude, that's all. We are normal.' Her voice is harsh and aloof. I hate her. His voice is an inkling, a sound in the distance, very faint."

EP14. IMAGE: HEARING BY PARENTS' EARS
"I am calling for my father outside, over the rise. He is not there. It is a lost cause. She hears me. She understands what I am saying but can do nothing about it. 'I have lost control,' she says. 'I am sorry.'"

EP15. IMAGE: UNDERSTANDING BY EARS
"He understands me somehow, but does not hear. She hears me but cannot comprehend."

EP16. IMAGE: PARENTS SNIFFING
"As she sniffs, she falls down. She is so drunk that she can't smell anything. But there is a faint recognition that someone is cooking an apple pie or making apple sauce and the cinnamon is very pungent. My grandmother must be cooking and it brings my mother to consciousness. She gets up off the kitchen floor where she was lying and sees her mother cooking in the kitchen. She is back as a young girl and everything has been put back to rights. Things are taken care of and she is a young girl of 18 or so, at their table. She is sober and enthusiastic about things that are hap-

pening at school and other interesting things. Her father is stern and grim. Though he loves her and his children, he is afraid for them. He knows that the world is a harsh place, as he has experienced the worst of it. My grandmother encourages my mother's enthusiasm and looks to the father for support. He says, 'Well, she had better be careful.' The discussion is about my mother working as a model. My grandmother, though a bit worried about the prospect, gets enthusiastic about the possibility. Her own life has been cut short by this grim man, the Depression, and the hassles of life."

EP17. IMAGE: WARMTH OF PARENTS' BODIES
"Mother drunk, no personal warmth. She is disgusting. Father is distant, though I want to be with him."

EP18. IMAGE: BODY ACCEPTANCE
"Skin of Father is thicker, much thicker, almost impenetrable. Her skin is frail, ruddy and marked, but very thin."

EP19. IMAGE: HEALTH OF SKIN
"Father's skin appears healthy. Mother's appears frail but fairly healthy genetically, but chemically abused."

EP20. IMAGE: ARMS GIVING
"My mother gives me a bottle of booze. She says, 'Have a drink. It will make you feel better.' Father says, 'Here is a gun. Use it if you need it. Take care to keep it correctly or else it can backfire on you.'"

EP21. IMAGE: ARMS RECEIVING
"I take the bottle from her and hit her on the head with it. I push her out of the way and step over her. I yell as I am leaving, 'You are a son-of-a-bitch.' I take from my father a set of keys, as if to a car or house. He has left them in an envelope for me, under the rug or on the table."

EP22. IMAGE: STRENGTH OF GRASP
"She is holding a bottle. It slips and crashes to the floor. She gets hysterical and frantically tries to mop it up but is helpless to do something or anything about it.

He is holding onto my hand. I am four, but the great wind comes and he can't hold onto it anymore."

EP23. IMAGE: SWALLOWING FOOD
"My mother is disgusting. She stuffs food in her mouth and washes it down. She is a pig and she has no ability to know what she is eating. She wants a five-course meal with all of the fixings, prime rib, pies, bread. It is making me sick. He is the same as before, the wooden figure, though he seems to eat but only as a function, eating only slightly."

EP24. IMAGE: DRINKING FLUID
"She drinks pails of water, drowning herself in it. Throwing it over her as if she were bathing in it. He becomes constricted when he drinks as if it would choke him."

EP25. IMAGE: JAW PRESSURE
"She is disgusting. She has so much in her mouth at one time she can't chew it. She stuffs her mouth because she is afraid it is going to be gone. He chews with more rigidity, tighter."

EP26. IMAGE: PARENTS' BRAINS
"Mother's brain, it is disgusting, lukewarm, all mushy, like vomit. Father's is still tight and efficient, but he has lost something. His brain has become rubbery."

EP27. IMAGE: BRAIN EFFICIENCY
"His brain is more efficient, but she still has some ability to be imaginative. There is still some music in there for her."

EP28. IMAGE: PARENTS' HEARTBEATS
"Mother's heart is exploding in the little chest cavity. It beats very hard, and as it beats it gets too big and pushes against the window, not having enough space to beat. His is sturdy but smaller than it was before."

EP29. IMAGE: PARENTS' INTESTINES
"Her intestines look like a penny arcade where you put the quarter in and it goes down the chute and

hits the bells along the way. Finally it gets to the end. Father's are the same but a bit less healthy."

EP30. IMAGE: PARENTS' GENITALS

"Father is okay with the process, but he says that we have no time to play today. We cannot be frivolous. Then when I ask again, he says, 'Sorry I was preoccupied. I always have time to explain things.' He then bends down and picks me up and I become a little child again. He sits down with me in the chair, and says, 'Okay honey, what do you want to know today?' His genitals feel warm and accepting and I feel secure that he is with me again. My mother says, 'Oh, sure,' and she also feels warm and I feel like I am connected with her again. It makes me feel safe and secure, like she cares about me."

The material reported while using the filter of a drinking parent as an activation filter revealed mental structures and fixations that were at a different level of consciousness than the previous test had yielded. The parent who is not an alcoholic may also be imagined as alcoholic and kept in mind that way while doing the test. The imagery changes as a result. For instance, in the previous administration of the EPT, EP30 had pointed to an age level when there was a positive feeling. Here, under the filter, the natural strength and security indicative of early childhood were, in fact, brought forward and experienced with both parents. Another indication or cue directing attention to an earlier, more positive state was found in EP22 where the father was seen holding the patient's hand while the mother was holding a bottle. Prior to this, the patient fixated in early adolescence when the image of the drinking parent overshadowed the strength. There was a further indication of this level and the trauma associated with it in the third testing, in EP20, when the mother was seen giving a cup and there was a sense that she was shaking. Further exploration revealed that there was also brandy shimmering in the bottom of the cup.

Throughout this testing, the father was seen with positive qualities. For example, the father's vision was intact though he was seen as wooden (EP8 and EP10); the father gave her a gun as a means of self-protection and a source of philosophy (EP 21); and she said, "He is holding onto my hand" (EP22). A tactic at this point was to use the non-drinking parent as a filter in order to activate some of the natural strengths and positive resources that the child has absorbed from the positive parent. The patient was instructed to see the drinking parent's image while keeping the other parent in mind with the following results.

Alcoholic Mother Images (EP1, EP2, EP24) with Positive Non-alcoholic Father Filter

These particular images were selected to use with the non-alcoholic parent's filter because they would provide concise material about the parents in the context of the home, their relational aspects and further dynamic information about the addiction.

EP1. IMAGE: HOUSE
"When I see my mother in the house, drunk in the chair, and keep my father in mind, he comes into the image, bends down and says, 'What is wrong? What is troubling you so much?' I feel very moved when I see the image. She looks at him and is first very angry and then says, 'It is your fault. You had to go and ruin it. You ran away from the field and all of the good things that could have happened.' He says, 'Let me help you,' and they go outside into the yard and sit together on the swing and watch the sunset. He is rocking her and she is getting more secure and comforted. They both understand that it has been a hard life. It has not been kind to either of them and there is a tacit understanding between them that transcends their differences."

EP2. IMAGE: LEFT-RIGHT POSITION OF PARENTS
"She shrinks down to her size and becomes the mother in the third EPT with him smoking his pipe, her with her hair braided. It is very positive."

EP24. IMAGE: DRINKING FLUID
"He comes in and helps her put the pail down. He says, 'Come on, this is foolishness. Let's go and relax and talk about what is bothering you.' She looks at him helplessly and follows his instructions. It is obvi-

ous that she was out of control, not able to take control for herself and he was able to intervene in her favor."

EP24 Repeated
"Now I see her drinking at a bar, slumped over the bar, drunk, miserable. She is in her cups. It looks like a western bar. Father comes in through the swinging doors, sees her there, and says, 'Oh boy, this is no good. I wonder what got into her.' He takes her back to the room which is over the saloon, puts her in bed and puts an ice pack on her head. She wakes up and sees him and says, 'How did you get here?' He says, 'I got here late.' She says, 'What a mess. I have been so depressed, not knowing what to do or how to do things without you.' He says, 'That is all over now. We can go home again.' She smiles and they hug."

EP24 Repeated
"I see her staggering down the street and holding onto a lamp post, trying to stand up. I see him walking down the street with a cigarette in his mouth and a hat on. He stops next to her. She is enraged at him. She says, 'Where were you, you bum? You are never around when I need you.' He says, 'What can I do? I do the best I can, but I can't be here enough to meet your needs.' She says, 'I just want a nice home like my mother had with nice Sunday dinners and the good life.' He says, 'You can't have a full plate if someone else is starving. I can't live with it.' She does not give a damn about anyone else's problems. She has her own needs and those of her child and they come first, after all. She says, 'We all have the things that will make us happy and you need to be there too.' He helps her home and says that they will talk about it tomorrow."

The Eidetic Parents Test revealed the underlying qualities of the alcoholic mother as well as the character of the non-drinking father and the strength that his image brought to the imagery scenarios. This strength ultimately provided a resolution for the emotional conflict between the parents in the patient's mind. When these images were allowed to interact, they revealed a deeper emotional layer and each parent's hidden desires, values, conflicts, and strengths. The patient reported a feeling of emotional release and relief at knowing the parents' natures more fully. The anger toward the alcoholic mother that was indicated in the test while seeing her images dissipated over repeated projections, and the patient reported a feeling of resolution and closeness with her that had not been experienced previously as well as a more open feeling in consciousness. Overall, intimacy in the internal relationship with the maternal figure created a greater sense of emotional stability and self-confidence.

Positive Parent's Eyes Filter Under Various Situations

1. *See an image of your alcoholic parent. It is a negative image.*
2. *Now see your nonalcoholic parent watching the alcoholic parent while courting. See the alcoholic parent through the nonalcoholic parent's eyes. It is a positive image of your alcoholic parent. You are seeing through the positive eyes.*
3. *Now see an image of your spouse. You feel like you did with your alcoholic parent. It is a negative image.*
4. *Now see your nonalcoholic parent seeing your alcoholic parent when they courted. See through the nonalcoholic parent's eyes and watch the person this parent courted. Then see your spouse. It is a positive image of your spouse.*
5. *The previous image of your spouse was based on your negative image of your alcoholic parent and could cause your spouse to fail.*
6. *With this negative image of your alcoholic parent in mind, your spouse could not succeed.*
7. *This negative image has negative power.*
8. *When the positive eyes are withdrawn, your child also has a negative aura.*
9. *When you see through the nonalcoholic parent's positive eyes, your child looks positive.*
10. *When you see through the negative eyes, your spouse and your child fight.*
11. *When you see through the positive eyes, your spouse and your child don't fight.*

In the following case, the positive parent's eyes were used as a filter to counteract the negative alcoholic filter that originated with the patient's alcoholic father and had been transferred to her alcoholic husband and to their son. She reported that due to this she took things out on her son because she believed he had a negative alcoholic aura. In order to remove the fixation on the father's image, she was instructed to see her father through her mother's eyes prior to their marriage, when they were courting. This tactic revealed the positive qualities of the father that had been obscured by the negative alcoholic filter and lifted MD's negative fixation on him. When a more positive image of the father was revealed, the negative fixation on her father was lifted and the impact of his alcoholic filter was able to be removed from her husband and son as well.

MD, Female, Age 30

MD had been married to SD for nine years and had experienced family and marital difficulties because of his drinking. She reported that her father had also been alcoholic and at this point, she feared that her son, age seven, was showing signs of alcoholic behavior and would ultimately become alcoholic as well.

In the first administration of the Eidetic Parents Test, MD reported: "I see my father as angry. He makes me feel badly about myself and I now regard him as pathetic. I remember a lot of fighting in the house, I always walked around on eggshells; everything always revolved around my father. I do not remember having any sense of myself or that I was important."

In the second administration of the Eidetic Parents Test, more positive feelings were revealed regarding both parents. However, there still remained a negative fixation on her father. Through deeper exploration of the parental figures, an image was developed in which the parents were seen when they were courting. MD was instructed to look at the courting scene and to see her father through her mother's eyes. This tactic revealed the positive qualities of the father that had been obscured by the negative alcoholic filter and lifted MD's negative fixation on him. It also removed the negative alcoholic filter that had been projected onto her husband and her son. MD responded to the Positive Parent's Eyes Filter images as follows.

"When I see the image of my father, it is a negative image. I feel hurt, angry and frustrated. When I see him through my mother's eyes, when they were courting, I see a happy, charming, fun-loving, handsome man, who is very much in love with my mother. I like that man that I see in this picture. He is the father that I like. I still have mixed feelings. It is a happy feeling, but I wonder why he didn't stick around. The negative still stays, I wanted him badly, why didn't he stay? The child in me is still there. A part of me did not grow up. My needs weren't met. I feel that half of me grew up, my good points, my strong points, but the little girl is still in pain.

"When I see the image, my mother is so happy. She knows right away that this is the man that she is going to marry. She has finally found him. I feel that this is all well and nice but I know what he is really like, and I know the pain he is going to bring my mother in the future. The future is grim. The picture is tainted. When I have difficult moments, I immediately have an instant replay of the past. But if I am feeling good, it is fine. I do not dwell on the past. There are times when I look to the future and I think positively, but then I think it is just a fairy tale.

"When I see the image of the positive father again, I can sustain it a little longer. I am happy with it. The first few times I saw the image, it felt like a trick picture. I thought to myself, I am trying to trick myself into saying that I had a happy father. I am too sneaky for this and I know what is up. Now when I keep seeing the image, it is probably the happiest they both have ever been. I am happy they are both happy. Her eyes are shining, she is so happy. The eyes are bright. She is very gay, she looks so pretty.

"If I see my mother seeing my father when they were courting and then look at my husband, I remember that when my mother first met my husband, she adored him right away. I think she saw a lot of what she saw in Daddy in my husband. She always says kind things about my husband, how sweet and sensitive he is. He is a nice man. My husband likes her very much and senses her sweetness toward him.

"I love my husband. He is the man I wanted to marry. He is wonderful. He is kind and good and amusing and exciting. Everything I always wanted. I still have those feelings for him. My feelings for him have not deteriorated that much. I just think that I bring a lot of my feelings of my father onto him. My father's alcoholism caused me a lot of anguish and pain. My husband is an alcoholic and he will cause me anguish and pain. I must have been operating off that premise even though I love my husband very much. I have to get rid of that image of my husband based on my father. What attracted me to my husband was the magic child in him. My magic child sees his magic child. I don't think that either of us could have been happier. We were so madly in love for so long. We were children together. We had so much fun, it was almost as though we were addicted to each other. I love my father. My mother loves my father and I love my husband.

"When I see my father negatively, I feel guilty that I imposed this on my husband. I have to undo it. The negative image has a lot of negative power. It is very strong. It is draining. I will turn that around. It will be equally powerful, strong and supportive and encouraging. With the negative image, even my son has a negative aura. He fits the pattern. I was thinking today that sometimes I take my feelings out on my son the way I did on my brother. I realized that I took out on my younger brother what I felt about my father.

"When I see the positive image, with mother seeing my father when they were courting, and then I look at my son, he looks wonderful. He is sweet and adorable, bright eyes, he has the magic child in him. It is definitely easier for me to have the more positive eyes with my son, more difficult with my husband and still more with my father.

"When I see my son with the negative image, I am so angry, I think, 'Typical alcoholic behavior and early signs of alcoholism.' When my son fights with my husband I think, 'There go a couple of drunks at it.' I grit my teeth; it never ends; a vicious cycle. I feel drained and helpless. Then I have bad feelings about myself and I go right down.

"When I see the positive image again, when I see with my mother's positive eye, she is very happy, very animated. I can feel her physically very excited. My father is her knight in shining armor. I feel the excitement in my chest. Now when I see the image of my husband, it is such a nice picture. I am happy, content, nothing is wrong. The future, it looks great. Since we started this I have had positive memories of my father. Until this point, I had him labeled negatively and put him up on the shelf."

Parental Filters with AA-VVIQ Images

The VVIQ (Vividness of Visual Imagery Questionnaire) was originally developed by Marks (1973) to measure imagery in terms of vividness and to discriminate between poor and good visualizers. Marks contended that vividness was the essence of imagery experience and did not change during test-retest. However, Ahsen (1985a, 1986a, 1987, 1988b, 1990a) found that vividness of mental imagery was not, in fact, a constant but changed under different conditions as illustrated in the previous examples of parental images as activation filters. Ahsen's adapted version of the VVIQ (AA-VVIQ) measures the variation of change in mental operations when the parental figures are kept in mind while viewing the sixteen items presented in the AA-VVIQ.

AA-VVIQ Imagery Items

In answering item 1 to 4, think of your father/mother separately and consider carefully the picture that comes before your mind's eye.

1. *The exact contour of the face, head, shoulders and body.*
2. *Characteristic poses of head, attitudes of body, etc.*
3. *The precise carriage, length of step, etc. in walking.*
4. *The different colors worn in some familiar clothes.*

Think of your father/mother in your mind. At the same moment, visualize a rising sun. Consider carefully the picture that comes before your mind's eye.

5. *The sun is rising above the horizon into a hazy sky.*
6. *The sky clears and surrounds the sun with blueness.*
7. *Clouds. A storm blows up, with flashes of lightning.*
8. *A rainbow appears.*

Think of your father/mother in your mind. At the same moment think of the front of a shop which you often go to. Consider carefully the picture that comes before your mind's eye.

9. *The overall appearance of the shop from the opposite side of the road.*
10. *A window display including colors, shapes and details of individual items for sale.*
11. *You are near the entrance. The color, shape and details of the door.*
12. *You enter the shop and go to the counter. The counter assistant serves you. Money changes hands.*

Think of your father/mother in your mind. At the same moment finally, think of a country scene which involves trees, mountains and a lake. Consider carefully the picture that comes before your mind's eye.

13. *The contours of the landscape.*
14. *The color and shape of the trees.*
15. *The color and shape of the lake.*
16. *A strong wind blows on the trees and on the lake, causing waves.*

The measurement of the differential impact of the parental images on perception yields a wealth of information regarding current identifications and issues relating to the parents. This is of particular value in cases of parental alcoholism and drug abuse. In the reports of "normal" populations, the father figure has emerged as a highly problematic image, dramatically inhibiting mental operations and the processes related to imagery ability (Ahsen, 1990a, 1991). In one group tested, when the subjects kept the father in mind while seeing certain images, imagery ability was reduced up to 380% as compared to when the mother was kept in mind (Sussman, 1993). Interestingly, however, in some clinical populations, these results showed a tendency to be reversed, indicating that imagery ability tends to be more obstructed or inhibited when the mother is kept in mind (Ahsen, 1985b).

The underlying dynamics involved in the suppression of imagery functions when under the mother's image have been found to correlate to difficulty with the mother figure in early developmental history, giving rise to a compensatory and often defensive identification with the father figure. Difficult and entrenched emotional problems seem to arise when there is inhibition, lack of connection or unresolved negativity regarding the mother's image. The most basic emotional needs essential for sustained mental and emotional health are innately rooted in the image of the mother. When these qualities are absent or inhibited, neurosis and impaired functioning result. Compensatory attitudes toward other figures or objects do not resolve or replace the need for this primary relationship. The ultimate goal, therefore, is to retrieve the mother's image and restore her ability in consciousness to provide supportive and life enhancing qualities.

In the following case study (Ahsen, 1990a), the AA-VVIQ was used as both a diagnostic tool and a therapeutic tactic. The questionnaire was utilized in this manner to document the therapeutic change that took place over that period of time regarding both the mother's and father's images. It also served to elucidate the progression of therapeutic change and provided a means of analysis and integration of the material.

SS, Female, Age 43

SS was administered the AA-VVIQ on three separate occasions during a two-year period in Eidetic Image Therapy. The first administration occurred at the beginning of treatment; the second administration in the mid-period; and the third administration near the end period. A comparison of the results is provided below. The results of each administration are compared and discussed in light of various subjective reports and other experiential data.

Before presenting the comparison and the analysis and retrospective view of the material, scores for vividness-unvividness for the three test administrations are provided in Table 1. These scores reflect the comparative degree of vividness over the sixteen items while keeping the father or the mother in mind.

Comparison of Results

In comparing the results, the most striking feature in SS's AA-VVIQ is the difference between the ratings of first and the third administrations. In the first administration, SS reported ten of the sixteen items as more vivid when the father was kept in mind; five of the sixteen items were more vivid when the mother was kept in mind; and one item was rated the same under both conditions. The third administration indicates a reversal of these ratings: fourteen of the sixteen items were rated as more vivid when the mother was kept in mind; only one item was more vivid when the father was kept in mind; and one item was rated the same for both the mother and father. Thus, in the first administration, mental operations are obstructed more under the image of the mother, while in the third administration, mental operations are obstructed more under the image of the father. The second administration appears to represent a transitional phase between the first and third administrations.

The following material includes a brief description of SS's mother and father images from a report given prior to beginning Eidetic Image Therapy and before the first AA-VVIQ administration as well as the report from the third administration to illustrate the differences in perception that transpired.

Table 1

Comparison of AA-VVIQ Vividness Scores over Three Administrations in the Case of SS

Item	First Administration		Second Administration		Third Administration	
	5F	10M1	9F	2M	14F	1M1
	F	M		5	F	M
	1	2*	F	M	1	2*
1	1	2*	18	1	83	1
2	1*	1	2*	2	*5	1
3	1	4*	1*	1	1*	1
4	1	2*	1	2*	*3	1
5	1	2*	*4	1	*3	1
6	*3	1	*3	2	*4	1
7	1	2*	2	3*	*4	1
8	*2	1	*2	1	*2	1
9	*3	1	3*	3	*2	1
10	*2	1	*4	3	*5	1
11	1	4*	3*	3	*3	1
12	1	2*	*4	3	*3	1
13	1	2*	*2	1	*2	1
14	1	2*	*2	1	*3	1
15		*4	*2	1	*2	1
16			*2	1		

Note. The scores reflect the comparative degree of image vividness over sixteen items, while keeping the father or mother in mind. Dimmer scores are marked by an asterisk on one side. Scores that were the same for both parents are indicated by an asterisk in the middle. At the top of each column are the total scores dimming under father (F) and under mother (M) for that administration, and the number of scores equal under both father and mother appears immediately below.

Rating Scale

	Rating
Perfectly clear and as vivid as normal vision	1
Clear and reasonably vivid	2
Moderately clear and vivid	3
Vague and dim	4
No image at all, you only "know" that you are thinking of the object	5

Report Prior to Treatment: Mother

"My mother was alcoholic. She was diagnosed manic depressive when I was a kid. She did not express her depression much. The alcohol overshadowed everything. If you were to ask her, she would say, 'I am okay.' She would never go into a dialogue about how depressed she was. It was business as usual. When I would try to think about her, it would space me out. Her whole thing was about being normal. She was crazy and she kept saying we were normal, so I never knew what was happening in my environment. This is connected to my paranoia. She would say that it was one way, and my experience would say that it was totally different, so I never knew what was happening.

"She was, indeed, a very angry woman, angry and bitter. The tone of her voice was lethal. She was not a screamer. I think that my existence annoyed my mother because she could not cope with her own life. I never doubted that she loved me, but it was almost like I was not there. She had a lousy life; it was so disappointing. The whole family had lousy, tragic lives.

"If I focus on Mother, she becomes a monster, a vampire. There are a lot of physical feelings connected to it, an element of holding my breath, tightness in my chest."

Report Prior to Treatment: Father

"He had commitment and concern. He had his life purpose to do and he did it. I think that he was a tough old bastard, that is for sure. He was a real fighter, social commitment. He cut his losses, like with my mother. He went so far with her and that was it. He was moody. I have seen photos of him where he looked very intense and Mother would say I was sullen, just like he was. Finally, he became disillusioned, very disillusioned. He was a visionary, that's my take on it. He said to me, 'Well, what do you expect? You have to take care of yourself, you have got to learn that.' I learned that the hard way. When I see the image of my father spontaneously, he is very vague, almost ghostly."

Third Administration: Parental Images with Mother in Mind

1-4. "I see my mother more vividly than I see my father, whose vividness is not uniform."

5. "When I see the sun rising, I can feel the sensation of warmth on my skin. It is a damp heat which gets warmer as the sun comes up. I have the image of a day at the beach with Mother."

6. "As I see the sky clearing, I feel the sun tanning my skin. The image develops into positive images with Mother playing at the beach. I am about three or four years old in the image."

7. "When I see the clouds in the sky, I feel the temperature change. There is a coolness in the air which precedes the storm. As the storm blows, the sky becomes dark and awesome. My mother and I huddle together, she has her arm around me, points to the sky and tells me to watch for the lightning. It is very exciting. There is a magical quality to it."

8. "The rainbow appears as if by magic. It is enormous and extends over the horizon. The colors are vivid and seem to almost envelop everything."

9. "My mother kneels down next to me and points to the shop across the road. She says, 'Let's go over there and see what they have in the shop.' It is very exciting."

10. "As we approach the shop, all of the items in the window become bigger than life. The colors, shapes, and textures appear amazingly brilliant and I am mesmerized by them."

11. "The door seems very, very large. I am holding my mother's hand. As she holds the door open, a little bell sounds our entry. The door is a screen door with wood that is painted dark green. As we go inside, it hangs shut and sort of bounces on its hinges as it closes behind us."

12. "We enter the shop and go to the counter. My mother buys me one of those big round lollipops that

looks like a spiral of a million colors. I am very excited about it. I can taste all of the different colors of the
lollipop. It is a terrific image."

13. "When I see the contours of the landscape,
there is a sweeping quality to it. There is a sense of
panorama. My mother is kneeling down next to me
and pointing out different things to look at. She is
showing me things."

14. "When I look at the trees, my mother describes
different qualities of them to me. She tells me about
how birds make nests in the trees, and how the squir-
rels live in the trees. She takes my hand and says, 'Let's
go and get a closer look at things.' There is a feeling of
expansiveness in the image, and a positive somatic
feeling. There is almost a mystical quality about it."

15. "When I see the color and shape of the lake, my
mother and I are swimming in it. First we look at it,
and then run over to it and put our toes in the water to
test it out. There is a raft on the lake, a rowboat, a rub-
ber inner tube to float around in. I float with my arms
around my mother. It is a very warm experience."

16. "When the wind blows up on the water, I can
ride on the little waves, as if surf riding. The colors
are vivid. I see other swimmers with brightly colored
suits on, and bright bathing caps on. There is a lot of
activity and excitement in the image."

Third Administration: Parental Images with Father in Mind
1-4. "I see my father less vividly than my mother."

5. "When I look at the sun rising in the sky, I am
observing it when I keep my father in mind. I see
myself watching the sun rise. I see my head move
from the horizon up toward the sky as the sun rises.
There is a distinct separation from the body sensation
experience, unlike when my mother is kept in mind."

6. "It is again an observation. My father and I sit
on the beach and watch the sun rising and the sky
clearing."

7-8. "The image obliterates and there is a feeling
that I would have to work at it to get it again."

9. "Seeing the shop, I have an image of a hardware store. My father puts his hand on my shoulder to help me cross the road. We are going to the hardware store to buy something. It feels like a routine thing to do."

10. "We go toward the store and I see the items in the window. There are saws, hammers, paint cans hanging in the window. The things in the window look pretty interesting. I feel like standing there and looking at things."

11. "My dad holds the door open for me. He still has his hand on my shoulder. It is comforting that he holds on to me. The door seems very stiff to open, as if the springs are tight on the hinges to keep the door closed properly. I keep looking at the window as we go inside. I turn my head around so that I can keep looking while we enter the store."

12. "We go inside. The store is kind of dark and musty. We walk over to the counter. My dad buys some sandpaper. I look up at the counter man as he talks to my dad. Dad hands him some change for the paper. I can smell sawdust all round. There are a lot of things to look at, bins of nails, screws, all kinds of doorknobs, very interesting stuff, but for some reason we have to leave."

13. "There is not the sense of panorama that there was with my mother. This image with my father in mind is close up. There is very little distance when looking at the landscape. He squats down and picks up some dirt in his hand and tells me something about the landscape like, 'You see that tree over there?' and then he directs me in a specific direction to look at something with focus as opposed to seeing the whole landscape."

14. "Looking at the contours of the trees, he is showing the measurement of the trees, pointing out the variations in height of the trees. The image lacks color. It is black-and-white."

15. "The lake tends to be a steely gray and has a vague shape."

16. "There is a protective quality of my father here. He says, 'Stand back here behind me so you don't get wet.'"

Analysis of Responses and Integration

In SS's third AA-VVIQ administration, one of the most distinct differences in the experience of keeping the mother, as compared to father, in mind is the very positive somatic component connected with the mother's image. Not only is the image of the mother that appears in the scene positive, but the body feelings associated with her image and with the scene itself are positive. There is a feeling of potential in each scenario. Each part of the scene has the potential of being expanded and further evolved to evoke more positive imagery. This quality is juxtaposed to previous images of the mother which were extremely negative. The father, on the other hand, creates a cool and detached feeling, black-and-white, which is at some variance with his earlier images and the feeling states connected with him. However, he resides more as an idea in the earlier images, and although the idea is positive, he appears ghostly and vague.

The intensity of the positive somatic experience associated with the images when the mother was kept in mind came as a surprise; also, each image revealed qualities in the mother that had not been previously experienced. Her magicality and her ability to impart that quality to objects and events were new, as was the experience of her physicality. During the AA-VVIQ, her image evoked feelings of love, support and care, which was a contrast to the earlier states associated with her. The image of the father was more flat and static than had been experienced previously, which suggested that the depth of these qualities had not been fully experienced and required further exploration. The image of the father, when compared to SS's ideas about him, underscores the experience of objective detachment with which the image scenarios are seen when keeping the father in mind. For example, while seeing the sun rise into a hazy sky, the image is observed rather than experienced, as it is with the mother. There is an idea of the father as a visionary, yet the image reveals that he is short-sighted, as illustrated by his lack of perspective and distance in the landscape scene.

In evaluating the scores by clusters, the greatest change can be seen in the images concerned with Nature (items 5-8 and 12-16). In both (the rising sun image and the landscape image), in the third administration results, all of these items were rated most vivid while keeping the mother in mind whereas, previously, six of the eight items were rated most vivid while keeping the father in mind. The later images were more vivid under the mother than they had been under the father because of the added, new somatic component. The mixing of sensory modalities is a quality discussed in detail by Ahsen elsewhere (1987). However, suffice it to say that there was a richer, "thicker" and feelable (Ahsen, 1991) quality to the most vivid rating under the mother's filter than had been previously reported under the father's filter. Much of therapy had been focused on exploring a compensatory identification with the father which, when resolved, enabled the image of the mother to emerge with new positive strengths and characteristics that had been previously repressed.

The cluster of items related to the shop showed the greatest variance during the transitional stage. While the items were rated as more vivid under the mother in the first and third administrations, in the second administration dimming occurred under both the mother and the father. This can be attributed to the evolving positive image of the mother. In the first administration, the shop was a clothing store in which the subject and her mother were shopping together. The items, though positive, did not have the same depth as the later images. There was also an age difference between the first administration in which the self-image was perhaps twelve or thirteen, and the later administration in which the self-image was a much earlier age, three or four. Though the first image was most vivid, the third contained the positive somatic quality, evoking a sensation of release and well-being.

In reviewing the results of the three AA-VVIQ administrations, the mother's image emerged with strengths and characteristics that were previously unavailable, providing a sense of support and a feeling of wholeness. The subject experienced a feeling of having access to new-found strengths and abilities. The father's image, on the other hand, left the subject with a feeling of wanting to know more about him. There was a lack in his image which required further investigation.

Thus, future directions for therapy were clearly indicated in the results yielded in the AA-VVIQ.

The analysis and retrospective review of the material also serve to elucidate and clarify changes in consciousness that have transpired during the last two years of therapy. Retrieval of the mother's portrait provided a stabilizing influence, engendering the experience of primary rootedness in her image. There was also a growing sense of a separate identity with distinctly different attributes than those possessed by the father or the mother which gave a feeling of a unique and autonomous self. This progression illustrates the goal of the eidetic process: "The progression in pictures is a progression in perspective, a shift in self perspectives, a new birth of self image and identity" (Ahsen, 1977a, p. 140).

Expectation High Parent Image and Filter

In each of the Eidetic Parents Test image scenarios, see your alcoholic or addicted parent (mother/father) in a high state without alcohol or any other addictive substance.

Keep the Expectation High Parent in mind while seeing an image or experiencing a life event.

When an addicted parent is seen in an Expectation High state and also is used as an activation filter, aspects of the parent's personality that have been obscured by the addiction can be revealed. The parent's essence becomes activated and his or her natural capacity for euphoria, elation and the expression of imagination can provide the patient with a new level of awareness of the parent's potential. This tactic is illustrated in the following case. Here the patient is instructed to see an image of the alcoholic father in an Expectation High state, without alcohol, in each of the Eidetic Parents Test scenarios. This tactic evoked a positive free feeling and revealed an aspect of the father that had been previously hidden. It provided the patient with the feeling of contact and intimacy with the father and a more relaxed somatic state.

LB, Male, Age 26
Expectation High Father without Alcohol

EP1. IMAGE: HOUSE
"I see my father mowing the lawn. He just starts pushing the lawn mower in the street and wandering around in the neighborhood, pushing the lawn mower. He is mowing everything, not destroying, but not differentiating what is lawn and not lawn, just going along with the lawn mower. I feel open and very clear and free. It isn't that funny; it is normal for me. There is relief that he is behaving the way he should."

EP2. IMAGE: LEFT-RIGHT POSITION OF PARENTS
"I see him a little to my right. Now he just moved to my left. I move him a little closer maybe. He doesn't bother me. His energy is much more fluid. It has harmony with everything else that I am feeling. The left side of my face is warm."

EP3. IMAGE: PARENTS SEPARATED OR UNITED
"It seems to be ever changing mixtures of colors and temperatures and overall fairly warm and bright. They are almost like being playful and teasing. Now I feel it on the left side of my face. I feel the heart beat on the left side of my face and my muscles seem to be relaxing."

EP4. IMAGE: ACTIVE-PASSIVE PARENTS
"He is very open to his environment and his level of activity is in accordance with what harmony is. Now the warmth in my face is expanding a little bit all over, still pretty subtle."

EP5. IMAGE: RUNNING FASTER
"He runs all different ways, whatever makes him feel good. He is open and aware and has a sense of pleasure in community."

EP6. IMAGE: PATTERN OF RUNNING
"He is running for pleasure and community. The style is about enjoying sensuality and pattern; it is just like the patterns of the wind. There is no pattern, but there is a pattern."

EP7. Image: Freedom of Limbs
"Father's limbs appear relaxed, very relaxed. I can almost see him flying. Watch him fly around. It is fun, very freeing, open and free, playful."

EP8. Image: Brilliance of Parents' Eyes
"They are extremely brilliant. They are like baby's eyes, bright blue."

EP9. Image: Object Orientation
"His eyes are just object oriented. He looks at things for the amount of time they should be looked at. It is pleasant. I feel the warmth on the left side of my face."

EP10. Image: Story in the Eyes
"I see the story of the beginning of things, newness, openness and all essence. Father looks with wonder the way that babies look, looking around for as long as something catches its eye. Just looking at it for the way it is."

EP11. Image: Loudness of Parents' Voices
"It has a different loudness but has a nice tone, so it is all pleasant."

EP12. Image: Meaningfulness of Voices
"It is meaningful, as meaningful as voices get, very meaningful."

EP13. Image: Story in the Voices
"It tells the story of primordial thunder and the sound of creation."

EP14. Image: Hearing by Parents' Ears
"He hears me very well. I feel free and unobstructed."

EP15. Image: Understanding by Ears
"He understands me perfectly. He understands through the energy rather than the words. This is interesting. All of a sudden he is processing legitimate psychical information for what it is. That is odd. It almost brings up a sense of vulnerability. I feel almost a little naked. For the first time he can

see me. When I see that he accepts the information as information, it makes me sort of want to trust him, which I haven't really done since I was about three years old."

EP16. IMAGE: PARENTS SNIFFING
"It is pleasurable. He is happy, interested, playful. A lot of tension in my butt is opening up."

EP17. IMAGE: WARMTH OF PARENTS' BODIES
"It is nice, sort of soft and friendly. Nice vibration, warm. It feels pretty masculine. Thank God, my body is opening up. It is frustrating, my body hurts, when I get to the edge, it is like bouncing up against the wall."

EP18. IMAGE: BODY ACCEPTANCE
"It accepts me. It is inviting almost, very touchable. I feel more fluid, softer, warmer."

EP19. IMAGE: HEALTH OF SKIN
"The skin appears healthy. It has a nice active, growing glow to it. My right arm has a burst of warmth."

EP20. IMAGE: ARMS GIVING
"He gives me that rose; actually, he knows this state and he wants me to do it again and have fun with it. More warmth in the body, things opening up.

"I have times when I wake up and I don't know how to let go of the blankets, like they get sort of soldered together in my hands and other times, like when a kid holds something and doesn't want it and lets it go. Like real clean, you deal with what you deal with and when it goes, it is gone."

EP21. IMAGE: ARMS RECEIVING
"I feel sort of giddy, laughing."

EP22. IMAGE: STRENGTH OF GRASP
"His grasp is firm, there is a feeling of union. He was holding a sword, union. I have tingles above my eyes, there is loosening up in my face, jaw and neck. My muscles are tight, the tightness goes out of them and I stretch them out."

EP23. IMAGE: SWALLOWING FOOD
"Father is eating a rabbit. He can taste it, swallowing it, playing with the food. I feel it in my jaw and cheek bones, opening, growing, moving up."

EP24. IMAGE: DRINKING FLUID
"He is drinking from a lake. He drinks all different ways. He is very sensual about it. He wants to feel different ways, playing and making noises. My skin feels warmer and is opening up. I feel closer to that state of harmony with the environment at the mystical level. My chest and lower back are still tight. These are my worst places. I still hold my breath since my chest and back are connected to the breathing."

EP25. IMAGE: JAW PRESSURE
"Father is chewing on a big bone. He is very open about being animal-like. Opens my peripheral vision. I feel wider. I can focus on an activity and expand my view at the same time."

EP26. IMAGE: PARENTS' BRAINS
"My father's brain is warm. I feel giddy. It feels like he is laughing inside his brain. Back of my head feels like it has opened up."

EP27. IMAGE: BRAIN EFFICIENCY
"It looks like a movie screen for ideas and images that come from that and are independent and around in the air and they show themselves on his brain and leave. It is always really clear what is going on."

EP28. IMAGE: PARENTS' HEARTBEATS
"Father's heart beats very strong and is active and seems to be aware of itself and fully conscious. My breathing feels a little better, quieter."

EP29. IMAGE: PARENTS' INTESTINES
"They look healthy, almost muscular. They look clean and sort of shiny almost.

"I feel muscular in my lower abdomen, but sore. When the tension gets released the muscles get sore there. Then it starts to move in ways that it did not move before."

EP30. IMAGE: PARENTS' GENITALS
"He looks healthy, warm. I can touch his genitals because he is my father, but it does bring out a little bit of male competitiveness, but it is not bad. There is a bit of dominance, like how male hierarchies go. Like rutting season when the rams butt heads.

"It is a little playful, like maybe getting away with something, fun in that way for both of us. Now it is competitively playful. I pretend that I will kick him there, like when the rams square off before butting heads. We don't butt heads but play the game of squaring off. I feel more open, more aggressive in a relaxed way."

Unvivid Filters and Images

Keep the vague person (parent, grandparent) in mind while seeing an image or experiencing a life event.

Concentrate on the the vague object in the image and allow the details to emerge.

Ahsen (1985a, 1986a 1986b, 1987, 1990a, 1991) has extensively investigated and discussed the role of unvivid and vague imagery in mental operations. He has emphasized the importance of this aspect clearly. As evidence indicates, unvividness is a special quality of the imagery experience that is necessary to the achievement of a goal which cannot be otherwise attained through vivid imagery. Subjects invariably go through clear and vague images as necessary and critical steps in arriving at the total experience. Thus, a vague image may be associated with a psychical need or trauma or it may be vague simply because it is supposed to be vague to create the effect it is designed for. Interestingly, in regard to issues of addiction, he reports that the experience of hope often emerges from vague imagery, growing dimly at first on the periphery of consciousness and only later giving rise to clear images. Thus, attention to what may at first appear as unvivid or vague has particular application to retrieving the qualities of hope and positive Expectation High states of futurism.

In the following example, several positive filter images appeared initially as vague or dim imagery that, when concentrated on, provided the person with a sense of relaxation and comfort and allowed deeper involvement with the material.

SD, Male, Age 35

SD reported that he was having marital difficulties due to his drinking. His wife had asked him to leave the house on three occasions because of the problem. He also said that he had problems with his son, age seven, and with his father, who was also alcoholic. SD said that he had been drinking alcohol and using drugs since early adolescence.

SD showed a great deal of impatience during the Eidetic Parents Test process. His responses to the images were sparse and lacked detail. He often misunderstood the meaning of the images, which resulted in incorrect conclusions about his parents and his life. For instance, he stated:

> "My father still does it to me. He still thinks that I should get some success and get somewhere and settle down. It revolves around impatience, not having the ability to let the creative thing flow. He has the mentality of the conservative person, which serves him well. He tries to force that on me and I yield. It doesn't make me feel good. It creates bad consequences. I sense a frustration on his part and it makes me uncomfortable. This has been going on over the years. I think I have hurt him and disappointed him. I see how this carries through on how I interact with my son. I am impatient with my son, like my father was with me. For instance, I interrupt him and force my thoughts on him and he reacts badly. I am sure that scenario has repeated itself many times; it makes everything fall apart. It creates a reaction, chaos. Against this tendency to repeat what my father did to

me and what I do to my son, there is the image of my grandfather who let things flow, let it happen."

To further explore the image of his father, SD was administered image scenarios from the AA-VVIQ. He was instructed to keep his father in mind and see an image of entering a store and transacting business. He said:

> "I see that my father is very quick and gets it done; he does not spend time in transactions. Sometimes I am that way too. There is not much detail as to what Father does in terms of transactions, it is too quick. It is just done. A lot of times, I will do it so quickly, so fast. People like to see how it is done. I have had the complaint about my non-attention to details. There is a loss of details. It has been pointed out to me later on that if I had paid attention to detail, something would not have happened. This has been often seen as a defect and a problem in how I did something. I often respond by saying it is not a problem, but people don't buy it and from that point, the deal goes sour."

Initially, SD experienced the image of his father as quite negative, not only in the observation of his father's impatience in the image, but also in the feeling of impatience that was evoked in him while he saw the image. SD said that his father's quickness and impatience had always created a feeling in him of being controlled. He also said that he had these feelings with his own son, with whom he was often impatient and controlling.

Grandfather Filter. The image of his grandfather, however, was quite positive and evoked an open and active feeling. In his grandfather's image, there were intimations of the Expectation High, connection with Nature and the ability to let things flow. When it was used as an activation filter, it provided SD with a more positive orientation and base of operations.

Parents as a Couple (EPT item 3) Filter. Through further exploration of the parental images, the impact of their separation at age twelve emerged as a major theme in development. SD was sent to boarding school when the parents separated and he reported that soon after this he began using drugs. When the parents were seen together as a couple prior to the separation, SD reported that his ability to see things was stronger and that the image had a positive effect.

When the positive image of the parents together was used as a filter, SD reported that the images appeared stronger and clearer. This indicated that the experience of his parents' presence as a couple had a positive effect on his ability to see things more clearly. When his parents were absent in the image, he reported that the images appeared dimmer. The clear picture of his parents together and actively involved with him gave SD a feeling of action in his mind.

Father's Clothing as Vague Image (AA-VVIQ item 4). The opportunity to understand and benefit from dim or vague images provided SD with a greater understanding of his present situation and enabled him to gain more skill in interacting with it. Further exploration of vague imagery revealed an underlying positive image of his father's conservatism represented in the clothing that he wore. SD reported: "Father's clothes are dull, fall colors. There is a feeling of nature in them; nothing special, casual and comfortable. It is a nice conservative look. I feel more comfortable when I see his clothing, more at ease. I am less in conflict with him. He also shows more ease and patience. It gives me a certain lift in my mind. I am more focused."

As a result of concentrating on the vague image of his father's conservative clothing, SD appeared to be more relaxed and attentive to the material and the issues involved in it. Prior to this he reported feeling impatient during the process.

SD was instructed to see an image of his father and mother and to rate differentially the degree of vividness of each parent concerning various colors worn in some familiar clothing. He said: "I was trying to differentiate between the conservative clothes that my father would wear and my mother, who is more brightly dressed and more spunky."

Concentration on aspects uncovered in the vague image provided access to an underlying positive quality in the father's portrait. The more obvious and vivid qualities of quickness and impatience that were initially ascribed to the father evoked a negative feeling for SD.

Quickness of movement was ascribed with vividness and a brighter image of the father, while less movement and dimness were ignored. The quicker movement and more dramatic action had captured SD's attention and suppressed the potential in the unvivid imagery. He also said that the terms "less movement" and "unvividness" were pejorative because they indicated weakness to him. Thus, while he attended to quickness and a flamboyant style because it was experienced as more vivid, he needed to secure the qualities found in vague imagery, that is, relaxation and a more comfortable feeling. When he had become too quick, he had missed the details in his business transactions and was unsuccessful. The quickness and flamboyance that captivated his attention in his environment were flawed because they prevented him from gaining the strengths and abilities he needed to be successful. By uncovering his father's underlying positive potential found in unvivid images and drawing on his grandfather's ability to let things flow, he began to discover his own unique style of action. He found that he was flamboyant in his own special way, more like his grandfather in essence, yet he also possessed his father's comfortable, conservative style. He commented:

> "This is the essence of what I was striving for, success in business, which will facilitate many other aspects of my life which have fallen in disrepair because of faulty mechanisms. The problems I experienced would happen over and over again, with everything going wrong in my business, personal life and with my health. If I see a flamboyant person in the office, I would now look at him with disdain. If there was no substance there, I would not stop to talk to him. I used to be attracted to that kind of person, the flash-in-the-pan flamboyant, and that attraction reflected a weakness in me. I was always vulnerable to them. I would think to myself, 'I am a bright guy, but I get into the same thing over and over again.' It would stump me, I was really confounded by it. Now I can see it clearly."

An Antidote Image

In some cases, an image will emerge during the imagery process that will be useful in correcting inaccurate projections and false positive associations with alcohol and other drugs. This particular image can be used to demystify the power of the drug and remedy the influence of autosuggestion. This type of image, which Ahsen calls an antidote image, surfaces from the patient's own imagery process and has meaning in that context. The following case examples illustrate this process. When repeated, the antidote image served to remove the fantasy of pleasure and enjoyment associated with the activity of drinking alcohol, and allowed the Expectation High to be restored to its natural expression.

Paul, Male, Age 21
(For a detailed presentation of this case, see Chapter 7)

In Paul's case, exploration of EP24 revealed an image of the mother drinking iced coffee which, when more deeply explored, provided remediation for the patient's alcohol involvement.

EP24. IMAGE: DRINKING FLUID

In the first projection, Paul saw his father drinking faster than his mother, who was drinking in little gulps. In a later projection, he saw his father drinking faster. He was drinking milk, which was reported to be a pleasant image. His mother was seen drinking iced coffee. Paul said: "Iced coffee is Mother's drink. I associate that with my mother. I never liked that. How can she like it so much? It is pretty positive."

Philosophy about Drinking

Paul's philosophy about his drinking and his current alcohol experience were developed. He reported:

"When thinking about my philosophy of alcoholism, I have a little bit of a problem. When I try to cut down I realize that it has become an unnecessarily unconscious part of my evenings out. Over the months, I have cut down. When I go out I have four instead of eight or ten. Sometimes I go out four times a week. When I was doing a lot of drugs I had to drink alcohol to keep balance. The drug speeds up the body and the alcohol brings it down. If I had not used alcohol, I would have died. I was using a lot of cocaine, at least three nights a week, for a few months. I stopped that when I got sick. My body was so worn down from drugs, I got sick."

Antidote Image: Self-Image Drinks Alcohol from Mother's Glass or Cup

The image of the mother drinking tea or coffee from a glass or a cup was introduced through the following instructions.

1. *See yourself drinking alcohol.*
2. *See an image of your mother drinking tea/coffee.*
3. *Which image is stronger?*
4. *Drink the tea/coffee in the image. How do you feel?*
5. *Now go back to the image of your mother drinking tea/coffee.*
6. *Smell your mother's tea/coffee and take a sip of it.*
7. *Take another sip and check your feelings.*
8. *Now see alcohol in your mother's glass/cup.*
9. *Smell and taste it.*
10. *When you smell the alcohol, what is that like?*
11. *Taste it.*
12. *Now pour the alcohol in your mother's tea/coffee and mix the two.*
13. *Mix the two flavors and smell and taste it. Drink it, the whole thing.*
14. *What is your reaction to drinking alcohol now?*

Paul responded as follows to the above image.

> 1. "It is a game. It is like when you are little, five or six, and you are with other little kids and say, 'Do you want to play a game?' Now we are older and you say, 'Hey, you want to go out?' It is the same thing.
> "I go out with a couple of close friends to one of the bars that we go to and hear whatever band we want to hear. We listen to music, have fun, get a buzz on and be silly. Everything flows. It is an unconscious

process. I feel set with the friends in the bar. It is like I have everything I need. It is cozy, nice, a little nest, a sanctuary. That would be a good name, 'Club Sanctuary.'"

2. "I go to the refrigerator and I see this pitcher of what looks like iced tea and it smells funny and I taste it. I don't like it. She says it is iced coffee. I see her sitting at the kitchen table and we are having lunch and she is sipping on this glass of iced coffee. She seems to be enjoying it."

3. "The image in the kitchen is stronger."

4. "I would rather not drink it. It doesn't totally disgust me. I don't particularly care for it."

5. "I am laughing because I am thinking about having lunch with my mother when I was little. I am paying attention to what I am drinking because it doesn't taste good. I am paying attention to what I am drinking in the bar too. It tastes so much better than the iced coffee. The bar image is weaker in comparison. I am more focused on my drink in the bar."

6. "My mother keeps asking me 'Why the hell do you keep drinking it if you don't like it?' It smells like cold coffee. It doesn't turn me on and it doesn't turn me off. I would rather not drink it."

7. "I just put it down and I don't want anymore and I wonder why anybody would take a whole glass of it or go out of their way to make some."

8. "Baccardi and coke. It looks good."

9. "It smells like rum and coke. It is nice. It smells sweet and I can smell a faint hint of rum. I can see the bubbles hanging around the ice cubes. I can even smell the straw. Straws smell. They smell like plastic or wax."

10. "It is nice. It makes me want to taste it."

11. "It is good. It is nice and cold and tastes good. It is just very nice."

12. "It doesn't taste good. I am not going to drink it. I tasted it but I won't drink it."

13. "It is gross. It is a good thing that it was a small glass."

14. "It doesn't taste good. It is gross. I wasted half a drink. Now I have to go get another drink. I sense the bitterness from the coffee and the syrupy sweetness from the soda and a tiny bit of carbonation left. Whatever rum is in there doesn't go well with the coffee. The whole combination is too funky to be enjoyed. I have that feeling in my mouth. I would rather not have this taste in my mouth. I can't wait to clean it out with another drink, without the feeling of coffee in it. I can't wait to get this taste out of my mouth."

In a later projection of the image, after it had been repeated many times, Paul was instructed to see himself drinking alcohol and asked what he got from the image at this point. He reported: "Not much. I am not getting anything, not much from the alcohol. What I get from it is disgust." The image was repeated again, as follows.

Repetition of the Image

1. *See yourself drinking alcohol in the image.*
2. *See your mother drinking tea/coffee. Which image is stronger?*
3. *Drink the tea/coffee.*
4. *Smell and take a sip of the tea/coffee.*
5. *See alcohol in a glass, smell and taste it.*
6. *Pour alcohol in the tea/coffee in your mother's glass/cup.*

Paul's response is reproduced below.

1.-2. "She enjoys it. My mother's image is stronger."

3. "I feel like I don't like it. I look at my mother and she is drinking it and I do not question it. Some people like it and some people don't. I can see more in the kitchen and the periphery is a lot clearer. I see the rest of the kitchen, the sun coming in the window, the cat by the back door, everything, the time of day. It is late summer. Everything is clear. The bar scene is weaker in comparison."

4. "I don't like it. It reminds me of left-over coffee in the coffee cup. What you do is pour ice cubes in and it tastes good all of a sudden. It doesn't."

5. "The alcohol tastes good and smells good."

6. "The alcohol in the coffee cup is gross. I am getting tired of drinking iced coffee and rum and coke. I drank it and it made me feel sick and I don't want it. I do not want more. No, I do not want to drink anymore. (Laughs) It is funny. It is an image, but I am not going to drink it. I will if you want me to, but I do not want to drink it any more."

As the image of drinking alcohol from the coffee cup was repeated over a period of time, Paul's drinking behavior gradually diminished until it ceased completely. At the same time, images that brought forth the primary imagination and natural high states were developed and enhanced, enabling Paul to retrieve these states without the use of alcohol or drugs. It is important to note here that the treatment evolved from Paul's own imagery process rather than from any external suggestion or reinforcement. Both the problem and its solution reside within the imagery structure, waiting to be retrieved. The power of this process is in the uniquely individualized eidetic image, which is highly personal, internally consistent and dramatic in nature.

KT, Female, Age 29

The following case example provides a brief description of the development of an antidote image. This patient came to therapy with a concern about her drinking. In her initial report of the problem, she stated: "Alcohol is affecting my life. It is a block that holds me back. I don't feel I can grow or get on with things as I should. I have a lack of confidence." She also reported having difficulty coping with a divorce that occurred two years earlier. She said: "I feel like my drinking has changed over the last few years. I feel guilty. I love the release and acceptance, being with a good friend, doing what I am doing, talking over things. It is a comforting, easy thing to do. It makes you feel all right. I don't have to deal with much. You don't really have to deal with things although you think you are. I have so many friends who drink."

Following the steps outlined in the core method, she was asked to recount her first experience with alcohol from which the antidote image emerged.

First Substance Use Experience (FISUE)

"I went to a dance in school. We made lemon gin. We brought cans of lemon pop and poured in the gin. I remember being in the school yard. We thought, 'Isn't this great?' I picture us in the washroom, laughing and giggling. It was contagious laughter.

"My first drug experience, I was smoking pot with a girlfriend at about twelve. It was a social thing to do. I was nervous about it. Apprehensive, but wanting to try it because the other girls wanted to try it. I was thinking, 'Should I do this?' We did and we laughed and giggled and had fun. Then we found out after that it might not really have been pot, but we thought it was when we smoked it. There was always something I did not like about it as I got older, would get into head trips, paranoid. After having a few experiences with drugs, got less social and more withdrawn."

EXPECTATION HIGH. The Expectation High was drawn out and enhanced, using the person's own words and segmenting the material in such a fashion that she could experience the high state more deeply along the following lines.

1. *See yourself at age twelve with your girlfriends.*
2. *See that you are all excited and giggling.*
3. *See that there is a little sense of nervousness and excitement.*
4. *There is a little danger and excitement in breaking the rules.*
5. *You all giggle and laugh and you sneak around.*
6. *You wanted to have fun and get high.*
7. *You had the fun, the excitement, and broke some rules with the girls.*
8. *The high was in the laughter and excitement and fun with the girls, not the drug.*

While seeing the image, the person reported experiencing a sense of expectation and excitement as well as evoking a feeling of involvement and belonging rather than withdrawal and isolation.

History with the Parents

The theme of isolation was further revealed when the parental images were explored through the Eidetic Parents Test. The patient reported that both of her parents had died when she was a child, her mother by suicide when she was six, and her father two years earlier in a train accident. She reported feeling a lack of emotional support and loneliness as a child and as an adult. While initially seeing the parental images, she experienced some difficulty entering the house and sadness upon seeing mother as helpless. However, as the images were helpfully evolved, a deep sense of intimacy and comfort was revealed in the early childhood images with the parents. The image of the house is especially illustrative of this. Although there was an initial inability to enter the house or see the mother, this quickly moved toward a positive interaction.

> *EP1. Image: House*
> "I see a blue door, gold brick house. I am coming home. It is a happy feeling, contentment. As I am trying to come closer and go in, I can't. I feel apprehensive. Maybe I had been bad that day and was afraid that I would be in trouble. Now I have entered the house. I turned right and have gone into the living room. I am going to the easy chair on the right side of the room. I feel that my mother is there and I am going to her, but I can't see her. It is really difficult. She is like a black film. I have a vision of her face, snarling out of this black film like a snake. Now the vision softens and I can see her in her chair looking so tired, so helpless. I am in her lap now and she is hugging me, crying. I cried when I had this vision and I held it for a while and I cried. It was comforting though. It is hard for me to just let it go. I could feel her holding me, rocking me, crying her sadness and loneliness and now I cry for mine too. I feel such a closeness with my mother and the connection is very strong. With my father, I see him in the kitchen. I like him. I am very young. I walk over and I am tugging on his leg. He lifts me and hugs me. He is big and handsome and warm. He holds me in front of

him. We laugh and giggle, then I am back down and wrapped around his leg. I love to be held and cuddled by him."

These and other early high states of consciousness were retrieved through the images of the Eidetic Parents Test. As these states were further developed and enhanced and linked with the Expectation High, the person reported a growing sense of well-being and expansiveness of perception. The excitement of the Expectation High, full of adventure and natural curiosity, was supported by images of loving intimacy with the parents.

Antidote Image: Expectation High Self-Image Sits with Father

At this point, an antidote image was developed to insure that no further misconception or misallocation could be made about alcohol's power to evoke these states.

In EP24 (parents drinking fluid), the father had been seen sitting at a table calmly drinking a beer. She reported: "He looks very calm, sitting back, sipping. I think that he is drinking a beer." Mother was seen drinking "...voraciously. She drinks faster, glass after glass of water." Father drinking beer was linked with the image of lemon pop and gin in the following manner following her own recommendation.

The patient said: "I see myself sitting with my father at the kitchen table; he looks calm. I feel a connection with him, there is comfort there. Seeing him drinking the beer, it feels like a relaxing thing to do." These statements were segmented into the following instructions and the experience of comfort was more clearly linked with her connection with her father, rather than with drinking alcohol.

1. *See yourself sitting with your father at the table.*
2. *Feel the connection and comfort between the two of you.*
3. *See that he is drinking a glass of beer at the table.*
4. *Take some of his beer and pour lemon pop and gin in the glass with the beer.*
5. *Smell the mixture and see what smells stronger.*
6. *Drink the mixture and taste the combination of the beer, gin and lemon pop.*
7. *It looks like a bubbling, steaming potion in the glass. It is disgusting.*

8. It gets all mixed together and warm as you drink the whole thing down.

9. Now focus again on your connection with your father, and feel the comfort. That is the high state; that is where the comfort really is.

Self-Image Technique

The Self-Image Technique is a variation of Ahsen's Age Projection Test. The Age Projection Test (also called the Symptom Oscillation Test) was designed to reveal "self-images at various age levels and their associated structures of imagery functioning useful toward the understanding of a presented problem or a symptom" (Ahsen, 1988a, p.1) Further, Dolan (1997) states that this test "detects, deciphers, reveals and expulses negative experiences and brings the original capacity for positive experiences to the forefront. The central thrust is to bring the individual to use diverse and positive sources of mind in response to the symptom pressure. As the individual concentrates and experiences the images revealed through the test, the drama of imagery reveals novel corners of mental life. The individual is brought to keen awareness of the natural potential within the mind itself and develops an incisive skill for new insights into elusive shades of emotion and thought" (p. 25). This test is useful for eliciting material about the symptom and any other emotions which the individual has evolved but whose cause is no longer available to consciousness.

The Self-Image Technique was designed specifically to uncover aspects of the self that have been progressively obscured by the addiction. The negative and positive features associated with the addiction are examined in depth at various age levels to provide the person with greater understanding of their meaning. The negative and positive self-images that are linked to the addiction and its symptomatology, both historically and in the present, are brought to the surface and developed in a bipolar fashion. As each end of the polarity is revealed and attended to, the symptom and its features begin to behave in a rather changeful manner, as Ahsen (1977a) points out:

> The symptom, which resides and floats in consciousness structures, obeys the rules of nature and of projection mechanisms in the same manner as the rest of consciousness. An individual usually settles himself in a life perspective which involves the pain, conflict, and his adjustment in a state of relative equilibrium. This state, however, is not altogether static because the symptom becomes alternately acute or ameliorated, according to the events and changes around the person. The symptom behaves like a pendulum...passing through the midpoints of extremes all the time.
>
> If, then, we make the symptom acute in some way, we will successfully create a state of amelioration spontaneously, as demonstrated by the pushed pendulum returning from the high point. Since the symptom shows a natural instability, we can always break fixity of the symptom by making it respond to artificial accentuation, followed by ideas of relief. This is a technique by which we push the symptom to its negative extreme and thus cause the positive side to come to the surface. Thus, by knowing the symptom's opposite positive relation to the past, we can deal with its structures in a curative fashion. The technique first involves deep concentration on any negative feelings, worries, or concerns you have about the symptom which cause the symptom to become acute. As soon as the symptom becomes acute, then let yourself relax and come back to a normal state again. As this happens and the mental states tend to become more positive, allow your mind to think of positive images from the past. As a positive picture emerges in your mind, you come to know the positive end of what bothers you. (pp. 99-100)

This process serves to demystify any fixed ideas attributed to the addiction, reveal and dramatize its negative impact and evoke and strengthen the positive self-image. In the final step of this technique, the relationship with family members is explored to determine individuals who are supportive or obstructive to the person's return to health. In this step, the positive qualities of the person and a better self-image can be utilized as well as the positive aspects of family members. The steps of this technique are described below.

Step 1. Preliminary Information

a. Basic information is gathered through administration of the first image of the Eidetic Parents Test. The person is instructed as follows.

EP1. IMAGE: HOUSE

Picture your parents in the house where you lived most of the time with them, the house which gives you the feeling of a home. Where do you see them? What are they doing? How do you feel when you see the image? Are there any memories connected with this picture?

Additional details can be gained when the following ten questions are asked, elaborating the image.

EP1 Image Elaborations

1. *Picture your parents in the house. Where do you see them?*
2. *Does the house give you the feeling of a home? Describe it.*
3. *See your father. What is he doing in the picture?*
4. *Do you experience positive or negative feelings when you see him?*
5. *Relax and recall memories about the place where father appears.*
6. *Now see your mother. What is she doing in the picture?*
7. *Do you experience positive or negative feelings when you see her?*
8. *Relax and recall memories about the place where mother appears.*
9. *Where are your siblings? What are they doing?*
10. *Now, see yourself in the picture. What are you doing?*

b. List the various names by which the person has been addressed (nickname, first name, last name, middle name, etc.). Note if both parents were present during childhood. Also ask the person to list the names and ages of siblings.

Step 2. Description of Addiction – History and Symptoms

a. ONE SENTENCE. The person is next instructed to give a brief statement (one sentence) about the addiction, as follows.

> *One-Sentence Symptom Report*
>
> *Tell me in one sentence only, and no more: "I drink (take drugs, etc.) because......"*

Example: "I drink because it helps me relax."

b. EXPANDED STATEMENT. Following this, the person is instructed to expand this statement to several sentences, providing a more detailed description of the addiction, including physical symptoms and any worries or concerns, as follows.

> *Several-Sentence Symptom Report*
>
> *Now, please describe why you drink in several sentences. Begin again with: "I drink (take drugs, etc.) because......"*

Example: "I drink because I feel anxiety and it helps me relax but I also can't sleep very well when I drink, so I have to drink more. I worry that I won't be alert enough to work in the morning after a night of drinking. I often feel exhausted and more anxious after a night like that."

After this step is completed, the person is instructed to expand the description to a paragraph or more, as follows.

> *Paragraph Symptom Report*
>
> *Now, please tell me about why you drink in as much detail as you would like, using as much time as you need. Begin again with: "I drink (take drugs, etc.) because......"*

Example: " I drink because I feel a lot of anxiety in my work. By the time I come home at night, I am really wound up. I feel caught in the problems of the day so I need a drink to relax. I tell myself that I deserve a break from the mess. After one drink I relax a little bit, but don't really feel like it makes much of an impact, so I have another. By that time, I feel exhausted, and I think I should have another drink so I can go to sleep. When I go to sleep, I don't sleep very well, so sometimes I will wake up a few hours later and feel anxious again. I sometimes have something more to drink at that point, hoping that it will do the trick. Then of course when I wake up for work, I am really exhausted and anxious that I will not be able to do my job well enough that day."

c. Next, a statement is developed following the above instructions, but this time beginning with:

"I would like to stop the drinking/drugs because..."

Example: "I would like to stop drinking because I think I could do my job better, I would be more alert, feel more energetic, and I would probably sleep better."

Through this process of assembling information, a detailed picture of the addiction is evolved with the negative aspects (I drink because) and positive aspects (I would like to stop because). The causes become more and more clear as the description is expanded.

Step 3. Age Drop Technique

1. *Now see an image of yourself at your present age engaged in the addiction. Where are you? What are you doing? How do you feel in the image?*
2. *Now see an image of yourself as younger, very young, when you were first engaged in the addiction. Where are you? What are you doing? How do you feel?*
3. *Now see yourself as a little older engaged in the addiction. Where are you? What are you doing? How do you feel?*
4. *Now again see yourself as a little older, engaged in the addiction. Where are you? What are you doing? How do you feel? (The instruction is continued in the above manner until the person reaches the present age.)*

Beginning at the present age, the person is instructed to drop back to the youngest age at which the addiction was engaged in. The person is then instructed to see his or her self-image engaged in the addiction at progressively older ages. Through this procedure the positive and negative features of the addiction emerge and provide perspective on the addiction and its meaning. Each image is developed in full ISM detail (Image, Somatic response and associated Meaning).

Step 4. Negative/Positive Self-Image: Bipolar Development

Ahsen (1987) describes the rationale of the bipolar procedure in terms of a natural inner tension, differentiating it from reciprocal inhibition but likening it to the forces in the consciousness field as follows.

> The eidetic image is a bipolar structure that has an expressive oscillating quality in consciousness. For any given event, it will manifest one of two opposite expressive possibilities. The image is assigned with either a negative value or a positive one. When there is a fixation on the negative end of the pole, it leads to a repetition of the original negative event giving rise to a negative result. Operationally, the image's bipolar configuration is like an opposing pair of muscles in which one muscle does not inhibit the opposite muscle, it merely expresses its own potential in the form of a tension, which means that it mechanically involves relinquishing the opposite possibility. This operation does not involve active inhibition by interference as suggested in the behaviorist notion of reciprocal inhibition, but rather is more in keeping with Hilgard's (1977) conception of the consciousness field, which offers a dynamic of the possibilities inherent in the interplay between the variety of forces operating in the person's current mental condition. (p. 167)

As a practical technique, both negative and positive self-images are evoked in a bipolar fashion. The negative end of the bipolar configuration is represented by the negative self-image and the addiction. The opposite end of the bipolar configuration is represented by the positive self-image and absence of addiction. As each end of the bipolar configuration is evolved and concentrated on, a bipolar swing is activated and the dynamic movement toward health and well-being is mobilized.

All the information is gathered and the emotions related to the addiction are applied to the present self-image. Similarly, the positive emotions connected with the opposite state are developed to enhance the positive self-image. This procedure is evolved in several stages.

a. *Relaxation*

The person is instructed to relax comfortably in a chair. When the person reports feeling relaxed, the next set of instructions is given.

b. *Activation of Addiction Symptoms*

By repeating the description of the symptoms of the addiction that the person has already given, the symptoms, emotions and attitudes are evoked. The names that the person is known by (assembled in Step 1b) are repeated along with the descriptions of the symptoms. This process builds the atmosphere of the addiction and its attendant feelings so that the person fully experiences the symptoms of the addiction. For example: "John is addicted to alcohol. Johnny feels tired, bloated and in poor health. Mr. A. looks fat and bloated. John A. keeps on drinking." This verbal instruction is performed repeatedly until the person shows signs of discomfort. When the person reports discomfort, the next step is administered.

c. *Negative Self-Image*

1. *Now see yourself at your present age, your present self-image, engaged in the addiction. Describe the image fully. Where are you? What are you doing?*

2. *Experience the addiction symptoms in the image. (The descriptions from the history of the addiction are added to the image after it is fully developed; e.g., "John, you are addicted to alcohol, you feel in poor health," etc.)*

3. *Experience the image deeper. (After this image is fully experienced, the negative features of the symptom are repeated to deepen the experience of the negative aspects of the addiction.)*
4. *Fully experience all of the negative details, symptoms, images and meanings. Do you feel you are seeing a complete picture of all aspects of the addiction now?*
5. *Now, what do you feel is positive about the addiction? See it in the image. (e.g., "I like the taste of alcohol.")*
6. *Experience it now fully in the image and describe it in detail. (e.g., "What is the taste like?" or "How does the taste affect you?"*

The negative self-image that is connected with the addiction has important features that need to be uncovered. By experiencing each aspect of the addiction, the person can begin to see the underlying dynamics of the addiction and its impact. In each of the following scenarios, the image, the somatic response and the meaning connected with it are fully developed. The various names the person is known by are repeated along with the instruction to enhance the experience and the attendant feelings.

d. Bipolar Swing to True Positive Self-Image

1. *Do you want to end this addiction? Why? Please see and describe the positive aspects of life without the addiction. (Example: "I don't want to use alcohol, I want to be healthy, I want...")*
2. *Experience ending the addiction. Please see that you are not engaged in the addiction. Describe how you feel. What are the positive features? (This process brings relief preparatory for projection of the positive self-image.)*
3. *Now see a new image of yourself at the present time. You are not addicted to (substance). Where are you? What are you doing? What do you look like? How do you feel?*

Through this procedure the features which were originally described as positive are revealed as negative. The faulty labeling and memory of the elements believed to be positive are brought into awareness. Each point appearing in Step 1 is repeated until the person clearly sees and experiences all of the negative aspects of the addiction and wants to do something about it. After this, steps 2 and 3 are administered. An experience of pleasurable and positive feelings should emerge at this stage. The false aspects attributed to the addiction as well as all of the negative experiences are seen in relation to this positive, healthy self-image.

Step 5. Practice and Homework

The new positive self-image with all of the associated body feelings and meanings should be repeated. If the desire to engage in the addiction emerges at home, the person is asked to repeat the negative images of the addiction without actually engaging in it and then to practice the positive images. The person is instructed to feel the gratification of not engaging in the addiction. If at any point the addiction retains any positive quality, the following tactic is added.

Step 6. Self-Image Dialogue

> See that your positive self-image is talking to your negative self-image, who is engaged in the addiction. What does the positive self-image say? Does the positive self-image tell the negative self-image to stop the addiction? Does the positive self-image understand your problem? Is the positive self-image being helpful to you? How do you feel as this positive self-image talks to the negative self-image? Hear and experience it. Describe the image.

This step utilizes the person's strength, compassion and good will toward his or her own self by helping the negative self-image become aware of the positive self-image. This is a totally internal process that makes use of the individual's own advice and helpfulness rather than another person's, and, as a result, the individual feels gratified and strong. The self-image may also offer a solution to the problem through advice.

Step 7. Sibling, Parental and Family Images

1. *See that you are engaged in the addiction with its negative features. You really want to stop.*
2. *Your sibling is there. See your sibling and look at the head and skull.*
3. *Now see that the sibling's brain is visible in the skull and that the brain is thinking about you, about your addiction and about your desire to stop the addiction. What does the sibling say to you?*
4. *What is the sibling's brain thinking as it sees you engaged in the addiction and wanting to stop? Does the brain think you can stop? Describe the image. How do you feel when you see this image?*
5. *Now see again that you are engaged in the addiction with all of its negative features. You want to stop. Your parents are there.*
6. *Imagine you can see your parents' brains thinking about you, about your addiction and about your desire to stop the addiction. What do your parents say?*
7. *What are your parents' brains thinking as they see you engaged in the addiction and wanting to stop? Do they think you can stop? Describe the image. How do you feel when you see this? (Alternate attention to your father and your mother, their words and thoughts. Use also images of the present family, wife/husband and children.)*

It is possible that a sibling or parent is hostile and that this person's attitudes perpetuate the individual's addiction. What the sibling or parent actually says in real life can be different from what the individual hears that person saying in the image. The individual may think that the sibling or parent is positive and compassionate about the problem when, in fact, he or she really is non-supportive and hostile. This imagery tactic helps discover a non-supportive sibling or parent as well as a supportive sibling or parent or a member of the current family who provides genuine help and compassion.

Step 8. Supportive/Non-Supportive Features in the Present Negative Self-Image

1. *Now see your present self-image engaged in the addiction.*
2. *You appear (previous descriptions of negative features). You feel (previous descriptions of negative feelings).*

3. *You want to stop the addiction.*
4. *Now see the most hostile parent or sibling in the image. What is s/he thinking and saying?*
5. *As you experience what s/he says, what do you feel? Describe the image and the feelings associated with the image.*
6. *Now see the most positive parent or sibling or current family member. When you see her/him, how do you feel? (Description should emphasize the positive features).*
7. *Describe what this positive person thinks about the negative person.*
8. *Listen to the positive person. What does the person say and think about you?*
9. *Listen to the negative person. What does the person say and think about you?*

This imagery tactic utilizes the most positive family members to battle the most negative ones who keep the person in a negative feeling state. Through awareness of the intentions of these family members and observing them interact in the image, the person gains feelings of strength. From this experience negative influences can be overcome and a deeper integration of the positive self-image occurs. When these positive feelings are experienced, return to step 4.

WL, Male, Age 30

Step 1. Preliminary Information
EP1. Image: House
"It is strange, when I see my parents in the house they are not in the same room. My mother is in the bedroom upstairs, father is in the kitchen downstairs. The house does not give me a feeling of a home. When I look at my father, he is hammering a piece of wood on the counter. I experience positive feelings when I see him. When I see him in the kitchen I remember sitting there having dinner and he was giving me a hard time about school. When I see my mother in the bedroom, it is weird; she is trying on a hat and she is feeling horny. That is really weird. It is

a positive feeling. I remember coming up the stairs when I was about 16, the door to their room was closed and it sounded like they were having sex. It was a weird experience but it made me happy at the same time; it was kind of a relief that they would be doing that. My brother is in his room sitting at his desk. He is doing his homework and there is also a bong on his desk. He is two years younger than me. I feel good when I see it. I am in outside in the back yard. I am just daydreaming."

Step 2. Description of the Addiction: History and Symptoms

a. ONE SENTENCE. "I drink because I don't know what else to do, because I feel crowded or thwarted."

b EXPANDED STATEMENT. "I feel like I am not getting anywhere in my life. I feel unsatisfied and bored. I just feel like the world has become too tedious and I go into a panic about it; I feel trapped. It is a good way to have an instant reality change. It is sort of a way to change what is happening. I feel worse physically afterwards. I feel fatigued and kind of weak and toxic. It doesn't cure the boredom, it just gives me a break from it so drinking is kind of like a distraction until things actually change."

c. *"I WOULD LIKE TO STOP THE DRINKING/DRUGS BECAUSE..."* "I would like to stop because I feel like it is a waste of time and there has got to be a better way to save myself from feeling bored and trapped. I feel like there is something that is more productive and satisfying. I don't get any satisfaction from drinking."

Step 3. Age Drop Technique

a. CURRENT AGE. "I am sitting on my bed drinking a bottle of Jack Daniels straight from the bottle. I feel irritable and crowded and repressed."

b. YOUNGEST AGE. "I am in the kitchen on the floor, taking nips out of all of the bottles in the liquor cabinet. I am in fifth grade, about ten years old. I feel disoriented, confused. It is not as exciting as I thought it would be when I first sat down to do it. I thought they were like potions or something but they just taste like poison."

c. *A bit older.* "I now see myself drinking beer. I am sixteen. I am in the den, watching TV, and I am drinking beer out of a can. I feel anxious and disoriented."

d. *A bit older.* "I am in the basement. I am eighteen and I am drinking rum and vodka. I feel manic."

e. *Current age.* "I am in a bar, I am drinking tequila and I feel ambivalent about drinking. I don't know if I should drink a lot more or if I should just stop."

Step 4: Negative/Positive Self-Image: Bipolar Development

Symptoms. "I am in a bar, drinking tequila. I look annoyed, restless, impatient, ambivalent." (Names: Bill, Mr. L.)

a. *Relaxation.* "I feel relaxed."

b. *Activation of addiction symptoms.* "Bill, you are in the bar drinking, you are annoyed, you feel restless. Mr. L., you are impatient and irritable, you look fatigued. Bill, you are annoyed, you feel weak, bored, you feel like your life is not going anywhere. Mr. L., you feel trapped and crowded."

This process was repeated until the symptoms were acutely experienced.

c. *Negative self-image.* "I feel very annoyed and restless, I see myself at the bar, just wasting my time, I don't really want to be there but I don't know how to get out of it; it is a hopeless situation."

d. *Bipolar swing to true positive self-image.* "I really want to stop this; it does not help me anymore. I don't get any satisfaction from drinking and I don't like myself when I am drunk. I want to feel patient, clear, healthy, strong, open and happy. When I see a new self-image of myself at this point in my life and I am not drinking, I feel good, clear, clean and happy. I am not bored, things don't feel tedious."

Step 5. Practice and Homework

WL was instructed to repeat the image of feeling clear, clean and happy and allow those feelings to be carried into other areas of life. He was to repeat the image several times a day until it was deeply experienced.

Step 6. Self-Image Dialogue

"The positive self-image says, 'I can see things better now; you should try it.' Things are not tedious; it is not as crowded; things are more open. The negative self-image says nothing, it just sighs. It knows the positive self-image is right, but it doesn't really know how to get out of it. The positive self-image says, 'I will help you, Bill.' I feel like the positive self-image can teach the negative one how to get out of the situation and how to change."

Step 7. Sibling and Parental Images

Parents (in this case there were no siblings)

"I see both of my parents there. They know I want to stop. My mother is all nervous. She wants to say something but she is too nervous. When I see her brain thinking about it, her brain is black. That means to me that she can't find anything to say and she doesn't feel good. She feels like bad things are going to happen. Father is kind of pissed off and he drinks himself. I don't know if he really wants me to quit or not, but I can see that he would rather hold it against me. When I see them like this, I know it is something I have to do on my own. It makes it easier, I feel clearer. It is something I have to do; they are not going to help me with it."

As these images were repeated, WL reported that he felt more strength and clarity in his life. He said that one of the most revealing aspects of the process was seeing the images of his parents, whom he had thought were supportive of his attempt to stop drinking. When he saw their images and their lack of support, he reported feeling a new sense of clarity and strength. He said that he now felt fully responsible for his own health and well-being. This quality was another aspect of the new self-image. This new self-image was strong, clear and energetic. He could accomplish things, get things done. According to Ahsen (1977a):

Mind works at many levels, yet in a completely understandable manner. As a person learns...the various processes involved in feeling and thought, he can differentiate the various aspects of mind. As he contemplates the various aspects of mind, he learns about how his mind behaves and develops knowledge of the psychological causation. The free flowing and changing mind is not an unstable chaos of feeling and thought processes, but a reliable sequence of imagery events....The reality of the self is equally distributed over the lines of imagery sequences and their bipolar configurations. True identity is formed out of these possibilities, whereas mistaken identity is an image nucleus merely accidentally formed. Realization of the self is realization of the perspectives offered by all the image nuclei. (p. 98)

Early Ego States

Introduction

One of the strategies developed by Ahsen (1988b, pp. 43-46) pertains to strengthening of the personality by mobilizing strength from early childhood states. The strategy speaks of a saga of the mind which is waking up in the morning with all the abilities at the person's disposal.

How does a person feel when getting up in the morning? Ready to face the world? Happy, unhappy, neutral, alert, active?

Such questions lead us to determine how one's current mood while getting up in the morning gives the day a positive or negative orientation. From where does this mood come and permeate the life of a person? Obviously, from the past. And since this is the case, can't we also transform the mood to the person's advantage?

The essential ingredient we are searching for in this transformation is happiness. To achieve this, one needs to be brought from the sleep of the night to an alert and goal-oriented awakening in the morning.

Experience has shown that we can recover the positive mood and the constellation of actions which operate in it. Through interaction with certain positive traits, we can encourage consciousness to push through obstructions. We can expect the person to finally appear happy alert, active, eager for new adventure, excited concerning the future, interactive, hopeful, taking initiative and not fearing risks, explorative, battling so that opposition can be overcome, open-minded and resourceful. These traits finally appear together as the Expectation High, a feeling of life force directed at the world.

Now let us begin with the following instructions. Each instruction brings out a different positive trait relating to awakening in the morning and greeting the new day with feelings of happiness and sense of direction.

States of Experience

1. HAPPY. *Now relax and listen and experience along these lines. It is morning time. You are waking up from sleep and you are still drowsy. Feel drowsy. Relax and feel drowsy. Rock back and forth between sleep and wakefulness. As you do so, glide back to the past, when you were still a child. See that you are waking up from sleep and you are happy. Now rock back and forth in drowsiness again and see yourself as that child, happy and alert. Describe what you see.*

2. ALERT. *Now relax and feel drowsy, rock back and forth and see that you are waking up happy and you also feel alert.*

3. ACTIVE. *Relax and feel drowsy, rock back and forth and see that when you are waking up you are also alert and active.*

4. EAGER. *Relax again, rock back and forth between sleep and wakefulness and see that when you are waking up you are also eager.*

5. EXCITED. *Now relax and feel drowsy again, rock back and forth between sleep and wakefulness and see that when you are waking up you are happy and also excited.*

6. INTERACTIVE. *Now relax and feel drowsy again. Rock back and forth between sleep and wakefulness and see that when you are waking up you are happy and also interactive.*

7. HOPEFUL. *Relax and feel drowsy again, rock back and forth between sleep and wakefulness and see that when you are waking up you are happy and hopeful.*

8. Initiative. *See that as you are waking up, you are happy and also show initiative in doing something.*

9. Explorative. *Now relax and feel drowsy again, rock back and forth between sleep and wakefulness and see that you are waking up happy and also explorative.*

10. Battling. *Relax and feel drowsy again, rock back and forth between sleep and wakefulness and see that you are waking up happy and also battling.*

11. Open. *Relax and feel drowsy again, rock back and forth between sleep and wakefulness and see that when you are waking up you are happy and open.*

12. Resourceful. *Now relax and feel drowsy again, rock back and forth between sleep and wakefulness and see that you are waking up happy and also resourceful.*

In order to recover the mind's natural ability to be expressive and energetic, early emotional events and their eidetic representations need to be explored for areas of strength and positive orientation. Imagery research has revealed that in states such as sleep, drowsiness or negative imagery, the qualities of anticipation and expectation are largely inhibited and attention is minimally activated (Ahsen 1988a, 1990c, 1993a). When attention with all of its potential is not heightened, the individual becomes disengaged from reality and acts like a drugged or narcotized subject. The essential difference between negative, narcotic attention and high consciousness imagery is manifested not only in sleep and some twilight forms of consciousness, but also in forms of imagery which do not allow the full potential of consciousness to come into play, such as in negative memory images and images with negative symbolic potential. Images like those of the Expectation High that generate heightened expression and engagement in reality are of central importance in the treatment of addictions, but the individual caught in addicted, habitual behavior takes flight from reality into a temporary state of elation where he progressively loses contact with the natural high potential in the mind. The need, then, is for a progressive and positive attunement toward genuine and fulfilling engagement with reality through the utilization of the psyche's natural and powerful resource, the Expectation High.

The power of the progressive engagement toward reality is represented in the state that precedes full waking consciousness, when a person rises from a night's sleep anticipating the day's activities. During this process, there is usually an alternation between a retreat into deep sleep and the emergence from sleep into full awareness. On one side there is an expectation of reality and thoughts about success or failure in the day. On the other side the fear of reality and engagement with the world cause anxiety and conflict, bringing a sense of foreboding and a desire to retreat. How a person finally approaches the day will determine his or her confidence, or lack of it, while moving into reality. People report that if their energy and vitality are missing upon waking up, they cannot gather enough strength to start the day. The need for more rest is essentially created by tension and conflict during sleep at night.

To participate effectively in reality, high states of consciousness need to be activated and utilized. In the strategy of early ego states, the person enacts early states of consciousness prior to fully awakening from sleep in order to progressively bring forward positive states of anticipation or the Expectation High. The introduction given above is read to the person and this is followed by administration of the twelve experiential steps given above.

The following example demonstrates how the primary imagination of childhood is activated, creating the feeling of energy and enthusiasm. From this state, the natural resources of the mind can be utilized to enable the person to engage in the challenges of life creatively. When this primary creative ability is falsely attributed to alcohol or drugs, the individual's natural dynamism is suppressed, reinforcing the idea that the substance is needed to achieve high states of consciousness. Unless these false notions are uncovered and the Expectation High is linked to the proper mental structures for expression, the person remains caught in the cycle of addiction. The mind is haunted by the desire for the high and unable to achieve it in a fulfilling way.

BK, Female, Age 60

1. *HAPPY.* "I am at my Great Grandma's and am in this deep feather bed. When I rock back and forth I am forced into wakefulness. I am forced out of the feathers and then down again into sleepiness, I go back and forth. I think about my day in the hammock and in the attic and the piano. I think about feeding the chickens and the pigs and reading in the summer court in the honeysuckle trellis and exploring the gully. I feel happy."

2. *ALERT.* "I become more alert as I think about those things. I am gearing up to do this and that and it makes me feel alert."

3. *ACTIVE.* "I stretch and I yawn and I wiggle around and scratch my head as my body starts to gear up to do all those things."

4. *EAGER.* "I feel a smile start to happen and I feel anticipatory. I feel like hopping up and getting to it, I feel so excited."

5. *EXCITED.* "I say, 'Hi, Granny, I am hungry.' She says, 'Your breakfast is ready.' I am getting dressed and I am hurrying. I hurry and eat my breakfast because I have a busy day planned."

6. *INTERACTIVE.* " I help my Granny clean up the breakfast dishes and get her bonnet so we can get going".

7. *HOPEFUL.* "I am hopeful that my Granny is going to take me out in the rowboat and we are going to go and pick berries on the other side of the creek."

8. *INITIATIVE.* "I am eating my breakfast in a hurry and I start to clean up and get the dishes off the table. I am helping her do the chores so we can get going."

9. *EXPLORATIVE.* "I decide I am going to explore the gully and stream today. I feel excited about the possibility of a new adventure, about the new things I will

find when I go down to the stream."

10. BATTLING. "I go down into the gully. It is really steep. The trees are very tall and the tree trunks are exposed. They make a little bridge across the water. I cross over on these branches to the other side where the stream starts to curve as it goes under the road bed. I walk through a pipe that goes under the road bed. I have to crouch down to walk through the pipe. I come out on the other side and go down the hill to the other side of the creek. I walk down to the creek and out onto the dock. I lay down on the dock with my head over the water. The sun is shining and the water is clear. I can see all of the fish in the stream; I get really lost in it."

11. OPEN. "I see the fish in the stream, then I notice leaves, rocks and branches; my eyes are seeing everything in the stream."

12. RESOURCEFUL. "I decided to take a rock home to Granny, maybe I can make something out of it. I see one shaped like an egg, I think I will paint it for her when I get home to share my adventure with her."

The Eye Patch

The hemispheric behavior of the eidetic image was reported in the classic studies of Klüver (1928) and Meenes (1933), where the eidetic image was seen with only one eye. More recently several researchers (Ahsen, 1959, 1972; Freides & Hayden, 1966; Leask et al., 1969; Stromeyer & Psotka, 1970 and Gazzaniga, 1972) have reported bilateral differences in imagery. The evidence suggests that hemispheric access to eidetics under specific conditions may reveal more information than by using a total brain approach. (Ahsen, 1977b, p. 27)

According to Ahsen (1993a), the focus of each eye contributes to the overall perception of the image. When one eye is covered during an imagery instruction, the imagery process is affected and the quality of the image changes. In the Eye Patch procedure, the subject is instructed to see an image of the parents

standing directly in front and to determine their left/right positions (Eidetic Parents Test item 2). The subject is then instructed
to observe which parent is more amenable to taking a substance
(alcohol, drugs, cigarettes). Then the subject is told to cover one
eye with an eye patch, to draw a picture of that parent with the
non-dominant hand and to hear the parent say something
about the person's involvement with the addiction. The subject
is then instructed to do the same thing with the parent who is
more negative toward taking the substance.

The Eye Patch

1. *Picture your parents standing in front of you. Who is on the left
   and who is on the right?*
2. *Which parent is more amenable to drinking/taking drugs?*
3. *Cover the opposite eye with an eye patch. (If the parent appears on
   the right, cover the left eye and vice versa.) Now draw the parent
   who is more amenable to drinking/taking drugs with the non-
   dominant hand.*
4. *Hear what this parent says about your addiction.*
5. *Which parent is more negative to drinking/taking drugs?*
6. *Cover the opposite eye with an eye patch. (If the parent appears on
   the right, cover the left eye and vice versa.) Now draw the parent
   who is more negative to drinking/taking drugs, with the non-
   dominant hand.*
7. *Hear what this parent says about your addiction.*
8. *What is your reaction to what each one says?*

The person should repeat the image and the drawing until
full knowledge of the parents' influence on the person as well
as his or her response to them is gained. In what ways does each
parent affect the person? What is the person's attitude toward
them and what do the parents actually say? How have their attitudes influenced other experience?

Futuristic Dot

The subject practices with a small dot to change severely
obstructed consciousness originating in a parent. This maneu-

ver, explained by Ahsen (1993a) is geared toward releasing creativity and expression.

> ...many unusual effects can be enacted when a small round dot approximately 1/4 in diameter is presented to the subject's left or right eye while the other eye is covered by an eyepatch...when these effects are related to the mental images of the parents, various states which are connected with negativity or a tendency toward inhibition or lack of control can be transformed. This is achieved through creative revision of parental images from recalled history as the subject follows the above procedure. It has been demonstrated that the image of either parent, regardless of whether it is the one who is more amenable to drinking or the one who is negative to drinking, can be used by the subject in order to relate to otherwise useful but unavailable creative capacities and resources in consciousness. The procedure procures feelings of release which can be used to enhance positive effects in treatment. (pp. 22-23)

Futuristic Dot

1. *See your parents standing in front again. Who is on the left and who is on the right?*
2. *Which parent is difficult or obstructed in your consciousness? On which side does this parent appear?*
3. *Place a dot on the side where this parent appears and cover the other eye with an eye patch.*
4. *Concentrate on the dot as you think of this parent in your mind.*
5. *Now remove the dot as well as the eye patch.*
6. *See the two parents standing in front again.*
7. *Note that the difficult or the obstructed person appears less negative.*

In the following case report, the subject reported a problem with anxiety and difficulty expressing anger. She had smoked cigarettes for forty-five years and had been unable to stop. She stated that throughout her life, she always attempted to suppress her anger and be pleasant and agreeable.

Smoking was a way to cope with both the anxiety and the anger she had experienced in her life. As treatment progressed, she reported that she was able to stop smoking and express her anger more directly.

LT, Female, Age 63
Smoking

Symptom Report
"I feel like I smoke because there is a lot of anxiety in my life. I have anxiety. I think smoking is an expression of my anxiety. I don't feel like I have very much control over my life. I just thought that now. I think it is an old feeling. Now that I am looking after my granddaughter, she is a controlling factor in my life. A comfortable day for me depends on a comfortable day for her. Sometimes, I find that I get up and think, 'I hope this is going to be a good day for her, then it will be easier for me.' When I was raising my own kids, because of my own mania I was sort of happier, peppier. When my daughter calls me and she is in trouble, it flashes into my mind, 'Do I need this?' It comes from wanting things to be nice. I want my kids to be happy and successful. This is a hangover from taking responsibility for everyone else's life. I hardly ever feel really relaxed. I don't know how to do that. Drugs made me feel like that, but otherwise never since I have had children. I used to feel carefree and rallied. Part of me knows that I can be relaxed, but it seems like this stuff makes me not able to relax."

Response to the Eye Patch
"I see my father on the left and mother on the right. My father seems to be more amenable. My mother seems to be more negative. She say, 'Honey, I do wish you would try to cut down, you could die from it you know, and with my asthma.' I feel bored when she is saying it.
"I cover my left eye to block out my father and I draw a picture of my mother with my non-dominant hand while hearing what she says to me. I wish she

would just shut up; I am feeling really bored with what she is saying."

"Now I draw my father. He says, 'Honey I quit. The doctor told me to and I just quit. It didn't bother me too too much.' I feel jealous of everybody who has been able to quit smoking. The drawing of my mother appears to be more haunted than I meant her to be. Dad is not bad.

"When I repeat the image, Mother is still more negative to it. As I draw her, she is coughing and she is saying, 'It makes me so mad that I got this asthma at this factory, there is no compensation for it. They don't care.' I feel bored when she says it to me. I am wondering if it is possible that she had asthma and I feel bad for her and I wish she would just shut up. I am trying to think of something to change the subject from her asthma and my smoking. It is an old familiar feeling. I wish I could go home because she is boring.

"When I draw my father again, right eye covered, he says, 'Yes, honey guess it is a pretty bad habit and people seem to have a hard time to give it up.' I feel like there is no way I will be able to quit smoking. I recognize that noncommittal, noncritical, slightly detached observation is very like him. He wouldn't say, 'You poor thing.' I feel like I will never be able to quit. Now I see that my mother is bigger, my dad's shoulders have shrunk. As much of a pain in the ass as my mother was, she would address the issue. He would never address it, but my mother was so mealy-mouthed, it pisses me off. My mother is a boring, mealy-mouthed victim. I wish she would shut up. I want to get away from here. Father is noncommittal."

Drawing Repeated

"My mother could easily pop over to the other side now. It would be very easy for me to switch their positions. Now I put pants on her, and this tie. She is quoting statistics, how many people died from smoking-related illnesses. I feel like saying to her, 'You stupid asshole, don't you think that I know that, don't you think I would quit if I could?' I am still bored.

"Now when I draw my father again and I hear what he is saying, he is telling me about Norville, his brother, who got cancer of the throat. He is saying, 'What a shame.' I feel sorry for Norville. The image of my father keeps shrinking. As my father gets small, his eyebrows are still expressive. Mother is still boring. I wish she would shut up. She is clearer and more orderly in the last drawing. My mother was more scattered in the first drawing and looked more victimish. There is more humor in the third drawing. She is looser and stronger. Father is weaker. My mother played at being calm but I know she was very anxious. Sometimes I would have a cigarette with my mother. It was like bonding with her, being with my mother while smoking, spending time with her relaxing and having a cigarette."

Response to Futuristic Dot

"When I add the dot to the experience, my father has aged in the image. This is the first time that this happened. When I try to switch them, my father is still less willing to switch but not as immovable as before. Now when I put the dot on his side, he becomes younger. The dot is helpful. When I see the dot on his side, he is smiling. When I see him like that, he doesn't want to stay on the right. It just seems wrong for him to be there. When I see my mother on the right she is looking kind of pleasant, not troubled. She seems a little more tolerant toward my father. Anxiety is not far from the surface though. When I put the dot on her side, I get an anger response. The more I do this, the drawing and the dot, the angrier I get."

SP, Female, Age 33

Drinking

Response to Eye Patch

"When I picture my parents standing in front of me, my father is on the left and my mother is on the right. When I think about who is more amenable to drinking, my father seems more easygoing. He says, 'Oh well.' Mother is standing behind Father, receding behind. You can tell there is discomfort with it, like she doesn't want to discuss it. There is tension around the whole thing. Mother is gray and she is removed and set back from it. Then she rushed forward and is now clearer. He was clear at first. She came forward, beaming defiance, not sincere, weird face. When I draw my father who is more amenable to drinking , he is cool. It is a strange feeling. I don't know if it is real or not. When I draw my mother as more negative I think she is on the left. They kind of hop back and forth. He is set back on the right, she has more of a reaction to it. My mother is on the left, and my father is on the right. When I finish the drawing and ask my parents about drinking, my mother is screeching, 'You know this is bad.' There is a negative sadness about it, all black and negative energy. My father is cool, he is just laid back, he says, 'Just relax and enjoy yourself. It is no big deal. Be cool.' The image that comes to me is my father is a cool cat. I never saw that before.

"When I repeat this image, I see my father more amenable. He still is wearing a hat. My mother is right out of the picture now. She is so vague, it is almost a feeling that he is more amenable. When I draw my father with my right eye covered and with the non-dominant hand, there is concern from him. He says, 'Look after yourself, be healthy, happy.' There is a real concern about the whole idea. He was thinking of my mother; he does not want me to be like that. As he says it I can feel a lump in my throat. I feel just sort of sad and heavy and lethargic. It is sad, maybe a little angry. It is just a feeling I have in my stomach. It just flashed that I am just a little angry; there is more sadness there.

"When I draw my mother with my left eye covered with my left hand, my mother says, 'You have to be a good little girl, do the right thing.' She is much softer than the first time around. It is vague. There is something uneasy about this. I feel nauseous as I am drawing this. I feel kind of hot. The first drawing is more clear, it felt more clear. I do not know it if was real. The second drawing, there is more distance, it is probably closer to being real.

"When I repeat the process again, it is vague. My father is on the left, my mother is on the right. I have to say that my father is more negative to drinking. She has a gentle face, calm flashes in and out. Father is not really negative, but less positive. When I draw my father with the non-dominant hand, he is really sad. He is crying little tears in the drawing. He is saying, 'I don't understand. I don't get it.' Maybe that is directed toward my mother. It makes me feel really sad, feeling that my mother is bad. I feel it in my stomach. I have a lot of anger as well. It is directed at my mother. She is a slut, a tramp. There is a lot of angry feeling by him toward her. Sadness, bitterness. I feel angry and sad, defiant. Sort of angry. I guess part of it is directed at me as well. It is like a doubled-edged thing as well. I feel angry with him for saying it and I feel angry for the whole situation. I feel sad.

"When I draw my mother with my left eye covered, she is really sad, a beaten person. Mother says, 'It is ugly, sort of sad, black.' I feel black, heavy. It is heavier with her, there is a different kind of reaction. He is sad, but she is getting to the end of her rope. She is sliding. I have the feeling that I can sympathize with both of them. It is a real pull. It angers me to hear him speak so badly of her, especially because I did not hear her speak badly of him. It makes me feel guilty hearing my father say those things, like she was like that. There is a strange sense of guilt about it. I am sure I identify with my mother. Probably the third drawing feels more real. Number one is more surface than reality."

Response to Futuristic Dot

"When I see them standing in front of me again,

he is on the left and she is on the right. My mother switches more easily, like she is tiptoeing around my father, giggling, like a game she is playing. When I try to place the dot on his side and concentrate and then look at him again, he is sort of soft. He is melting. Later on he becomes excited, and becomes more animated, alive. There are changes in him. He will move now.

"The image is quite positive now, there is a glow around the whole thing, a rosiness in the color. It is very calming for me. My mother looks quite content, rosy and warm and comfy. They are both quite clear now. Now I can see them both. Now when I see the image, there is freedom in it. I feel energy and curiosity."

AR, Female, Age 43

Response to Eye Patch

"When I see my parents standing in front, Father is on the left, Mother on the right. My mother hits my father on the head with a newspaper and tells him to stay in his place when he attempts to move. She kicks him so that he stays on the left. She pokes at him and tells him to smile for the camera."

Response to Futuristic Dot

"When I put the dot on the side of my mother, who is not yielding, and concentrate on it, and then see Mother again, she becomes very playful and runs to the other side. She is playing hide-and-seek; she is playful. She is very flexible about it. She is very animated. Father looks static. He is lifeless. When I put the dot on his side and concentrate and then look at him again, nothing happens. Mother looks at him and has an expression on her face like saying, 'Oh well.' It does not affect her attitude per se. She is like a school girl laughing, shifting around on the right.

"When I repeat the image, Mother is on the right, Father on the left, he is lifeless, she is a free spirit, I see the wind blowing in her hair as if she is in a boat and the wind is up from the water. When I put the dot on my father's side, and concentrate, and then look at father, this time he becomes instantly animated, turns to my mother, gives her a big kiss on the cheek, picks her up and they run off together. When I see the dot again on her side and concentrate, and then look at her again, she becomes more centered, mature and almost mythic. She is wearing some kind of long dress which is blowing in the wind. The gaze of her eyes is steady, sure and intentional; there is wisdom there. I have a feeling in my chest and throat when I see this image. It is a very expansive feeling, very emotional. When I put the dot on my father's side again, I see him step forward and fall down on his knees with his hands in the air. He says, 'I am free at last.' This is an image of resurrection. I can see the sky clearing in the background, the sun is breaking through. This is a very powerful image. There is energy and power in it. I feel eager to learn things. There is curiosity."

The multilevels of this process—covering one eye, drawing the image and placing a dot on the side of one of the parents—bypasses rational thinking and immediately reveals various levels of perception of the parental figure, moving from the more superficial layers to deeper ones as the process is repeated. It quickly and graphically depicts the developmental conflicts and themes. The process evokes information at the imaginal level as well as the emotional states connected with it. As the experiment is repeated, the underlying situation is revealed from a different perspective. The use of the dot placed on the side of the parents evokes a positive potential in the parent who is most obstructed, as indicated by the degree of fixity or resistance. Ahsen (1985b) reports on this phenomenon: "Do the parental images themselves, due to their prolonged association with development, cause the medial hemispheric spaces to behave in an asymmetrical way, or is the underlying genetic tendency responsible for these asymmetries? The evidence that the positive potential in these medial hemispheric spaces can be enhanced and changed resulting in the change of parental imagery in the positive direction is an interesting piece of evidence. That enhancement of neural potential through concentration changes the quality of negative images of the chronic type suggests a possible psychosomatic attribute embedded in hemispheric asymmetry" (p. 7).

Eidetic Heart and Expectation High

Ahsen's eidetic imagery of the heart involves mindbody experience which binds emotions and experience of the flesh through a centrally important life-giving organ. In this special tactic, the eidetic heart experience accompanies the Expectation High as its "physiological counterpart" (Ahsen, 1997, p. 32), to help remove negative viewing of the world.

Eidetic Heart and Expectation High

1. *As a child you were loving and enjoyed life. Your heart was open.*
2. *Now see your heart beating inside your chest on the left side of your body.*
3. *Experience the Expectation High as you do this.*
4. *As you experience the Expectation High, imagine that you are doing things with your heart in it*
5. *Become aware of the heart as essence (feeling), and as a physical organ (flesh).*
6. *Feel the heart pumping and experience the strength and feeling of life in the heart.*
7. *See the heart as an image, experience the somatic feeling of the heart, and allow an awareness of meaning to emerge as you also experience the Expectation High.*
8. *Touch the left side of your body all over and feel the flesh. Let the flesh of the heart join with the flesh of your body. Feel the presence of the heart everywhere in the body—skin, limbs, organs, bones— as you experience the Expectation High.*
9. *Feel the pleasurable heartbeat everywhere.*

For the true function of nature to evolve fully in life, activation of high states of consciousness found in the Expectation High need to be addressed in a positive and meaningful way.

Rather than withdrawing from the world into the desomatized haze of addiction, the person needs to reinstate the natural vitality of the soma through activity and dynamic engagement with life. Toward this end, the imagery exercises presented in this chapter and the next elucidate, beyond the Core Procedures, the various persistent elements and symptomatology found in the addiction syndrome. They assist in elaborating self-awareness connected with negative and positive experiences to develop and enhance the nourishing aspects of life. Because the issues of denial, resistance and defensiveness are so pervasive in the addiction syndrome, it is essential to deal with the symptoms progressively through the deeper layers of the mind in order to reinstate healthy functioning, as Ahsen (1977a) elucidates in terms of memory and Nature:

> It appears that the symptom is always related to a problem with the parents in a direct or indirect manner and originates from an unknown part of the relationship with parents. This unknown is guarded by the inertia of habit. This inertia of habit is further engirdled by myopic behavior. The myopic behavior is fenced in by a form of "pseudo-imagery" which provides a sense of "pseudo-reality." This "pseudo-reality" is defended by "pseudo-reasoning." Finally, the original "unknown" relationship is replaced by a conscious relationship which has so many superficialities that it frustrates the natural functions of the mind...
>
> Return to the unknown part of the relationship with parental figures involves rejection of the "conscious," the "known," and its various memory manifestations. This can be done by generating past reality afresh through eidetic rules of imagery projection which gradually cut through the "habits" of memory and pseudo-thought processes, allowing the "original" experiences to emerge again. It is precisely in the dissolution of the outer shell of superficial life and in the understanding of one's precise relationship with the original capacities endowed by Nature that the favorable outcome of emotions is insured. (p. 99)

Chapter 7

The Somatic Connection

"The drug came and set up a false state of being for me, who I was, a certain type of person with certain abilities. That was the self-image under which I lived, but that is not who I am. The drug was a mask which was hiding me from myself. When I looked in the mirror, instead of seeing who I am, I saw this facade which is brought about by the drug state. So I have to break away from the drug state to be really free to be me. The hard part of it is that I stopped doing drugs twelve years ago and I still have the drug in me. I don't understand why, but it is there and I have to begin to give it up in a new way. I have to learn to be really free from it. I don't have a craving for drugs, but it has affected so many facets of my life."

The Memory Trace and the Soma

When a drug or substance is ingested, the Expectation High associated with the drug as well as its pharmacological effects combine and create an experience of the event. When the mind recalls the memory of the original event, the experience of the effect of the drug is re-interpreted. Even if the drug is no longer ingested, the mind will recreate an experience similar to that of the drug through recall of the memory. In essence, the memory of the drug experience retains a mental connection to the drug itself or what may be called a "drug connection." When the mind releases a "memory trace" of the drug into the body, it evokes a desire to retrieve the physical state attributed to it at an earlier period, when the drug was taken for the first time. The person's true ability to achieve this state independent of the drug gets lost in the game that the memory trace plays on the body, resulting in a psychosomatic state. Within the network of events, the memory trace of the drug is released by the mind into the body. The memory trace, however, is not from the drug but originated within the mind in a condition of pure intentionality. When the positive elements of the personality that are believed to be released by the substance are brought forward and separated from the distortion caused by the drug experience, the high is recognized as a primordial aspect of Nature in which the soma plays a more prominent role as a mediator between the image and the meaning of the universe, the influence of the external world and the positive strength of inner biological reality.

The Role of Nature

For Ahsen (1977a), Nature represents the fundamental experience of biological stability and positive psychic power. It is, in essence, the ultimate high. Especially in the case of drug addiction, Nature represents a backdrop against which the artificial high effects imparted by the drug can be known and its negative addictive effects on the body can be fully realized. In this context, the positive soma grounded in Nature becomes a bipolar choice that can be achieved through the ISM act. For Ahsen (1993b), the image is a biological act and becomes a full presence in the mind which enacts its own reality in a powerful way. The following case explores this dynamic in a clear way.

NJ, Male, Age 36

The patient reported that he felt the strained relationship between his parents during his childhood had violated his nature. He withdrew into himself and was fearful about things happening in the family. He reported feeling somewhat scattered and that he needed to relate to friendly objects. Initially, experience of Nature had helped him dispel these negative feelings, but later the drug replaced Nature, "but the drug was never the same as being outdoors." He reported that he took drugs after he was no longer going to the woods: "I was hanging out with my friends. The nature experience was not their thing."

In his account of his first substance use experience (FISUE), the patient reported that he did not achieve a high the first time but only later while on a Nature trip. In this case, the intertwining of the drug and the elements of nature is very evident. In the images, he is not under the influence of the drug but under the influence of the mind, which proved, indeed, to be the genuine experience. He reported that he really enjoyed the experience and that "It was real." The experience of well-being and enjoyment was retrieved from this memory and intensified through the image process, presented below from Step 2 of the core procedure outlined in Chapter 5.

First Substance Use Experience (FISUE)

IDENTIFYING THE EXPECTATION HIGH. "The drug experience was an attempt to retrieve a better self-image through a better feeling of being. It did make me feel very good about myself. In that state, I liked talking to people, especially my family. I felt good about everything. I started to smoke marijuana when I was in tenth grade and it took a long time before I started to feel its effects, to get high, of being stoned. When I am very stoned I begin to laugh, a powerful laugh. The laughter makes my whole body feel good.

When I am not stoned I have wider peripheral vision, and when I am stoned I have a more focused vision. It is a very strong concentration and there is also a lack of memory involved. I do not hear what is around me. My eyes become much sharper and I catch details much quicker. The colors are also emphasized. Everything merges. My family then looks happy and peace comes all over and they become totally, totally in contact. If I could always feel like that without the drug experience, I would be flying high.

"I used to sit in the woods all by myself when I was eight years old. I could not wait to go to the woods. Sometimes I used to take my younger brother and go there. I used to love to be alone and go to the woods even during the night. I would try to make peace with my fear, learn to deal with the animals and not fear them. My ears and eyes at night in the woods are twice as sharp as in the city. Everything is magnified. I am able to pick up details very well at night. My eyes are good, not only my ears. Anything I saw worth climbing, I would start climbing. It could be a tree, anything. When I smell the outdoors, I feel good and I go wild."

SEGMENTING ELEMENTS OF THE EXPECTATION HIGH: THE DRUG CONNECTION. "It is a good feeling. I can easily relate to it. I am feeling the wind, smelling the plants, the flowers. There is that nice cool breeze at this high altitude. The wind is blowing through the tent, the wind is howling. There is thunder and lightning.

"When I combine the image of the drug with the image of the storm, everything is strong and powerful. It takes over your whole body. Everything is clear. The sound of the wind. You lose the sense of time. It separates you. You just feel good. The drug emphasizes the wind. Without the drug, the interest in the wind only lasts a few minutes. With the drug, it is longer, more drawn out, like listening to music. When I am stoned I really hear the song of the bird.

"How can I experience the same exhilaration without the drug? Life is so boring. At times I am able to achieve the same exhilaration by making people laugh at the office with me. When I have accomplished something and am happy, I rub my hands together and I feel good. It is difficult to have those feelings without reality or without drugs.

"When I am stoned, I use more of my ears than normally. I never used to enjoy music, but I discovered it through drugs. The music was heavenly. I begin to enjoy the ears. Now the dizziness is less. I combine the exhilaration of the drug experience with the sound experience and it feels good. It feels like I am away from reality. In fact, my ears are so sharp when I am stoned, I can hear my own voice. It releases me. I can hear from the smallest to the loudest animals. I can even hear fish jumping out of water. I am looking at the stars now. Somehow I went up to the stars. It is so quiet with the stars. I hear the wind blowing through the tree, the rustle of the leaves. I look into the stars and it is quiet again. Then I hear the coyote howling. There were several of them. I have got to understand what they are saying. I am tired now. It is funny. My head feels like numb."

He was asked to repeat the experience and summon up the "stoned" feeling again and hear music in that state.

EXTENDING AND ENHANCING THE EXPECTATION HIGH: THE SOMATIC CONNECTION. "The music is filling up all of the space and the air. It has really reached an apex, like you have climbed a mountain. You are so taken by the experience, it does not let you down. In the climb up, I was lost in the music. There is a feeling of excitement. The music fills up every available space. I hear every vibration. You become part of the music. The music is always vibrating. It wants to make you do things. It makes you want to run. You want to release the energy by running. I used to release my energy by running or riding my bicycle. I always used to ride my bicycle when I was stoned. The wind picks up as you go fast. Your body feels so good. Whatever you are feeling, you feel the good side of it.

The houses are passing. I'm going through the time machine. I am in a very constant peak."

As the imagery process was repeated, he was asked to enjoy the vibrations of the music.

"I am listening to the music. The music is going through everything. It just lifts your spirits up. There is a real shift. As the vibrations get louder and louder, it tickles you. You become part of it. I see it. I see the music, the vibrations, the sound waves. It really touches you, touches you all over. It makes you numb. The feeling of numbness is at the back of my head now. There is no dizziness. It has moved as numbness to the back of the head.

"The voice makes me feel numb. The vibrations make me feel exhilarated. The human voice I do not hear as clearly as I do the music. I can't recreate the human voice, but I recreate the vibrations of the music. It is also hard for me to listen to the person and what he says, stoned or not stoned.

"I want to use the wind on the mountain. I can also see the wind. You become part of the wind. You see how high you are. You can scan everything around you. When you hear the wind, you can also hear the animals. Everything is so clear. I feel very relaxed to the point that I could go to sleep."

Disruption of the Psychosomatic Unity

As demonstrated above, the memory of the drug experience is linked to the original high body feeling or somatic state which it has falsely linked to itself. This body feeling is activated when the drug experience or the original memory is recalled. The memory itself is maintained through the drug link and, therefore, both aspects of the experience must be attended equally in order to successfully disentangle them. Attending to only the body feeling or somatic experience confirms and supports the link rather than providing distinctions that are useful.

The importance of the somatic connection cannot be underestimated as a final understanding of addiction, especially if one is dealing with ordinary recollection and not with the eidetic images. Although attempts to change the somatic state by altering the memory in some fashion may, indeed, result in some change, ultimately no real change is achieved. All that is actually achieved is a movement away from one memory experience to another condition. Although a new memory and its associated image may show some potential for development, it still remains an enforced memory structure based on autosuggestion dependent on twisting of the actual event. It is not an eidetic image. Thus, the drug link has the ability to reactivate itself and its associated body feeling by releasing just enough of the drug from the memory trace to retain power over the individual.

In fact, a new structured condition with a weak recollection of the original somatic state is ultimately more insidious to an individual's true state of health because it will silently deplete his or her energy resources. Because the miniscule amount of somatic potential goes virtually undetected, the false memory continues to exert a negative influence. Over time the function of a negative memory is to become more economical to insure efficiency of recall while retaining the same pattern and working toward the same negative original goal. Thus, though out of awareness and out of context, the memory trace still retains powerful effects. That is the lurking danger. In this light, it is clear that attempting to combat the influence of the memory of the drug experience by converting it to a purely verbal memory is ineffective because the somatic base still remains intact and exerts influence from the source. Although helpful to a certain extent, the verbal instruction does not alter the memory.

The Drug Link

As we have discussed, when a person takes a drug, the drug releases high states of consciousness such as exhilaration and euphoria. In effect, the drug experience opens a window in the mind to these states of consciousness in the mind. However, because the person has never truly exercised the mind's natural ability to achieve these states, the drug becomes the only means by which to achieve it. Thus, the person becomes quickly attached to the drug while at the same time becoming more alienated from its reality and its demands. In time the drug state becomes more highly valued than external reality because it provides a false self-image and illusions of confidence.

Ultimately, however, since the drug cannot provide the abilities and skills that reality itself offers, it leaves the person with a feeling of inferiority, alienation and failure. For instance, an adolescent using drugs during school may skip classes and not do homework, resulting in a failure to perform according to the school's standards and eventually a loss of self-image. The experience of exhilaration and euphoria that is connected with the drug soon becomes tied to failure and over time becomes tied to feelings of inferiority. At this point the drug connection is tied to a failure of performance but eventually it will generate a host of other symptoms.

A drug disrupts the innate balance of the entire psychosomatic unity because it persistently intervenes, usurping normal functions. Rather than receiving stimuli and information and, in turn, enacting healthful ways of engagement, the drug acts on the weakness of the person, resulting in his or her withdrawal and lack of engagement with the world. In effect, the drug state is parasitic because it insidiously takes over the individual through a vacuum at all levels of existence.

The Somatic Connection

Clearly, recall of a drug memory brings forth a negative parasitic pattern of physiology which takes precedence over the body's positive potential. It enforces negative connections consistently and without any change, thereby retaining power over the body.

As previously stated, the eidetic image, composed of its ISM structural components — the visual image (I), the somatic response (S), and the meaning (M) – is a torch bearer of healthful expression. The unity between the image and the body take precedence over the meaning, which is ultimately derived through the union of the other two. When this natural process is interrupted in any way, as in the case of ingestion of a drug, both the memory trace and the somatic state live independent of one another though tied falsely together. As a result, the body's natural balance and dynamism are obstructed, and the soma becomes unable to perform or express itself in a healthful and biologically correct way. Euphoria and elation, reduced to a dependence on the experience of an actual drug, become a closed emotional circuit, feeding off themselves in a vacuum, with no concern about unreality, creating an illusion of positive accomplishment and omnipotence.

By upsetting and altering the deceptive somatic connection with the drug at its eidetic source, the original positive somatic state can be gradually reconnected with it, releasing healthful expression of the biological operations. To accomplish this, both the memory and its somatic base are attended to equally in order to rid them of the drug connection. For instance, a person seeing the self-image (I) in the drug state creates a body feeling or somatic response (S) which is very specific to that image of the drug state. If another image is added, such as the person walking in the image ($2I$), it creates a second somatic response ($2S$) and another awareness of the body with a different sensation not coming from the drug. The meaning of the first image (I), and the meaning of the second image ($2I$), become different as a result. If the person breathes out while seeing the image, the image slightly changes again ($3I$). However, what changes most is the somatic response ($3S$), and not the drug, and the meaning follows through as a result. This helps restore the original nature of the somatic response apart from the drug.

Breathing Out: Activating Somatic Power

The innate strength of breathing out, when accompanying the imagery process, upsets the negative somatic base in a powerful way. As the process is repeated and enhanced over time, the natural high states develop to enable the body's operation to function in a more relaxed, less stressful manner.

In any physical activity, spent breath (breathing out) rather than earned breath (breathing in) creates more power. While breathing in brings oxygen to the body, breathing out uses it to mobilize the force of the organism and leads to an active body state. Breathing in results in a shallow breathing pattern within a few cycles, causing the chest to tighten, the body muscles to tense up and an overall feeling of somatic rigidity to develop. When the breath is constricted or held back there is less room for air to be taken into the body, which ultimately leads to choking and causes anxiety. Breathing out is the converse of all of this.[1]

The following diagram illustrates the differences between in (*earned*) breath and out (*spent*) breath in connection with operations of the ISM.

---

[1] For Ahsen, coughing exemplifies the function of spent breath. The function of the cough is to clear away debris in the throat or lungs, and in the process to release muscular congestion in the body. During coughing, the abdomen contracts, the chest expands, and the anal area becomes expulsive rather than held in tightly. Brief coughing spells often occur at night during sleep as the body begins to relax and expel congestion, or before a person makes a speech as a means of releasing tension. The cough is welcome even during intervals of musical or theater performances when the demand for total attention is relaxed. Ahsen (1984) puts yawning in the same category although he connects it more closely with positive recall.

Many forms of yoga recommend coughing as an exercise, and coughing has been observed during some imagery exercises as a spontaneous somatic expression. Coughing can be an effective exercise while seeing a troublesome negative image. The person is instructed to see a negative image, breathe out and cough at the end of the spent-breath. Often the person reports feeling a strong, pleasant jolt as the body gives up the muscular controls and opens up. Sometimes laughter follows the cough, creating a childlike feeling.

Ahsen utilizes breathing in many ways in conjunction with eidetic imagery exercises. A detailed application of his breathing-out technique is found in Bent (1995), who describes this process in the treatment of multiple sclerosis. She has also presented many other Eidetic Physical Therapy exercises combining images and physical expressions of the body.

ISM AND BREATHING

IMAGE (*I*)

↓

SOMATIC (*S*)

Breath In	*Breath Out*
fatter	slimmer
stuffed	compact
dull	sharper
weak standing	strong standing
diffused	targeted
memory repeats	new thinking
recall	ideation
static	dynamic

↓

MEANING (*M*)

(From unpublished case report, Ahsen, 1990)

Note. The comparative descriptions given above provide an idea of the difference between the active breathing-out state and the more passive breathing-in state. The addictions resemble more the breathing-in state.

The images below emphasize the somatic connection and can be used during the course of therapy, especially when a person does not initially report the symptom of drug or alcohol abuse but during treatment, the addiction is discovered in the past or even the present. These images help activate and strengthen the somatic power. The therapist looks for the Expectation High within the experience along the lines described in Chapter 4. The instructions given here are, however, self-explanatory.

Breathing Out with Negative Drug Image

1. *You feel that there is a drug inside you.*
2. *You feel like you are floating.*
3. *Now dig your feet into the ground.*
4. *Intensify the feeling of planting your feet into the ground by breathing out.*
5. *As you breathe out, lower your eyes and feel your feet being planted.*
6. *You see yourself in the place where you usually take the drug. There is anxiety and fear in you as you take the drug.*
7. *You are floating.*
8. *Now breathe out and plant your feet into the ground again to recapture your strength.*
9. *Keep your breath out a little longer than usual.*
10. *The breathing out period is to counteract the negative drug.*
11. *The negative drug is a nondescript life situation in which the body produces a chemical that at one time seemed to have a positive effect.*
12. *The negative drug needs to be overcome by the Self.*

Breathing Out with Positive Drug Image

1. *Now experience the change in your body feeling as you breathe out more and keep your feet on the ground.*
2. *The change in the body feeling give you a positive chemical feeling. This is a positive drug experience from your own body.*
3. *Roll in this positive drug experience. It is normal.*

Breathing Out with Parental Images

1. *See yourself/your friends doing drugs in some place.*
2. *Now see yourself in your parents' home and you are not doing drugs.*
3. *Experience the feelings. Then deepen them.*
4. *Breathe out as you do the image.*
5. *Bring this image into the present time.*
6. *Are there any connections with your symptoms?*
7. *When there are parents around and no drugs are there, it feels better.*

In the following example, the patient's account of the drug experience was segmented and enhanced using the breathing out exercise.

PQ, Male, Age 36

As the image was repeated, the patient reported a feeling of strength and an increased ability to handle situations in his life. He reported that he wanted to be rid of the drug state "because there is so much strength without it." This strength was observed to extend into other images as well when he reported the experience:

> "I see myself in another place where I used to take drugs. I get up and leave. I have no need for the drug. I am myself. The need for the drug is a way of being accepted. I wanted to fit in. I wanted to be a cool guy who everybody liked. There was a lot of insecurity coming out of Catholic school into public school. The public school had tough guys in it. The environment was competitive. I went to public school in the seventh grade. I was thirteen years old."

The original drug state was controlled through the process of breathing out. Following the exercise he reported that the effects of the drug had been removed and that he was able to recover a feeling of strength and a positive experience.

Latent Drug Connection in Somatic Symptom

The following case offers an in-depth illustration of a latent drug connection in a recovered addict which caused symptoms apparently unrelated to the drug experience. The patient presented with an initial symptom of severe headaches which seemed to be connected with job stress. Upon deeper exploration, however, the symptom was actually found to have a drug connection. The patient had taken drugs from ages twenty-three to thirty-three and he had desired them again only once, one year after stopping them, but had not succumbed to the temptation. Although the patient no longer took drugs, there was a residual link which continued to persist through the symptom of headache. The drug experience had connected the mind to the high state of exhilaration, but when drugs were no longer used, the high state was no longer available. The lack of this state left the person with a hollow feeling that tended to create a headache.

Although relating to a drug image did result in removing the headache, according to Ahsen (1993a) a person would not normally recall the healing Expectation High image on his or her own because of the fear that it might create a temptation to take the drug if remembered. Ahsen calls this a "reality resistance," being rooted in a normal respect for reality. Many alcohol and drug treatment programs promote the notion that any memories of the drug or alcohol experience, except for the most negative aspects, be resisted lest they lead the person to temptation and relapse. However, buried under this fear within the experience itself resides the Expectation High with all of its life giving and curative gifts. Therefore, it is only through recalling all aspects of the original experience that the natural high state can ever be retrieved. As reported earlier, methods that attempt to suppress the desire for these states by denying their existence or attempting a solution without retrieving the primary strength of the Expectation High that lies there are ultimately doomed to fail.

In the next case, resistance in recalling even the memory of the drug experience resulted in resistance toward the experience of exhilaration in its fullest sense. The core procedure outlined in Chapter 5 was applied along with the breathing out technique.

PF, Male, Age 39

Step 1: Initial Symptom Report

"I have severe bilateral headaches. I feel it really crushing in, strong pressure. It feels like I am under strong pressure when they come. Aspirin does not help. Nothing helps. Sometimes I wake up in the morning with them, other days they are negligible and I don't feel that I have them. I feel good. I do not feel any nauseating sickness.

"I have had physical tests. The headaches started when I took a job in a real estate development company. I started my own company recently but I have lost the confidence that I used to have. Now there is a feeling of failure."

Step 2. First Substance Use Experience (FISUE)

"I had been doing drugs, marijuana, cocaine, since I was twenty-three, then I quit. When I was about twenty-nine I had an inflammation of the heart lining. It felt like a heart attack. I was put on codeine.

"When I see myself snorting cocaine in the image, it feels good, exhilarating. When there is exhilaration there is no headache. At the same time it is an uncomfortable feeling because of what it did to me. It knocked out my nervous system. The experience in itself was exhilarating, but the body consequences of the experience were shattering.

"Just before I started with the new company I had a car accident. I see myself driving. I was having a good time driving with a friend of mine. It was a day off. I am joking and talking, feeling good in my body. Then the other driver drove left into my car. I slammed on the brakes and tried to avoid him. If I had not slammed the brakes, I would have hit him hard. I hit the brake and I experienced a jolt.

"As I see myself snort cocaine I experience exhilaration and I experience some relief from my headache. I am feeling better. The headache has gone. The reenactment of exhilaration brought back some memories. I was driving fast, eighty, ninety miles an hour the other day and the headache went away. I said to myself, 'It is the same feeling of exhilaration.'

"I remember when I was about seventeen I used to get the high feeling of exhilaration when I would race a motor bike. I fell several times, and once I sprained my ankle. I was driving down my driveway too fast. I flipped the bike over. Another time I tore the skin off my leg on the right side and on my arm on the right."

Regarding the temptation to take drugs again, he said:

"It was more a curiosity than anything. It was uncomfortable to overcome. It made my nervous system very hyper and I did not like it. Now there is no temptation. If I open myself up to the temptation, it is like a hassle. It is tough to go into temptation again. I know what it did to me physically. I don't think I can take it anymore. When I think of the excitement of making drug deals, it was fun thing. Everyone wanted to know me. There was quite a return on your money, which was a big thrill.

"I get a headache sometimes while I am reading. That is an old thing with me. I was never a big reader. I never received great news in the mail or in the reading. I get a headache when I sit down to pay bills."

Breathing Out with Negative Drug Image
IMAGE 1: SCHOOL

"I see myself in school. It is boring and there is anxiety. I am uncomfortable. I was not prepared a lot of the time. I hated the work. I could not write long reports. I would condense them. I was good in math. I always failed English. I used to come stoned to class in the morning. I would do the same thing after lunch and after school. It was happening more and more in school. I was cutting school also. As I am saying this, I feel some pressure in my head now.

"If I see myself in the classroom and I am high, I can't pay attention. I don't want to hear. My attention is pulled off. It floats. My feet are on the ground only to the degree that I can get around. I am experiencing it right now. It is releasing. As I breathe out, it makes me focus more on the relaxation. It seems to diminish some of the school anxiety. I feel less pressure in my head. When I am stoned, I'm happy but I am a little weaker, more vulnerable."

"When the anxiety lessens, I feel that I was more anxious in the stoned state than I thought I was. I was always anxious about being caught and so forth. There was a lot of anxiety. I smoked marijuana a lot more than I did cocaine.

"I can see that when I was high I was also anxious but I was overriding the anxiety. As I breathe out more, I am more relaxed and less anxious. Things become clearer and sharper. Now I feel I can learn and succeed in the classroom.

"I feel that if I give up this strong drug identity, I will be this flat, middle-aged nothing. I am afraid of being this nothing. I have a feeling that there is another side of my personality, the exhilarated side which is there but the drug identity says that it is not there. It is saying, 'I am the drug identity, the only exhilaration.' That is the thing which holds me back. It is set up as a Catch 22 situation. Not really, but this is a challenge. Do I accept it? I have to be helped to snap out of this thing. It is the fear of what is on the other side that locks me up in the drug identity. What shall I find if I go through it and completely eliminate the drug identity?"

Breathing Out with Positive Drug Image
IMAGE 1: SCHOOL

"I go into the drug state again and I breathe out and keep my feet on the ground. Before my self-image was bad. Now it is strange. It is improved. I feel more like I was hiding before behind a facade. As I do the breathing exercise I feel more clarity, more me and self-assured. As I breathe out, the bad self-image changes to a good self feeling. There is a positive body chemistry. I am more interactive in the class in the image. There is more participation and a better relationship. A part of my mind is still saying, 'This is bullshit,' but I am getting the feeling of a better chemistry. I am on the other side of it now and I feel much better. I was always afraid of looking back at the drug and now I am really seeing why I did the drug. I realize how much anxiety it was producing and how much I was hiding behind it.

"There is no need for the drug. I am myself. I want to be me and I won't be like anyone else I know. I see myself walking around by myself, not with the group of people who were on drugs. I feel strength. I am walking around erect with my chest out. I will take classes in the school and still have fun. I will laugh with my friend. I will be a better student. I will excel. I will not feel afraid of the class assignments and will not be put before others as an example of what can go wrong. I believe that these images existed all along. I know that they have existed all along but I was never aware of them. There must be tons of images that I am not aware of but they exist inside me, definitely. The drug state covered up everything, all these images of confidence. The drug perpetuated the loss of confidence by giving me a false confidence in a kind of a floating state.

"I see myself much more relaxed and I am carrying books. I never used to carry books. I breathe out and look at the books. I am just looking at the books. I am looking at the blue book. I am a little bit curious. I feel comfortable with the books. I feel I can excel in academics. I feel free with the books and feel good with them.

"Just recently I was driving my car and it was raining. The windshield wipers were going and I was feeling uneasy about the movement of the wipers. I was doing the image with the breathing out, thinking about why I wanted to stop the wipers. Then a memory came up. There was a time when I took mescaline which was laced with something like strychnine. I saw cars melt in my driveway. It was pretty intense and crazy. I was pretty freaked out with a stomach ache. We knew something was wrong and called for help. We were told to drink a half-gallon of milk and it brought me down."

Breathing Out with Negative Drug Image
IMAGE 2: TAKING MESCALINE

"As I combine the image of mescaline with the breathing, I see myself drinking milk and laughing. I remember that one of the guys with us at the time was a scary guy, crazy. He pulled out one of the kitchen knives as a joke. He was dancing around with the knife. I tell him to put it down, put it away. With breathing I am a little more objective and in control of the situation. Still not completely in control though, but I do not feel the edgy nervousness which I felt before. I remember making a conscious decision not to do psychedelic drugs anymore because I lost control of my body. I remember I used to enjoy psychedelic drugs before that."

Breathing Out with Positive Drug Image
IMAGE 2: TAKING MESCALINE

"When I am instructed to breathe out and see the positive mescaline experience, it feels good. I feel exhilarated but nervous also. I always feel nervous in my body when I talk about drugs. Talking about it elicits a nervous reaction in me. It is not that I am anxious. It creates an anxious feeling in my body like a strong emotional response.

"Some of the drug experiences were fantastic. Mescaline made me see things in a different depth, with a different clarity.

"I feel a knot inside my solar plexus while I am talking about this and the pressure in my head seems to have localized around and above my right ear.

"I remember a friend of mine who used psychedelic drugs ended up in a mental hospital and never recovered. I have heard stories of people freaking out and never coming back. There was always a fear that you could freak out and never return. When I experience this as real, freaking out and never returning, the pressure gets much stronger at the back of my head. When I go from the exhilaration to freaking out, it is real strong. It is a strong physical reaction. The pressure is much stronger in the head and I get this nervous feeling.

"It is exciting to be at this point of losing your mind and never returning. I am yawning and yawning. The pressure is different now. It feels lighter. It has moved.

"The memory of the cars melting and the breathing out takes all of the hallucinogen effect away. So instead of the cars waving and melting, they are just there in line, as they would be in reality."

Breathing Out with Parental Images

"I go into my parents' house where we were doing these drugs and tell the two groups to get out of the house. I am free of the drug state. I get a great sense of freedom and of being myself. I bring the image here, to the present time. I don't need the drug. I don't have to hide behind the drug state. In the image I threw them out, purified the house and restored it to my parents' home and to my house because it is my home too. The house is cleaner and lighter now. There is a sense of order.

"I was hurrying this morning because I was running a little late. I had a little pressure in my head as a result. I tried to look for the image. What I finally got was an image of a clock. Then I saw an image of my father pointing at it and yelling, 'Don't be late for dinner! You know what time you are supposed to be here.' As I started breathing out while seeing the image of the clock, I gradually saw myself yielding, thinking that he could be a little flexible. That relieved the feeling of haste and removed the pressure from my head.

"I again attended the image of the boys taking drugs in my parents' house while I breathe out. I do not like the attitude of the guys who are there with me. One guy is freaky, weird. The other guy is taking pleasure in the whole thing. I feel an irritation with them. I just do not want to do it anymore. When I am instructed to develop this feeling of irritation and anger, I get angry with the situation and with the exercise, that I have to deal with this stupid drug image so much. I had to stop breathing because it was making me uncomfortable."

At this point the person was told that he was overcompensating for his drug life and the pain he had said it caused his father. By being overly concerned about his schedule, he was using anxiety as a secondary compensation for the main drug state. He appeared to use pressure as a way of expressing anxiety in a real life situation.

Although it is normal to experience anxiety as a somatic pattern, its highly individual character should be explored. Anxiety exists in a real person in a real body and is, therefore, expressed somatically, however, in this case, the real situation was not critical enough to warrant the degree of pressure and anxiety the person was reporting. When this was pointed out to him, he responded, "I do feel that it is excessive, definitely." As the imagery process was repeated, residual anxiety was absorbed and he was able to approach daily situations in a more realistic and appropriate manner.

Developmental "Freeze" in the Symptom

The following two cases graphically illustrate the problems which arise when the Expectation High and the associated somatic states are obstructed and lost to awareness. When the body's natural expression is repressed or blocked during development due to fixation or trauma, somatic states of well-being become inaccessible. Essentially, a developmental "freeze" occurs in which the developmental muscular base is closed down, causing the somatic response (S) to disconnect from the ISM structure and become repressed in consciousness. The person, driven to recover these states, often turns to alcohol and drugs as the potential vehicle for their retrieval. In both cases below, we find a developmental freeze and the resulting somatic repression. In each case the somatic repression manifested its own unique symptomatology, yet both subjects reported feeling miserable, suffering from feelings of depression, isolation and aimlessness.

The aim of Eidetic Image Therapy is to retrieve natural states of well-being and wholeness present in the Expectation High and make them available to consciousness. The pace of treatment, however, must also involve opening up the body's channels and unfreezing the muscular base which has been developmentally inhibited and has separated the S from the ISM. When it is discovered in the course of treatment that alcohol and drugs have been falsely attributed with the ability to achieve these somatic states, all misconceptions and erroneous references must be cleared from the mind and the true states must be linked with their natural physiological base.

Paul: A Case of Pressure Versus Expression

Initial Symptom Report

Paul was a 21-year-old college student when he entered therapy. In his Initial Symptom Report, he said:

> "I don't have a problem really. I do not push things to the limit or go full force at anything. I push energy into a thing to a certain point and then drop it. I only work when it comes to finals. I do a little bit of everything in the meanwhile: play music, play around with my friends and socialize, do minimal work. It annoys me or frustrates me later on. I have been working on my relationship with women. I have a hard time treating them as equals. If I start some relationship with a girl, I don't want her to get too close or something... I am feeling curiosity, now that I am here, about what is going to happen. I am feeling comfortable. It is an open eagerness to learn something that I do not know already. I am not sure what I am going to learn. It will be about myself. Change, progress, learn, mature. It sounds good."

After further discussion, Paul reported that he was often unable to accomplish the things he set out to do. He said that as he approached the end of a project or course assignment, he would become angry and resent the fact that he was expected to finish it. At this point, he would procrastinate, change direction or drop the project altogether, only to face the same problem over and over again. He often blamed his inability to accomplish things on the demands of society and the expectations of his family. When he did work, he did well in school and reported that his professors often acknowledged his talents, encouraging him to do more. This only added to the experience of pressure and the cycle would begin again. The time was spent drinking and socializing in bars with friends.

Administration of the Eidetic Parents Test

In the first administration of the Eidetic Parents Test, Paul saw an image of his current house in which he had lived since he was twelve years old. He first reported a pleasant image of his parents sitting on the couch in the living room, drinking cocktails. However, as he continued to look at the image, he began to experience some claustrophobia with his mother and a bit of uneasiness with his father. He said, "There is a feeling of coldness in this house."

As the imagery progressed, Paul saw an image of his father being playful and teasing him. As this was developed further, he was able to see images of the earlier house in which he had lived from ages two to twelve. In this house, Paul again saw an image of his father playing with him. Although he reported the experience of playfulness and excitement upon seeing this image, he said there was also a feeling of fear and anxiety. "I have no control... He would play a game with me and sneak up the steps and just before I could see him he would pounce on me, grab me and tickle me. He had it down to a science. Each time it was new, the anticipation." Paul reported that there was more intimacy in the earlier house.

Looking for the Expectation High and the Positive Somatic Base

In this image there was more activity and an intimation of the Expectation High with its special excitement, but there was also some fear and anxiety associated with the image. As Paul concentrated on seeing his father teasing, he was able to see an image of the first house in which he lived before age two. Of this house he said:

> "I can see the kitchen. I see a linoleum floor. I am on the floor next to my mother. I was always talking. I am talking in the image. My mother is cooking and I am talking and asking questions. I ask everything and anything. 'What are you doing? What is this and what is that? Why do you do this? Why do you do that?' I expect everything. I want answers to all of my questions. I want to see everything. I want to know everything. I ask so many questions. The baby has a good mind. He is filled with curiosity. It is this 'I exist' feeling. I see everything and not one thing. It

was there in me then, but somewhere along the line I learned that it was not good. I have been trying to get it back. This must be the real self. This self is not cold and detached. This self says, 'I exist'..."

In this house image the baby was fully engaged, curious and active, and Paul recognized that this must be the "real self." This self wanted to know things, expected everything and was confident that he would achieve it. He recalled two more events from this house.

"I remember going with my father to a house on the street that the landlord owned. He had just painted one of the rooms. My father said to me, 'Don't touch,' and I knew that I wasn't supposed to touch and I lost my balance and I put my hand on the wall and got paint on it and my father got mad at me. I felt bad. I did not mean to do it. Another time, I am in a car. The landlord's wife found this squirrel that was hurt with a broken leg. She sewed up the wound. She had it in a bird cage. It was there and they were holding up the squirrel for me to see. I'm just looking."

In these early images from the first house, the child was curious, excited and interested in everything. He expected everything. Here were all the elements of the Expectation High and the positive somatic muscular base: energetic and forward moving. However, at the same time, there was a sense of prohibition and holding back, as when he was told, "Don't touch." Here we may speculate that the child's natural curiosity may have gotten the better of him when he lost his balance, and this was followed by a bad feeling when his father got mad even though Paul felt innocent. As Paul looked at the squirrel, there again was a sense of his curiosity and awe.

Paul subsequently reported seeing images of the second house where he lived from age two through twelve. In the second house there was still a sense of intimacy although there was also a sense of anxiety and fear. The father's playfulness was exciting but also was tinged with a little discomfort in the play. In this house, images revealed tension or disagreement between the parents. Although Paul stated, "It is not on the surface. It is repressed," the father was seen repressing the aggression. The mother was seen holding back something that "...she wants to give or something that she wants to say." In this house, the father was seen as accepting Paul conditionally: "My father's image gives me a sense of work, that I have to do some kind of work or put forth some kind of effort."

Finally, Paul described his experience in the third, current house, which he had originally reported as having a feeling of coldness and flatness, saying: "There is a lot of holding back, both negative and positive." It is interesting to note that it is in this house, at age twelve, that Paul started experimenting with alcohol and drugs.

At the completion of the EPT, Paul commented that he felt tense, fatigued and a little guilty: "Like I am giving my parents a raw deal with the images. I don't think my father is as cold as I see him in the images." He also said that he felt guilty for seeing his mother as inferior to his father, and "I have a hard time not protecting my mother all of the time." When the images from the first house were repeated and he was asked to see the child as curious and engaged, he reported that his feelings of fatigue went away and he felt more energetic.

Enhancing the Expectation High and the Positive Somatic Base

As the early states of consciousness are revealed through the parental images, there are two signals in the mind: one positive, with a sense of curiosity and openness; and one negative, with the feeling of prohibition and constriction. This is clearly illustrated when Paul said that the positive feeling he had when he did the images did not go away, and at the same time he felt guilty for seeing his parents in a certain way, particularly seeing his father as cold and detached.

Earlier, Paul had said that his "real self...is not cold and detached." It is also important to note that with the passage of time, the images of the parental houses get progressively colder and less intimate. Because of this, images of the first house when the child in him was full of curiosity and adventure were selected to retrieve high states of consciousness and a somatic feeling of well-being.

As the imagery process continued, rich states of consciousness flowed in a literary fashion. Paul's eidetic ability, highly imaginative and poetic in nature, emerged as his "real self." In the first house he saw the garden outside, and there was feeling of adventure to it:

"It was a long, narrow garden on the side of the house with bushes on one side and the house on the other. The other end had a little wall of hemlock. It was secluded and the soil was always loose because it was cultivated. There were all kinds of different things growing there. It would change constantly. There were little bugs all over. I can remember a cat we had that would sometimes follow me into the garden, and he had big, fat, white paws, and I would like the way they looked, walking through the dirt, through the soft dirt."

As this state was developed and brought forward in his mind, Paul was instructed to use his baby images to "warm up" the images of the later, colder houses. As he did this he reported:

"I feel the little baby inside of me. I have absorbed him. I see me now inside the other houses. I am melted into him. I am as I am not. I am in the sun and warm. I feel like a cherub. I can feel the wind going underneath my legs and through my fingers. I can see my hands. They are fat, little hands. It is like a glow too. I am glowing in the soft sunlight. I roll around a little bit on the carpet. I am just rolling my head from side to side. I am watching the ceiling and the legs of the table. Things are just going back and forth. I am doing it faster and faster and watching it go. The wind, I can almost see it pouring in through the window. It rushes down the hallway and goes through, then goes back. It is playful. It is like a genie coming in. It takes me up in the current, almost like I can get lifted up off the floor, out to the kitchen and all over the place. The wind is like another person, like a spirit."

In a later projection of this image, Paul was asked to experience the details of the things around him. He reported the following image.

"I am standing in the kitchen facing the window. It is summertime. I feel the heat from the sun coming from the window. I can see the dust down in the air from the sunlight. The light coming from the door. I can feel the tiles under my feet. The tiles — I can feel pieces are broken off and missing at the seams. I can see the hedges out the window. I can see the leaves. I can see the trees and everything outside, the grass, hedges, the leaves. Everything is clear and it is all one thing. I can see myself as a baby. I see florescent lights on the ceiling. I see the space between the stove and the cabinets. I see the dust at the edge at the bottom of the refrigerator. There is a metal strip between the edge of the kitchen and the carpet. It looks like it is gold. It is wobbly and bent up a little bit. I see the table again and my highchair. My father is there. My mother is there too. I just see everything. Everything is clear. I feel the oneness. I see clarity in everything. I don't see everything clear at once. The eyes see one thing and then another. The other things are there but not in the center.

"When I look outside from this home, I see bushes, strong sunlight on the bushes. Those little birds flying. There is a cat on the ground watching the birds. I see the back of the cat. I can see his fur and feel the fur and the sunlight on the edge of the fur. The end of the cat's tail is switching back and forth. He is flexing his paws straight out. I can see the muscles on his shoulders. I can feel the ridge of where his shoulder goes down to his back. I can feel the energy in his back. He is storing up all the energy in his back legs, waiting. I put my head out the window. I can feel the warm breeze on my face. I can smell all the grass, the trees, and flowers. I can feel the pollen go into my nose. I can hear the birds' wings when they fly in and out of the bushes. I can hear the noise when they land on the tiny twigs and the branch bounces up and down a little bit. The cat didn't know. He wanted to look at them all at once, but now he is just watching one. The bird is chirping. It has no idea what the cat is up to. The cat thinks he is invisible.

The bird seems so stupid. The cat is totally open, but he is real still. I can feel the fur on the cat, the breeze when the bird flutters around. I can feel the cat breathing in the grass. I can feel the cat's whole body, like a compressed spring.

"I am hanging out the window. I have my arms out the window. I am hanging there and looking. I don't have a shirt on. I can feel the sun on my skin. I can feel my muscles, loose and smooth, and my weight on the window sill. I feel where the paint is chipped against my skin. I feel the breeze going through the hairs on my arms. I can see the skin starting to get flushed from the sun and the heat. I feel the hair on my shoulders. Sweat in my armpits; the sweat rolls down the inside of my arms. It kind of tickles. It feels like a spider. I feel all of the blood going to the ends of my fingers. My veins are swelling on the top of my head. It is hot under my hair. I feel the sweat starting to bead under my hair and my temples. I am waiting to bead up enough so it will drip down my face. I can feel the side of the house. It is hard. When I move my fingers back and forth, little bits of dirt and sand come off. I can hear them fall on the leaves and plants below. It sounds like sandpaper when I move my fingers back and forth. I do it for a while. Maybe I will do it forever and make a hole through the wall. I can do it all day long.

"I can feel the sun hitting my arms and my shoulders. I can feel that it is strong. I can probably get burned if I stay there for a long time. I feel a soft sunlight around. It is soft and it is warm. It is warmer than warm. It is almost hot, but it is not unpleasant hot. It is just like the perfect temperature. The sunlight softens everything, but it does not blur it.

"I can experience the wind going through my hair. There is life in the wind. It gives me the life that it has in it. It is life. It is like energy, life energy. I see this power in the wind. I feel the little baby inside me. I have absorbed it. I am melted into him.

"I am in the sun and warm. I feel like a cherub. I

can feel the wind going underneath my legs and through my fingers. I can see my hands. The wind has water qualities also. It has strength to move objects like water does. It can pick things up, like a flow. It is picking everything up. It carries everything very lazily, but very securely. Nothing will break. Nothing will hit anything. It rolls around, the wind rolls off. Just rolls off.

"I feel myself outside. I get carried out the window and outside, rolling along in the dirt. It is almost like when a sea plane lands and pushes the water. I am making a wake in the dirt. I can smell it. I feel my feet and my toes go through it. I could just go — dive into the earth like it was water, and come out again. It is like I am swimming through the ground. Everything gives. I can touch everything and swim through everything. It is like I can go down to the earth and go up again, like a flower blooming, like a rebirth. Yes, it is like a rebirth. I am doing it over and over again. When I go down I can see some rocks down there. I went through the strawberries. I grab them and I bring them all down with me and then come up again and they are all over the place. I am sliding along in the grass. I am feeling the grass go against my body. I am gliding and sliding along fast. I put my hands out so that I can feel it."

Analysis of EPT and Expectation High Responses

The power and richness of high states of consciousness were completely lost to awareness through a progressive shutting-down over the course of years until, by the time Paul was thirteen, they were obscured by feelings of inferiority. He was now living in the third house, which he described as the "cold house," and he said that up until that time, "I was still a good kid, doing whatever I was told to do, like getting good grades and being on the honor roll."

At thirteen, however, when he began experimenting with alcohol and drugs, he was having an adversarial relationship with his father, conditions which imply that he was "not being a good kid" as he had reported. Paul saw his father's acceptance as conditional, contingent on putting forth some kind of an effort or work on his part. The baby's natural expressive qualities of curiosity and adventure were gradually repressed and, as Paul said about these qualities: "Somewhere I learned it was not good." Being good involved doing what he was told and putting forth some kind of effort; natural curiosity was not seen as being good.

Thus, the energetic and dynamic states of consciousness indicative of the Expectation High had been lost to awareness, frozen or obstructed in the process of development. Somatic well-being was no longer available, so that therapy had to gradually recover the repressed muscular base. As early positive developmental states were uncovered through the eidetic process, they were brought to the forefront of awareness and systematically reconnected to their proper mental setting and associated somatic states. They were then joined to the Expectation High to bring Paul to a natural state of activation and engagement in the world.

When Paul reported that he started drinking and taking drugs in junior high school, it became clear that the experience of the Expectation High had been misallocated to alcohol and drugs and not to his real self, which further diverted his mind from the source. At this point, specific steps were taken to disentangle the true source of pleasure from the illusory pleasure in the alcohol and drug experience, all in the context of his developmental material thus far revealed.

Alcohol/Drug Experience: Misallocation of the Expectation High

Paul said that he wanted to try everything that life could offer. This connected with his EPT responses of the baby who wanted to do everything and see everything. He reported:

> "There is also the element of danger in trying everything. Doing things that you were not supposed to do. There is danger in being spontaneous because you do not know what is going to happen. That is part of the fun and excitement, being daring and being a little nervous. In the marijuana high it is interesting. Things are more interesting. It is a new experience and all new experiences are interesting.

> With the marijuana I tried to lose control. In a way I was kind of looking forward to losing control. I guess I lost control a little. I remember being a little silly and saying, 'I am not going to school anymore and I am not doing my homework anymore.' It seems like these two things are very innocent. Even the high was innocent. Drinking seems to have been more of a quest for a new sensation. The marijuana high was more a quest for knowledge and it seems even more innocent."

Paul is curious, looking for new sensations, knowledge, and things to be interesting, yet these things seemed to be beyond his immediate reach without the use of drugs. He said that "things look dull and boring," and that he was "waiting for something to happen, something to change when I used alcohol or drugs." He did not know how things would change, but he expected that they would. He also said if he drinks now, he drinks himself up to a point of reaction in which he reacts to things that need to be done, for example, cleaning his room.

Action and activation became reaction and passivity, waiting for something to change while at the same time doing nothing to change it. The pattern of holding back development is apparent here — shutting off the natural state of curiosity and moving instead into a state of no action. Paul reported that drugs and alcohol produced a numbing of sensation and inactivity: "I am totally aware that I am voluntarily sedating myself and dulling the world."

There was a gap in consciousness in this statement. On the one hand, Paul wanted to be engaged and interested in things and said that drugs make things more interesting; on the other hand, he acknowledged that taking drugs and alcohol sedated him and dulled the world, evidencing a thinking style along the lines reported by research subjects: "More drinking, more euphoria."

Thus, only by examining memories and beliefs about the drug and alcohol experience in precise detail could it be determined where the distortions and misallocations occurred so that Paul's true high states of consciousness could be separated out and rescued. The philosophy, the somatic and emotional states, the social values and life style related to drinking and drug use needed to be critically explored so that all of the illusions and misconceptions could be removed from the mind. Accordingly, the Expectation High was separated out so that it could be joined with the developmental muscular base that had been repressed. An antidote image was used toward this end.

Antidote Image

In Paul's case, the use of an antidote image proved effective in helping to remove the lingering fantasies related to the bar scene (see the section "An Antidote Image" in Chapter 6 for Paul's case).

Impulse: An Aspect of the Expectation High

At this point, an important theme that Paul described in his opening comments emerged: the quite complicated and drawn out issue of action/reaction, waiting/impulse. Since these were related to the muscular freeze from development related to the Expectation High, the theme was now taken forward. Paul was asked to see an image of himself waiting in a situation, and he replied: "I am waiting. I am waiting. There is a feeling of impatience. There is extreme impatience. I have it." As the instruction was repeated, the feeling of impatience became very pronounced. "When I see that I don't have direction in a situation, I get annoyed. The annoyance builds and I feel like I am going to kill. It is dangerous, scary and frustrating." After repeating the image a number of times, there was a change in his perception and he reported seeing himself with more clarity:

> "When I see myself become anxious and angry, it is a knowledge of myself. I come to know a facet of my own person in a funny way, other than just living my life and not really seeing what makes you up as a person. Waiting has been a long time in my life. It is a running theme. There is a level of unnecessary pressure or undefinable pressure that will cause me to immediately do something. When I am waiting I just get really angry and frustrated. I feel like I have nothing to hold on to. It is like I'm being taken down a river and I am trying to get a hold on something and there is nothing to hold on to, but at the same time I am moving alone and I get frustrated and

angry. I think I have always been angry. I have a mean streak. I have always had it. Even when I think people don't see that I have it, it just comes up. It gets tiring and depressing after a while. I am a lot more relaxed that I used to be. I used to scare people a lot just being in the same room with them. I was like a bomb ready to go off. It amazes me when I think about these things. I was always on the edge. It some- one looked at me cross-eyed, I would slit their throat. I never really had to be violent because people knew that I was ready and willing to do it. You know when some people look for fights. I did not know what I was looking for. I knew that I needed to get rid of something, somehow, and other people can sense a directionless, confused anger. I was suicidal also. You could walk into my house when no one was there and you could see electricity all over the place. I am waiting for a direction, which seems like my entire life. I ask myself ten times a day, I ask myself, 'Now what do I want to do?' And then I say — maybe an hour later, I ask myself, 'Now what do I want to do?'"

In Paul's comments there was a signal of shutting down the body's natural inclination toward activity and curiosity. The baby's curiosity was clearly expressed at age two and he did not need to ask the ques- tion, "What do I do now?" He had interest in everything and every- thing was interesting, full of adventure and excitement. There was no room for impatience. When the expression of curiosity and action was held back, the body's natural impulse was repressed so as not to move forward. While Paul had a desire to move forward and to see and experience everything, he stopped himself short, resulting in a feeling of frustration and anger. As Paul experienced a build-up of pressure, he impulsively would do something in an attempt to get rid of it. As this theme was explored and developed, Paul realized:

"There are so many things that I would like to do that I really don't know where to start. It is like I can see myself standing in the middle of a completely messy room and I want to organize it and clean it up. There is so much stuff and I am standing there. In the

image I see that I have gone around and have gotten
a little done, but pretty soon I will make a dent in one
of the corners, clean up this corner first and then I am
going to do this and that. The time when I am cleaning up here and there, I don't know where to dig in.
It is frustrating. I don't get any satisfaction, don't get
any energy. It drives me crazy. What am I going to
do? When I do something I feel better."

Analysis of Impulse Response

Feeling better is a positive somatic response to doing something.
There is a sense of release and direction. Paul's case clearly distinguishes between the experience of mere impulse and action. The notions of
dynamism, engagement and purposeful direction are inherent in the
action, when Paul engaged in the adventure of the garden; the garden
drew him in, and he followed his natural curiosity each step of the way,
every aspect of his journey being rich in sensation. The impulse, on the
other hand, was evidenced in his reaction to the pressure and frustration
that built into an intensity when he was unable to get going. When he
thought more about this, he said: "Someday, hopefully, sooner or later, I
will free myself from unproductive anger." He was aware that something was needed to direct his misused energy.

When natural expressiveness is suppressed, it causes the body to
inhibit its organic responsiveness along with the ability to gain pleasure
from its actions. Negative emotions are then associated with expressiveness and the person begins to feel negative about the self. This further
results in an inferior feeling because natural bodily impulses are experienced as bad or wrong in some way. This is illustrated in Paul's case
when he says, "I never thought that I deserved anything. My whole life
my parents told me I was so great, but I never really felt that way." The
feelings of inferiority and a negative somatic self-image produce a
response of inactivity and waiting. Paul's statement, "I don't know what
to do," is coupled with the feeling of pressure to do something.

Paul's case shows a shut-down of natural expressiveness and the frustration and anger that occurred as a result. By age twelve, he saw in the
parental images, "...a holding back, both negative and positive." At this
point he began to use drugs and alcohol, which provided an element of

"...danger and doing something that you're not supposed to do." Up until this point he felt he was a good kid, "...doing everything that I was told to do." His natural desire and curiosity were held back "after learning along the way that it wasn't good." He did what he had been told to do – while he was still curious and drawn to new experiences (albeit the wrong ones, perhaps) – which meant excluding again his natural states of expression.

This eventually led to a developmental "freeze," resulting in repression of the somatic response (S) from current experience and the ISM memory structure. The results of this disconnection are very clear in Paul's case since there was increasing pressure or somatic build-up which propelled him to blindly attempt to discharge the energy in whatever way he impulsively chose. The somatic connection to well-being through the expression of natural curiosity and exploration was shut off and there was a negative feeling associated with the somatic base of desire to move forward and be curious about life.

The Ongoing Therapeutic Process

During this process, detailed examination of the alcohol and drug lifestyle was ongoing. Whatever was still left of the addicted personality was drawn out and replaced by activating source images that reconnected Paul to the Expectation High. The more these images were developed and enhanced, the more Paul rejected remnants of his alcoholic life. Any intimations of an indirect drug connection through the memory trace were also deeply explored. Interestingly enough, during a later period in treatment when the remnants of the alcohol and drug lifestyle had been all but removed and the Expectation High states developed, a memory trace of a cocaine experience emerged, unlocked through the imagery process and the seriality of image structures. This memory trace was dealt with directly by relinking the power associated with the drug to its proper somatic base.

Imagination: An Aspect of the Expectation High

As a result, Paul's deeply poetic, literary imagination was brought forward through eidetic imagery development, and he reported that some of his anger began to dissipate. After becoming more aware of this aspect of himself and working with it over a period of time, Paul reported, "Writing things down helps a lot. I have so many things in my head. Writing cools me off from the anger. A lot of the anger is because I feel like I am not doing anything. It does not take much effort, but I like it. I feel like I am getting something done." The "real self" earlier discovered in the baby became more accessible to awareness; these high states of consciousness evolved further through development of his literary ability.

To illustrate this process, at one point Paul was asked to see himself enter a mythical king's palace and describe what he saw.

> "When I enter the palace, I see the marble is like bloodstone. It is all dark and has veins like blood going through it. It is really smooth and cold under my feet and I can see these huge pillars running along each side going all the way down to the other end where the king is seated on his throne. The pillars are almost like thin pyramids, and far back from behind the pyramids on either side of the pillars are people in the palace. The sky is very open and reminds me St. Peter's in Rome, the courtyard there. I feel alone, but not lonely. Strong, but unsure of what is going to happen. Eager for something to happen, but wary at the same time. The king is far off, far away— seems very strong, sure of himself. He seems to know something about me that I don't know. I am waiting and he is waiting also. I see it as a game. It is a game you live. Like I said, when I walk in, I am wary. I feel that there is a lot of power, and if you are not aware of it you could get hurt. I see my tiger come in from the desert. I am standing in the palace and the tiger walks in through the gates. He walks in real slow and sure. He walks across the marble and I can hear his paws on the marble. I like the way it sounds. As I stand there, the palace gets full of smog, like smoke. The tiger seems to decide that he has some kind of purpose so he goes off to the side by one of the rows of pillars and kind of trots along, half crouched, pretty fast— going to the

other end of the palace where the king is seated on his throne. I can see the tiger's blue eyes going through the smoke and they light up a little bit of the smoke as he moves along. I take the other side, the other row of pillars in between where everyone is in the courtyard. I start the same way the tiger is, aggressively but carefully and kind of crouching and rushing through the smoke."

Analysis of the Imagination Response

Paul's literary imagination is obviously rich and expressive. Within the mythological story, the impulsiveness again played itself out so that the myth carried along a metaphor from his developmental struggle, unleashing his creativity and his literary talent while providing direction for its expression at the same time. He commented: "I was thinking that the way you make progress with yourself is going through experiences and dealing with them the best way you can. The problem is in normal life you have to wait for these experiences. I have learned that your mind does not really know the difference, so going through them in your mind you can deal with them, instead of waiting for them. It was real, vivid, intense. I want to go back and write it all down in detail." There was a strong feeling of enthusiasm and interest. In the writing he did not have to make things interesting; he was naturally engaged in the process.

Strengthening the Positive Somatic Base: Breathing Out

While the mind was becoming more activated and engaged, Paul's body was likewise becoming more involved as the developmental repressions were relieved through the reinstatement of the body's own sensations of well-being. Prior to this, Paul had not felt good about himself physically as a child. He said:

"I felt awkward, ugly, painful. Everybody thought I was cute but it did not matter to me. I thought I was ugly. I just wanted to be able to forget about it and have everybody forget about it. I was smart and polite, a total gentleman. I could be real serious. I thought I was an adult. I think that I was just a total composition of

> extremes. I knew that everybody thought I was cute.
> Everyone reacted that way, so I kind of fed their reac-
> tions, but it wasn't really conscious. I was being myself.
> I was not conning everybody. It felt bad because I
> thought that I was a person, but every time I had some
> kind of positive effect it was not really me. It was
> because I was really skinny and I looked really funny.
> It was like I was being treated like a little animal."

As this theme unfolded, he reported:

> "I see myself in junior high school, seventh grade. I
> am at my locker. It is metal. I see myself opening the
> locker. Everything is really, really hard. My body feels
> like metal too. It makes me so angry I start to clench
> my teeth. I can feel my body start to make acid in my
> stomach. It is very uncomfortable. I was always
> uncomfortable all of the time. It is like a wounded ani-
> mal. They get nasty. I feel sore in general, all of the
> muscles are tensed up. The breathing gets tight. I feel
> like I am going to burn myself up. It feels like nothing
> gives at all. Everything is real hard and nothing gives.
> There is no relief, release or satisfaction. If I struggle I
> am just going to destroy myself."

In this example the body's natural ability to experience well-being
was unavailable. Again, it was precisely at this time that Paul began to
experiment with alcohol and drugs.

Images that brought back the body's natural well-being into awareness enabled Paul to feel more comfortable with his physical body. He
finally felt "...vibrant, strong and weighty. I feel substantial."
Throughout treatment the body further developed along the lines of
strength and substance while the high states of curiosity and imagination were enhanced.

As the body was reintroduced to its natural states, attention to the
breathing process was found to be critical in order to break up frozen
musculature. While Paul engaged in various imagery exercises, he
said that he was now breathing better and better.

> "I felt like I had never taken a full breath. I feel like
> my lungs can expand more than they do. I did not

have the strength to fill them with air. A lot of times I will sit and try to take in more and more air until I feel like my rib cage is almost going to crack. I felt like, if I could cut my ribs open and put more ribs in, I could fill my lungs all the way. I would like to learn how to breathe fully. Right now I feel like I am using only half my lungs. I want to use my lungs 100% and then make them stronger than that. I know that when I do images for my body, my whole body opens up. I feel more relaxed and I feel healthier. Food goes through me easier. My whole digestive system opens up."

As illustrated in the previous case, breathing out brings power and a sense of activation. Paul reported:

"If I breathe out, my head feels more open. Everything is clearer. My voice feels smoother and more relaxed. I have more control over things. If I use breathing in longer, I feel like tension is building up again. When I go back to breathing out I feel a lot better. Breathing out makes me notice everything else in my body that is tight."

After Paul's body was introduced to proper breathing, it was mobilized during breathing out. When breathing out, the breathing processes gradually change in the body's favor and, in time, the person develops more strength. The neck muscles and the chest formation begin to change. The shoulders become more relaxed and become lower because they are not held tightly, as during inhibited breathing. As the shoulders lower, the rest of the body begins to adjust and the benefits spread to the legs and feet.

Review of Paul's Case

In Paul's therapy, the Expectation High states were retrieved and linked to their proper mental structures, the body was reintroduced to states of well-being, and the imagination sparked and engaged, all resulting in a general mobilization toward interaction in the world rather than retreat into withdrawal and addiction. When any negative cue surfaced during treatment, images that were engaging and releasing were further enhanced so that Paul could actively move toward reinstatement of the "real self." As the "real self" was brought forward and more deeply experienced, old obstructions and developmental fixations gave way to the emergence of Paul's new talents.

Alex: Choice and Movement

Initial Symptom Report

Alex was nineteen years old when he entered therapy. At that time he complained of nervousness and tension and felt that the circulation in his hands was cut off. He said that he felt like he had been floating since high school, not able to find a use for his skills. But he also said that "trying something new scares me." Alex was attending college and reported that he did well in his studies, though he found them unchallenging and uninteresting. He expressed annoyance and irritation at this and said he felt no commonalty with teachers or, for that matter, with the other students, a condition which added to his isolation.

Two Administrations of the Eidetic Parents Test

Images revealed in the Eidetic Parents Test brought Alex to age five where he saw his parents in the second house in which he lived. As he looked at the image (EP1), he reported:

> "As I look at my mother she keeps washing dishes. There is no feeling of attachment, nothing strong. I do not feel detached either, as if I am just there. As I look at my father, he is washing the car. There is no special feeling of attachment or even detachment... [Later he said] I don't think I ever sought either of my parents out. I guess I thought I will have to deal with things on my own, that is what I was supposed to do. I felt like this as far back as I can remember. Even now I do not become intimate with people or seek them out. I have gotten worse as I have gotten older."

In the first image, we find indication of a developmental repression and somatic "freeze" at age five. The natural feeling of biological connection, intimacy and security was absent from the image.

The initial responses to the parental images lacked detail, depth and feelingfulness. When the EPT was readministered, the images emerged at a deeper level. Alex saw himself as a baby, and he reported the following: "As a baby, there is attachment to my mother. It is a good image to look at but I can't feel it in my heart." Although he reported that there was attachment in this earlier image, there was still a lack of intimacy and somatic connection to the mother. When he looked at his father's image, he reported that there was a feeling of distaste when he came too close. He said: "I back off. It is like someone invading your space."

Alex was asked to repeat the images, this time keeping in mind that situations could be more open-ended than he may previously have thought. When asked to respond to each image in a more playful way and with a sense of openness, he said: "The idea that there is an opening is comforting." He was instructed to allow his mind to be more expressive rather than closed off and detached. Still, he showed a tendency to cut off the experience, when he said: "I am running dry on things in the image." There was resistance in him and a sense of having to draw things out of him with some struggle.

Theme of Control and Freedom: Bipolar Tension and Release in the Body

During the second administration of the EPT, the theme of control became clearer. Alex reported that he experienced tension in his body when he saw the images of both his mother and his father. When he saw his mother grasping something, he said: "She grips so tight to be in control that it makes my legs shake and my hands clench." On seeing his father stressed, he said: "I become stressed and tense." At one point he saw his mother make him wear a jacket he did not want to wear and he reported: "No matter how much I screamed and yelled, she still made me wear it." He recalled his father demanding that he do something in the house, and when he said he did not want to do it, "He grabbed my hair and started pulling it. I was crying. I held out for a while, and then I realized that he was not going to stop, so I did what he wanted. Then I ran upstairs and cried for about an hour."

In a later image Alex recalled that his mother used to overdress him as a baby and he would get overheated as a result. When he saw this image, he felt helpless and angry. He said that overheating made his mental processes "go a little berserk," causing him to feel "disoriented and helpless." He saw in the image that she overdressed him out of maternal duty, but he said that his father was more in rhythm with him when he helped him take off the jacket.

As the image progressed, Alex finally saw himself take off the jacket. He reported that he felt more free and that his mother was less in control. Here freedom was experienced as doing something on his own, something that he wanted to do.

Alex now reported that he often felt lethargic, tired and bored. He frequently slept nine or ten hours a night, only to rise feeling tired. Though he lacked energy, he said that he often felt like exploding. He said he did not enjoy socializing very much, preferring to remain at home alone or engage in more solitary activities. He admitted that his boredom came from not doing things. Doing things in the images created a feeling of more openness and release as opposed to the feeling of being overheated, constricted and helpless. Here was a more natural state of consciousness with an underlying sense of possibility and expressiveness.

This state was further revealed when the image of a younger mother emerged spontaneously and developed in the following way.

> "I see an image of this lady, my mother, younger. She has big brown eyes, almost Oriental eyes. It is a good person, but I don't know who it is. What the hell is this? I would like to dismiss her and find out where my mom is. This feels almost like a myth, like when you see something beautiful. It draws you to it and it doesn't let you go. It is like the Harpies for the Greeks. The song is so beautiful you can become blind."

Upon further elaboration of this image, he said:

> "She is beautiful, really powerful. It feels like my counterpart. She should be with me. She fits in so well. It explains and goes along with so many of my thoughts. She tells me I have to be strong against my dad. There is a cue of openness with her coming. She is my friend. She puts her hand on my shoulder and there is more of a feeling of contact. She is talking to me about strength, not weakness. When I see her and

hear her I have a cue of hope. When I hear her I have
in myself a cue toward strength."

In this image, there was evidence of release both in the body and in the
mind. Alex said: "There is no sense of control in the image."

Cues of the Expectation High and the Positive Somatic Base

The potential of the Expectation High resides within hope. The
image was already moving in this direction, as can be seen above. As
Alex continued to project the image, he further reported as follows:

"When I touch this woman and she touches me, it
feels like the part of me that is missing. When I touch
her skin, she accepts me and there is a strong emotional response toward her. There is a feeling of
attachment. She is very much part of me, my other
self. She is the very link in my development that links
me to who I am now with a sense of my past. There
are emotional feelings and normal sexual feelings.
There is a strong feeling of sexuality, my own sexuality. There is a powerful feeling there."

When Alex saw himself riding on horseback alongside the
"younger mother," he acknowledged that she was a symbol of
release and action and an invitation for new things in the future.
When asked to include his parents in this image, he could see them
riding on horseback in the same free way. He said: "Father appears
less tense and his thoughts are more free." These images released
Alex from his apprehensions, as they also removed the parents' lim-
itations in his consciousness: "There is a cure for my father too in this
image, in this new world."

Another strength emerged as well in the image, that of being playfully pesty and teasing. Alex was asked to bring the positive signals of
freedom and playfulness to the EP1 images that were previously seen
as obstructed. He reported:

"I start to do it and it feels that I am actually merging
more. I can see both selves, the obstructed one and
the other one. The other one is at peace with himself.
The obstructed self is walled off and introverted.
When I merge with him and play with him we are

both happier. This boy is friendly. Now he wants to run around and play. He is pesty. He goes in the kitchen where mom is and starts making all kinds of noises. He has a little plane and starts to fly it around. He runs in the kitchen with the plane and then runs down the hall and circles the house inside with the plane and makes noises. He runs all over the house. I run into a room and whipped the plane into the wall and made it crash. There is an explosion and I pick the plane up and fly it back into my room. I can see that he is into mischief, but not a big worrier. He doesn't worry at all. He is not worried about doing something bad. He wouldn't do something bad. He is adventurous. He is driven by his internal curiosity to do things. He doesn't let anything stop him if he is curious about something. He doesn't give up. He wants to do anything that is interesting. He wants to find out. My breath feels different when I feel more like that self. It is more stimulating. My whole being is more lively."

The "real self" that was now emerging had the qualities of being curious and a little provocative. His breath felt different inside and he was more lively in general. Alex now felt it was more in his nature to question rather than obstruct.

Analysis of the EPT Response

Images of freedom from overheating were important somatically as they allowed Alex to use his assertiveness and become free from his early bodily restriction. He had reported feeling physically overheated when he was annoyed and said that his head would be hot, but his hands would be cold. When the experience of heating up was linked to activation images, it resulted in an open feeling rather than restriction. Alex reported that these images cleared and expanded his mind as well as energized his body: "My body feels strong. I feel my blood flowing and my breathing free."

First Substance Use Experience (FISUE)

As the imagery developed, Alex reported that he experimented

with drugs beginning when he was thirteen. He reported that his
anger had gotten worse at age twelve:

> "I felt anger from guilt. I was bored and obstructed. I
> experienced guilt from my failure to use my skills. I
> was no longer worthy. I felt weak when I was not
> using my skills and that produced guilt which made
> me feel weak. I also felt anger because my parents
> did not teach me proper skills."

Alex reported that he tried drugs not only because he was seeking
an answer to his boredom – "I was bored because I was not doing anything." – but also because he felt that drugs were a way of defeating
his parents and their authoritarianism. Though he drank alcohol, he
said he never had any real interest in drinking, that he never thought
much about it and that he could not understand the motivation to
drink. While he did smoke pot and experiment with cocaine, he said
that he never liked cocaine:

> "I smoked pot pretty consistently from grade 9 to 11,
> every other day. I got the money for it from my par-
> ents, Christmas and working summers. This money
> went primarily for drugs. I also sold marijuana.
> When I started marijuana, I was bored and curious
> about it. I liked it."

Recalling the first time he smoked marijuana, Alex said: "I was
expecting something new and exciting. It is a very open feeling. The
open feeling is brought out by trying something new that I think I am
going to like." As the Expectation High was enhanced through concentration on images revealed in the FISUE, the new feelings of curiosity, excitement and openness gave him a positive somatic feeling. He
reported that he had no desire to smoke marijuana because he saw
that he was avoiding things by smoking; he became aware that the
feeling of openness came from within himself:

> "When I experience the Expectation High, I feel new-
> ness. I feel more open. The sky and the stars are very
> tranquil and give a very peaceful feeling. The more I
> think about it, the more it sinks in and the more pow-
> erful it becomes."

262   New Treatment of Alcohol and Drug Abuse

Strengthening the Positive Somatic Base

As Alex's mind progressed along the lines of enactment through images of freedom and strength, his body was activated accordingly. As this progressed, however, he began to complain of a leaden feeling his body. This physical feeling first began as the experience of annoyance and irritation, but it soon developed into an extreme form of physical heaviness: "A couple of days this week I have really felt exhausted when I woke up, like I just had to lay there and it took a lot of time to be able to clench my fists and get my muscles working. I feel like lead...there is something else in my soul that I have to get rid of. Something is keeping me stuck." As Alex's body was progressively activated and engaged through various imagery exercises, the somatic repression took on a separate character and life of its own, devoid of available developmental content and flooding the body with an unexplainable "leaden feeling."

This "leaden" feeling emerged as a somatic state (S) that was living on its own, disconnected from any image structure. It was not connected to any ISM structure and not related to an event. Psychoanalysis endlessly searches for causality, and in the process, seeks the roots or a cause. When approached through the eidetic, the somatic symptom is isolated and dealt with as a separate and discrete entity. Alex was instructed to view the symptom as an undesirable and foreign element, in a sense, an unwelcome visitor and, as such, subject to his command to remove itself. This instruction, coupled with the systematic activation of positive body states and images, resulted in obliteration of the leaden feeling in the body. At this point Alex experienced a dramatic overall change in his experience. His prevailing experience became one of unobstructed openness and somatic well-being. The disconnected S collapsed under the force of the Expectation High and the release, giving way to a true state of wholesomeness and well-being. As the newly retrieved somatic states were developed further, the repressed muscular base became strengthened and the areas of the body that had been weakened through the developmental "freeze" were once again activated. As a result, Alex reported that he felt eager to become more active and discover a direction for his skills and talents. He had overcome the somatic repression of energetic states and his obstructions in the mind, giving access to the energetic core of consciousness.

The "Real Self"

The central point in the above cases is a progressive attuning toward genuine engagement in reality. Fear of reality and negative anticipation regarding it cause a person to retreat and withdraw from active participation in the world. The quality of anticipation determines the basic character of activation and confidence, or lack of it, with which the person moves toward reality. A developmental "freeze" results in a general somatic repression which inhibits the person's ability to utilize natural resources and talents.

Dramatic results occur when high states of consciousness are returned to their rightful place in the personality functioning. When these energetic and buoyant images are released and activated, the person is able to evolve a fulfilling and effective lifestyle. Interaction with Expectation High images provides access to the deepest level of human expression, bringing the person back into balance and harmony with the "real self." Because talents are multidimensional, as the ISM demonstrates, they are dynamic, emotional, mythic and active, and they seek a means of expressing themselves in the world through interaction and engagement. As Ahsen (1988b) says:

> The loss of innocence through the demands of an increasingly mechanized world and the diminishing connection with the natural order of life makes retrieval of these states more complex and more essential at the same time. There are many ways of dealing with present reality. One of the ways is poetic. Other ways are adaptational. Clearly the world of loss, memory and adjustment is not the true world of feeling, except in the nostalgic sense. One way to find reality is to land in the very heart of the sun, in one's true self, which is to land in the truly poetic. There is

that grand, uttermost and ultimate power of Nature reflected in the poetic stance. From there one can proceed onward to current reality so that it is not isolated as a dark realm but accounted for in terms of light. The narrow reality is retranslated and reinterpreted through the poetic, which resolves the contradiction. In the true poetic journey, reality is not abandoned or scoffed at because any abandoned reality will surely come back to haunt us and no doubt finally defeat the merely nostalgic or superficially poetic participation in it. When the person takes inspiration from his true inner resource and brings out the "Expectation High" along with the sense of reality, we have a truly powerful encounter. The deepest victory of the self is not adaptation, but poetic participation. (p. 48)

Chapter 8

The Eidetic Imagery Intensive Treatment Program:
A New Model for Intervention

Ahsen has developed a unique protocol for therapeutic intervention that is designed to target a specific presented problem area in a highly concentrated manner. Called the *Eidetic Imagery Intensive*, this treatment program devotes an uninterrupted period of time and a singularity of focus to unearth deep information about the person's problem, including emotional and somatic symptoms. The Intensive extends over several consecutive days, uncovering the primary image structures related to the presenting symptom in a fast moving, concentrated fashion. Through such intensive investigation and extensive exploration of the symptom and its related issues, this model provides rapid entry into areas of difficulty and accelerated resolution to problems, such as those found in addictions.

The Imagery Intensive utilizes material yielded from the person's own symptomatology and core procedures described in previous chapters, to assess the nature and extent of the problem area. As specific information is gathered, extensive knowledge is gained and therapeutic experience is generated. Most significantly, the link between various experiential states and their related body processes is dramatically demonstrated through precisely targeted eidetic images that have been carefully gleaned from the material revealed in the process.

Throughout the Imagery Intensive, concentrated attention is given to the imagery structures. The person is instructed to apply newly acquired knowledge and therapeutic imagery to all routine activities. This insures continuity and depth in the process, which surfaces any underlying areas that require further elucidation. The atmosphere of the program is open and free flowing, thus allowing the mind to expand beyond its usual constriction and habitually limited view of the current problem.

The total milieu of the Intensive maximizes the depth of the probe. This process directly taps intrapsychic levels which are beyond routine thought and maintains them for a much longer period of time than conventional approaches. This quickly leaves the person's defense mechanisms behind and allows the matrix of interconnected images to surface more fluidly, revealing extensive and illuminating information.

Ahsen's Eidetic Imagery Intensive is particularly effective for breaking through blocked emotional areas that have remained elusive or recalcitrant to ordinary treatment approaches. Motivated individuals who have tried other methods without benefit or want to rapidly target and treat their problem have found it especially useful.

Program Format

There are three distinct phases of the program, each intended to facilitate deeper levels of involvement with the symptom area and to generate therapeutic insight and change.

Phase 1. Comprehensive Intake Interview and Testing Procedures

This phase consists of a comprehensive interview process during which extensive information about the problem area is collected. In the Initial Symptom Report, the person provides a subjective description of the symptom and any related issues in an open style. The Eidetic Parents Test and other core imagery procedures are administered at this time. When all of the information is gathered, it is extensively reviewed, carefully analyzed and used to establish the basic direction of treatment. Phase 1 may be conducted prior to coming to the Eidetic Therapy Institute.

Phase 2. Intensive Treatment

The Intensive Treatment phase is conducted over several consecutive days at the Institute. During Phase 2, key eidetic images that have been carefully gleaned from the information gathered in Phase 1 are used to unearth deeper aspects of the problem that have been hidden by the addiction and its related symptomatology. These images also represent a point of interpretive harmony between the test materials and the description of the current situation. They confirm the direction of the treatment strategy and dramatically demonstrate the link between various experiential states and their related body processes. When the images are experienced within all of the assembled response material, a plan or blueprint that spontaneously directs the person toward resolution of the symptom and problem area is revealed. It is the main task of the Intensive to uncover this plan and to initiate imagery action toward that end.

During the Intensive Treatment phase, extensive insight

into the problem area is generated, its underlying causes are revealed and the resources to resolve them are identified. As new material is uncovered, it is critically explored and added to the growing store of information. Uninterrupted attention is given to the problem, with time provided for rest periods, breaks for meals and other routine activities.

During the breaks, the person continues to concentrate on the imagery material while attending to other activities, an experience which is used as a teaching tool for applying imagery to real life experiences. Following these breaks, the person's comments and overall impressions are recorded because they reveal significant information about the impact of the process thus far and the future direction of treatment. For example, when the positive progress made during the session is maintained during the breaks, treatment will proceed in the same direction; however, if some negative aspects persist in the mind, further examination of the material is indicated; or, if the person regresses to the level initially reported, further elucidation of the imagery structures is taken up.

Each person needs adequate time for the imagery material to become active and emerge from deeper and more creative levels of awareness. With proper allocation of time, material will surface from the creative sources to resolve difficult issues. Most ordinary social interaction and discourse arise from superficial understanding and are the most familiar and obvious to the person. But time is an important, though often overlooked factor in eliciting a deep response. If there is inadequate time or a sense of urgency and hurriedness, imagery responses will come from surface levels. For instance, if a person grew up in a house where there were too many children and too little attention, if parents created a feeling of pressure and demand through an atmosphere of intolerance, or if parents were unresponsive to the child's needs, that person's imagery responses will tend to function at the surface level. As a result, his or her deeper core will remain isolated, and the person may exhibit a symptom of alienation from the self as well as from others. Physiological processes may also become disturbed because they have not been allowed to operate in a comfortable setting. This superficial response thus perpetuates the symptomatology because the symptoms remain operative alongside the mass of day-to-day routine structures.

The imagery response time will vary for each individual. Therefore, the atmosphere and pace of the Eidetic Imagery Intensive allows time for the imagery material to surface from deeper levels of consciousness and to evolve properly according to each person's needs.

Phase 3. Post-Intensive Treatment

Following Phase 2, steps for follow-up, maintenance and continued growth are established. As the material generated during the Imagery Intensive is reviewed and discussed, it is integrated more deeply. The person discusses any changes experienced during the Intensive and compares them with his or her usual symptoms and responses at the beginning of the process. This review also serves as an indicator for areas that need to be further strengthened after the Intensive is completed, as indicated in the following statement:

> "When I review the information, it is all accurate. It was possible for me to see the key images but I did not want to accept the feelings of compassion connected with it. I can do that now, I can accept understanding and compassion. I don't have the judgment: Is it worth it or not worth it? When I see the new image, the judgment lifts. I have a feeling of relief. Also, there is a sense that it is okay to have these feelings of compassion. Everybody in my family gave me the feeling that there was a price to pay for having these feelings. Now I have a sense of a new bargain: no price to pay for it. I am relaxed, not bothered.

I first said when we started the Intensive that I did
not want to experience certain feelings and thoughts.
That has changed. Now I would rather be a person
who resides in the heart and have the understanding
that it offers."

Follow-up imagery instructions and a strategy for maintaining and enhancing the goals achieved during the
Eidetic Imagery Intensive are finally outlined in detail and
reviewed prior to completion of the program. The Intensive
aims to provide the person with the tools required to sustain all the gains and integrate them into other areas of life.
Toward this end, practice schedules, self-directed homework and a plan for application of imagery structures are
all clearly defined.

Sample Imagery Intensive: Mr. "Z"

The reader may be already aware of the historical background, scientific evidence, and instructions for the therapeutic
application of Ahsen's Eidetic Image Therapy. Since its introduction in the United States, the success of practitioners who
have employed Ahsen's methods, and of individuals who have
experienced this treatment, has been so unique and expansive
that it may be termed profound. At the Eidetic Therapy Institute
and Ahsen's eidetic workshops, which are held internationally,
some for individuals and some for practitioners, one finds a
stunning integration of people from various walks of life, with
varying careers and interests. Appealing especially to those
who are fairly educated and achievement-oriented, his work is
simply known as Eidetics.

To provide the reader, who may be either a practitioner or an
individual seeking help, with a glimpse into the experience of
Eidetics as it pertains to the treatment of alcoholism, what follows is the sample Imagery Intensive of Mr. "Z." This is an actual case history which has been edited for brevity and readabili-

ty, but keeps Mr. "Z'"s true experience and remarks completely intact. What is revealed here is not only a typical Intensive, but also some of the terminology and colloquialisms, if you will, created by the many practitioners and individuals employing Eidetics over many years, in an attempt to convey the uniquely effective experience of Ahsen's methods. Scientific terminology can only go so far with these methods, and so here is further insight into the practical application of Eidetics and the real experience of Mr. "Z."

Arrival at the Eidetic Therapy Institute

Mr. "Z" decided to do the Imagery Intensive, chose the five-day program rather than the two- or three-day program, and came to the Eidetic Therapy Institute's main office in Manhattan. He arrived at the Institute each morning, worked intensively throughout the day and returned to his nearby lodgings in the evenings.

Phase 1. Comprehensive Intake Interview and Testing Procedures

Initial Symptom Report

On the first morning of his arrival, Mr. "Z" worked on reporting his problem and symptoms in detail. He gave a subjective description of the issues, as he personally saw them, to the eidetic therapist working on his Intensive. Some of what Mr. "Z" reported is as follows:

> "I have panic attacks that occur mainly at work, making my job very difficult. I am taking some medication to help the symptoms but nothing has really worked for me. Over the years, drinking has helped me cope with the problem, but my wife complains about my drinking. She says I am abusive to the family when I drink and she is worried that my health is being affected. I have given a lot of thought to what is happening in my life.
>
> "For years I was a social drinker and, on occasion,

I would drink too much, like everyone else. Part of the regular drinking I used to engage in would be to have a couple of drinks while my wife was preparing dinner. Gradually, the number of drinks increased, to three or four, then later to seven or eight. I became aware that I was probably drinking too much, but I also realized that there was a purpose to what I was doing. I have a very longstanding feeling of depression and lack of self-worth and I go through the day at work coping with the panic. When I arrive home, I feel that I have gotten through the day and, in some way, have earned the right to drink. I feel that by doing this, I will feel better and be more in control of the situation.

"Recently, I have developed a problem with my stomach, which acts up if I eat too much or drink too much. I have been taking medicine for it, which helps, but my wife thinks this is a medical problem related to my drinking."

Mr. "Z" also provided some information regarding earlier periods in his life that he felt had some bearing on his current problem. These comments were also noted by the eidetic therapist to be kept on record and further investigated later on in the program:

"My boss has been complaining about my job performance. I am very worried about this because I have lost several jobs in the past and really need to keep this one. I have always had problems completing projects, I generally get bored in the middle of the project and after a while, lose interest completely. I have always found it difficult to maintain my interest in things.

"When I was a kid, maybe in seventh grade, the teachers said I had a problem with concentration. Around the same time, I started using drugs. The problem with alcohol came later. Even though I don't use drugs now, I sometimes still think about it. These days I use alcohol. I don't remember being as bored then as I am now."

Core Imagery Procedures

After the initial step of reporting the basic symptoms was completed, Mr. "Z" was given the Eidetic Parents Test along with the imagery exercises designed specifically to deal with alcoholism. He found these images, along with the thirty images of the EPT, to be very full of insights and unlike any treatment he had ever experienced before. The testing left him with the feeling that he had reached a new level of consciousness where his problems revealed themselves readily to him. He was happy to find that the use of eidetic imagery was the most personalized therapy he had received. He also mentioned that he felt he had already made progress simply by going through the imagery testing and that this method put more emotional energy at his disposal, and seemed to be much more productive than talk therapies. In the thirty images of the EPT he found both the positive and negative experiences of his life, particularly in his childhood and young adult life, and he said: "I'm the type of person to remember most things and so I do remember the majority of all these events, but somehow the test has given me a new perspective on them and an opportunity to get better control over things with this new understanding."

Analysis of Information

After all of the information related to Mr. "Z"'s problem was uncovered using the Initial Symptom Report and core procedures, the material was carefully reviewed and analyzed by the eidetic therapist in order to develop the outline and clarity of what has been referred to as the eidetic "blueprint."

Eidetic Blueprint

At this point, the main goal of the Intensive was to uncover the plan or "blueprint" that would direct events toward resolution of the problem and relief of symptoms. The eidetic blueprint shows the primary images which reveal the source of the problem, many of which hold the keys to their resolution.

Phase 2. Intensive Treatment

Intensive Imagery Experience

Using the blueprint as a guide, Mr. "Z" went through a graduated but intensive experience involving the details of the images revealed thus far. The images which contained the negative experiences that were adversely affecting his life were deeply explored and core procedures such as the Expectation High were used to overcome his problems. Mr. "Z" commented: "I am amazed how frozen my mind was on these ideas and events. I tried to forget the events but couldn't, and they haunted me, but the images gave me a handle on them. I feel less stress and paranoia knowing that these memories and fears won't haunt me anymore."

Deeper Roots of the Problem Revealed

The Imagery Intensive experience led to deeper and deeper layers of illuminating images that explained the problem further and created the required clarity, precision, and understanding for progress of the treatment. Mr. "Z" reported: "I can sense that tightness in my chest, throat and shoulders is much reduced now. It is not at the level I find daily in my life, a level which is bothersome. I am much more relaxed. There is no longer a feeling of being accused of something, no more feeling of being found guilty. "

Allowing for Time

The time allocated to the various segments of treatment allowed sufficient space needed for important experiential points to be absorbed deeply. It also allowed for mobilization of the therapeutic effect. For example, Mr. "Z" initially was mobilized to experience routine anxiety, and would respond rather quickly at the surface level. His responses would come not only from an extra gift of intelligence but also from avoidance. He now allowed the time for the images to be absorbed and understood. He let therapeutic change take place in an effective manner.

Gains Are Tested

Mr. "Z" began to improve dramatically during the Intensive. The transformation took place in what he considered a "miraculous manner" and he wondered, "How long will it last?" In fact, as he found out later on as well, his progress and the positive changes he felt thus far were proving to be real because as improvements occurred during the Intensive, the solidity and stability of the transformation was also being put to the test. His gains were tested and challenged from every imagery angle to be sure that nothing had been missed or left unattended. His feelings and general condition were still somewhat new and unfamiliar to him but it was from here that healing eventually spread and became concrete. As a result, Mr. "Z" reported: "Now there is a very clear awareness in me regarding the problem. Even though we had discussed it in full detail in the very beginning, the imagery has much more meaning to me in terms of power and expression that I can develop through it. Now I want to apply my mind and work on it more fully."

Gains Are Confirmed

As the gains were tested and retested, the procedure led to a new phase of confirmation that the problem had been competently addressed using the correct imagery approach. Positive changes had already taken root and Mr. "Z's" healing was, in fact, already expanding on a natural course on its own.

Phase 3. Post-Intensive Treatment

Personal Imagery Tools

After Phases 1 and 2 were completed, Mr. "Z" left the Institute with an array of personalized images and imagery techniques which gave him the tools to sustain his gains and integrate them further with other areas of his work and life. The eidetic therapist had reviewed the use of these images with him so that he would be able to apply them successfully on his own. These, too, had originally been developed from the eidetic blueprint.

Post-Intensive Work

Mr. "Z" kept in touch with his eidetic therapist after completion of his Intensive. This Post-Intensive contact was designed to continue the growth made during the program, and allowed Mr. "Z" the opportunity to raise any new issues or problems outside of those which had already been addressed.

The Imagery Intensive is a concentrated and incisive approach to alcohol and drug abuse and its related symptomatology. It combines both short-term and long-term treatment goals. The immediate relief from symptoms and a return to stable functioning as well as the development of a successful and meaningful lifestyle are addressed through the program.

Dr. Akhter Ahsen's Eidetic Image Therapy offers a new approach to the treatment of alcohol and dug abuse based on the individual's innate potential for hope. Through the recovery of positive states of consciousness, especially the Expectation High, the natural enthusiasm for life is revitalized. As the results from other methods have demonstrated, solutions tried in the absence of this primary strength have limited results. Ahsen's approach has provided a much needed fresh perspective. Through his remarkable and innovative method, hopes can be translated into fruitful living, making life, once again, a truly high experience. As Ahsen (1979) states:

> Life, when healthy, moves in its own true grand style. Life in its natural form is made of a series of self-realizing events...when the psyche is so gripped by a high image, we are then talking of a truly high condition in the psyche. (p. 16)

Appendix A

Pilot Study: A Comparison of Three Groups of Alcohol and Substance Abusers Using the AA-VVIQ

[Excerpted from "Imagery Treatment of Alcoholism and Drug Abuse: A New Methodology for Treatment and Research" by Akhter Ahsen (Journal of Mental Imagery, 17(3&4), 1993, 1-60). I had the pleasure and the privilege of assisting Dr. Ahsen in administering the procedures developed by him and described in this paper for the first time.]

Subjects

The total number of subjects participating in the study was 58. The total from the Inpatient Alcohol Unit was 16 (Sub-Group 1); the total from the Inpatient Substance Abuse Unit was 31 (Sub-Group 2); and the total of outpatient alcohol and/or substance abuse subjects was 11 (Sub-Group 3). Twelve additional inpatient subjects were not included in the data because of their severe difficulty in responding to the test items. Their responses were calculated separately (Sub-Group 4).

The 47 inpatient subjects were drawn from the Yonkers General Hospital Alcohol and Substance Abuse Units. This hospital serves an urban population in the New York City metropolitan area. The 11 outpatient alcohol and substance abuse psychotherapy subjects were selected because of a reported history of addiction.

All inpatient subjects had been admitted to the hospital's Alcohol or Substance Abuse Unit for detoxification. They are assigned to either unit, depending on staff assessment of current primary addiction; however, there is very often an overlap of abuse history on both units. All admissions are initiated in the Emergency Room with an evaluation by a counselor and a nurse and are referred either directly to the appropriate unit or for medical treatment when necessary. Patients with a history of violence or psychosis are referred to other facilities for treatment. Length of stay for inpatient detoxification for alcohol abuse is 5 to 7 days; for substance abuse, it is 7 to 10 days. Following this period of detoxification, patients are referred to outpatient programs for ongoing treatment.

Procedure

Ahsen's Adapted Vividness of Visual Imagery Questionnaire (AA-VVIQ) was administered to Alcohol Unit patients in a single session. Patients were asked if they would like to participate and those who volunteered were seated in a small office on the Detoxification Unit with the tester. Since the detoxification period for inpatient alcohol patients is 5 to 7 days, they were tested at least one day following admission.

Staff reports indicated that, because of the impact of alcohol withdrawal syndrome and the types of medication used for detoxification, some patients' ability to concentrate might be better served by individual testing. For this reason, and also to eliminate problems of comprehension, the AA-VVIQ was individually administered to each subject, with the questions being read aloud by the tester. If at any point the subject was unable or unwilling to continue, the test was terminated and the results were omitted from the sample.

Treatment staff reports indicated that substance abuse patients would be capable of being tested in a group setting. The test was administered to subjects in a single session during a daily group meeting held on the unit. Test instructions were read aloud to the group and any questions were answered. Staff was available during the testing process to answer any additional questions.

Outpatient psychotherapy patients were tested individually in a single session. They were given the test instructions and asked to complete the test on their own and return it to the tester. The tester was available to answer any questions.

Results

The results indicate that outpatient subjects had a much greater inability to process imagery under the mother figure than under the father, a finding which correlates with other clinic populations tested (other psychotherapy patients; Ahsen, 1985a). Inpatients, on the other hand, had a greater inability to process imagery under the father, a finding which correlates with the "normal" population tested (Ahsen, 1990b, 1991). Out-patients demonstrated hemispheric inversion (mother on the left, father on the right: MF) significantly more than did inpatients, who more frequently reported the hemispheric position FM (father on the left, mother on the right). This result was also reported for the general population (Ahsen, 1977a, 1977b, 1985b.) Race and ethnic background did not seem to be a factor in that the Caucasian inpatients were more similar to other patients than to their outpatient Caucasian counterparts.

The outpatient group, which has the appearance of functionality, both in terms of a more functional lifestyle and a less debilitating dependence on chemical and alcohol so that they do not warrant detoxification, exhibits greater difficulty with the maternal figure, demonstrating both hemispheric inversion of parental figures and a greater inability to process imagery under the mother image. Inpatients seem to follow the societal norm, such as that demonstrated by college students who, according to Ahsen (1977b), projected the father in the left hemispheric space 67% of the time, and the mother in the left space 33% of the time. In her analysis of African-American groups who were administered the AA-VVIQ, Sussman (1993) noted that the maternal figure remains more intact in this community, providing more access to inner strength and abilities, because the father is often absent or his image in the mind is problematic. Our findings as well may imply a more sociological meaning for the issue of addiction. One inpatient, for instance, who was motivated to continue his sobriety after release from the hospital, reported that although he desired to remain abstinent, it was virtually impossible once he was back in his neighborhood. It was not a question of whether he could do it, but rather that the environment would not permit it.

Regarding the role of ethnicity in alcohol and substance abuse, as mentioned above, we found that Caucasian inpatients were more like other inpatients than they were like Caucasian outpatients. We might speculate that the more compelling issue is that they possess the same qualities that led others also to become inpatients.

Another possible explanation may be considered. Inpatients presumably have become out of control regarding addiction, leading them to hospitalization, while outpatients attempt to maintain control, potentially inhibiting whatever drives that might take them to the same end. This inhibition or attempt to control and maintain the status quo may, in fact, relate to some dynamic connected with the mother figure. They may be caught between two problematic worlds which they tenuously balance. The inpatients, on the other hand, are reported to have a very high rate of re-hospitalization. Within a fairly brief period of time, they resume the acting out behavior which warrants their reentry to inpatient status so that, for many, this is merely a revolving door situation.

Alcohol and Drug Abuse Questionnaire: Part I

Dear Participant:

Thank you for your participation in our study. The purpose of our study is to gather information that will help us understand how a person's abilities are affected under certain mental conditions. Your responses will help us determine how persons can use their abilities to live more productive drug-and-alcohol-free lives.

This questionnaire is anonymous! All of your responses are confidential, so please do not sign your name to the questionnaire. Your participation is voluntary and you are free not to answer the questionnaire if you wish. There are no right or wrong answers to the test and it is easy to do. Thank you once again for your cooperation.

Introduction to Imagery and Rating Scale

Imagery refers to a person's ability to see image in the mind, to form mental pictures, or to "see in the mind's eye."

In the following questions you will be asked to think of/keep in mind either your mother or father while you are seeing different pictures or scenes in your mind. The picture may appear more vivid, dim, or the same when you think about either your father or your mother. You will be asked to rate how vivid or dim each picture appears in your mind under these conditions. There are no right or wrong answers. Just take your time and see the pictures that appear before your mind's eye. Just relax and listen to the instruction.

Example   *Rate 1-5*

1. See, in your mind, a red apple. As you look at the red apple   (   )
    in your mind, rate it as follows, on a scale from 1 to 5.

Rating Scale

1 = The image is perfectly clear and as vivid as normal vision.
2 – The image is clear and reasonably vivid.
3 = The image is moderately clear and vivid.
4 = The image is vague and dim.
5 = No image at all, you only "know" that you are thinking of the object.

2. Now keep your father in mind, without seeing an image of   (   )
    him. If you tend to see an image, it is all right. As you do
    this, see an image of a red apple. As you think of your
    father, the picture of the red apple might look more vivid,
    dim or the same as before. Please rate this image according
    to the above scale.

3. Now keep your mother in mind, without seeing an image of   (   )
    her. If you tend to see an image, it is all right. As you do this,
    see an image of a red apple. As you think of your mother, the
    picture of the red apply might look more vivid, dim or the
    same. Please rate this image according to the above scale.

Now you are ready to do the test in which you will keep your mother and father in mind while seeing other images. You will be asked to rate the vividness of each image using the above rating scale.

Alcohol and Drug Abuse Questionnaire: Part II

Instructions for AA-VVIQ
(Ahsen's Adapted Vividness of Visual Imagery Questionnaire)

Complete all items for images obtained by keeping your mother or father alternately in mind and rate the image obtained for each item. The two ratings for a given item may not in all cases be the same.

VIVIDNESS RATING RESULTS

	Keep Father in Mind	Keep Mother in Mind

In answering items 1 to 4, think of your father/mother separately and consider carefully the picture that comes before your mind's eye.

Item

1. The exact contour of face, head, shoulders and body.   ( )   ( )
2. Characteristic poses of head, attitudes of body, etc.
3. The precise carriage, length of step, etc., in walking.
4. The different colors worn in some familiar clothes.

Think of your father/mother in your mind. At the same moment visualize a rising sun. Consider carefully the picture that comes before your mind's eye.

Item

5. The sun is rising above the horizon into a hazy sky.   ( )   ( )
6. The sky clears and surrounds the sun with blueness.
7. Clouds. A storm blows up, with flashes of lightning.
8. A rainbow appears.

Think of your father/mother in your mind. At the same moment think of the front of a shop which you often go to. Consider carefully the picture that comes before your mind's eye.

Item

9. The overall appearance of the shop from the opposite side of the road.   ( )   ( )
10. A window display including colors, shapes and details of individual items for sale.   ( )   ( )
11. You are near the entrance. The color, shape and details of the door.   ( )   ( )
12. You enter the shop and go to the counter. The counter assistant serves you. Money changes hands.   ( )   ( )

Think of your father/mother in your mind. At the same moment finally, think of a country scene which involves trees, mountains and a lake. Consider carefully the picture that comes before your mind's eye.

Item

13. The contours of the landscape.   ( )   ( )
14. The color and shape of the trees.
15. The color and shape of the lake.
16. A strong wind blows on the trees and on the lake, causing waves.

Alcohol and Drug Abuse Questionnaire: Part III

Instructions for Alcohol/Drug Self-Images and Parental Filters

The following questions concern your experience with alcohol or drugs. Please rate the images in the same way as you did before on a 5-point scale (1-5).

Rating Scale

1 = The image is perfectly clear and as vivid as normal vision.
2 = The image is clear and reasonably vivid.
3 = The image is moderately clear and vivid.
4 = The image is vague and dim.
5 = No image at all, you only "know" that you are thinking of the object.

	Keep Father in Mind	*Keep Mother in Mind*
1. Now see that you are drinking alcohol or taking drugs. How vivid/dim is the picture that comes before your mind's eye? Please rate the image according to the above scale.	( )	( )
2. Now see a picture of yourself enjoying drinking alcohol or taking drugs. Please rate the image according the above scale.	( )	( )
3. See a picture of yourself not enjoying yourself drinking alcohol or taking drugs. Please rate the image according to the above scale.	( )	( )
4. Now think of your father and see that you are drinking alcohol or taking drugs. How vivid/dim is the picture? Please rate the image. Do the same with your mother.	( )	( )
5. Now think of your father and see that you are enjoying drinking alcohol or taking drugs. How vivid/dim is the picture? Please rate the image. Do the same with your mother.	( )	( )
6. Now think of your father and see that you are not enjoying drinking alcohol or taking drugs. How vivid/dim is the picture? Please rate the image. Do the same with your mother.	( )	( )

7. Now see a picture of your father and mother standing directly in front of you. As you look at them standing directly in front of you, who is standing on your left and who is standing on your right in the space in front? Please check the relevant box.

	Left	*Right*
	❑ Father	❑ Mother
	❑ Mother	❑ Father

Personal Data

Please complete the following information.
❑ Male   ❑ Female

Age: _____

Ethnic Background: _____

With whom did you live while you were growing up?
❑ Mother   ❑ Father   ❑ Stepmother   ❑ Stepfather
❑ Foster Mother   ❑ Foster Father
❑ Grandmother   ❑ Grandfather   ❑ Other

Check if any of these had an alcohol or drug problem.
❑ Mother   ❑ Father   ❑ Stepmother   ❑ Stepfather
❑ Foster Mother   ❑ Foster Father
❑ Grandmother   ❑ Grandfather   ❑ Other

Are you right-handed or left-handed?
SELF: ❑ Left-handed   ❑ Right-handed

Is your mother right-handed or left-handed?
MOTHER: ❑ Left-handed   ❑ Right-handed

Is your father right-handed or left-handed?
FATHER: ❑ Left-handed   ❑ Right-handed

Any Comments:

AA-VVIQ Scores

Tables of Vividness-Unvividness Imagery Scores
Yonkers General Hospital Group
New York, U.S.A.

Key to Ratings and Symbols
Rating: 1 to 5 (1, 2, 3, 4, 5) Most vivid (1), Least vivid (5)
F = while father is kept in mind
M = while mother is kept in mind
*F = item rated lower under father in comparison to mother
M* = item rated lower under mother in comparison to father
F*M = item rated equal under father and mother, as *
    1m36A = serial number of subject (1), sex (m: male, f: female), age (36), ethnic origin
(A: African-American; H: Hispanic; C: Caucasian)
(L) = left-handed
(A) = ambidextrous
4F 3M = number of times father rated lower (4F), mother rated lower (3M)
 9 both rated equal (9)
FM/MF = Hemispheric position of parents when seen standing before the subject. FM
indicates the father is perceived on the subject's left, the mother on the right. MF indicates the mother is perceived on the subject's left, the father on the subject's right.

AA-VVIQ Imagery Items

1. The exact contour of face, head, shoulders and body.
2. Characteristic poses of head, attitudes of body, etc.
3. The precise carriage, length of step, etc., in walking.
4. The different colors worn in some familiar clothes.
5. The sun is rising above the horizon into a hazy sky.
6. The sky clears and surrounds the sun with blueness.
7. Clouds. A storm blows up, with flashes of lightning.
8. A rainbow appears.
9. The overall appearance of the shop from the opposite side of the road.
10. A window display including colors, shapes and details of individual items for sale.
11. You are near the entrance. The color, shape and details of the door.
12. You enter the shop and go to the counter. The counter assistant serves you. Money changes hands.
13. The contours of the landscape.
14. The color and shape of the trees.
15. The color and shape of the lake.
16. A strong wind blows on the trees and on the lake, causing waves.

Table 1

AA-VVIQ Scores for Subjects 1-16 (Sub-Group 1) in Inpatient Alcohol Unit (n=16)

	1m26A 4F 3M 9 FM		2m29A 5F 4M 7 FM		3m30A 16F 0M 0 FM		4m39H 16F 0M 0 FM	
	F	M	F	M	F	M	F	M
1	1	3*	1 *	1	*5	1	*5	1
2	2 *	2	2	4*	*5	1	*5	3
3	1 *	1	1	5*	*5	1	*5	2
4	1	3*	2	3*	*5	1	*5	1
5	*2	1	*3	1	*5	1	*5	1
6	1 *	1	*2	1	*5	3	*5	1
7	1 *	1	4 *	4	*5	1	*5	2
8	2 *	2	1 *	1	*5	1	*5	1
9	*3	1	*3	2	*5	1	*5	3
10	*2	1	2 *	2	*5	1	*5	2
11	2 *	2	1	4*	*5	1	*5	3
12	*2	1	1 *	1	*5	1	*5	2
13	2	3*	1 *	1	*5	1	*5	3
14	2 *	2	*2	1	*5	1	*5	2
15	1 *	1	*2	1	*5	1	*5	2
16	1 *	1	4 *	4	*5	1	*5	2

	5m27A 16F 0M 0 FM		6f47C 1F 11M 4 MF		7m32C 7F 3M 6 MF		8f34A 12F 3M 1 MF	
	F	M	F	M	F	M	F	M
1	*5	2	1	4*	2	3*	*4	3
2	*5	2	1	3*	2	3*	*5	3
3	*5	4	1	4*	*3	2	2	5*
4	*5	1	2	5*	3 *	3	*5	1
5	*5	3	2 *	2	*3	2	*5	3
6	*5	1	1	2*	1 *	1	*4	1
7	*5	4	3	4*	4 *	4	*5	4
8	*5	1	1	2*	2	3*	*4	1
9	*5	3	*2	1	2 *	2	1	3*
10	*5	4	3 *	3	2 *	2	1	2*
11	*5	3	2 *	2	*3	2	*3	2
12	*5	2	1	2*	*3	2	1 *	1
13	*5	2	1	3*	*4	2	*3	1
14	*5	4	1 *	1	*3	1	*3	1
15	*5	4	1	2*	*3	2	*3	1
16	*5	3	2	3*	4 *	4	*3	1

Table 1 (continued)

	9m23A 16F 0M 0 MF		10m34A(L) 4F 5M 7 MF		11m40A 2F 9M 5 MF		12m34A 13F 3M 0 MF	
	F	M	F	M	F	M	F	M
1	*5	1	1	2*	1	3*	*4	3
2	*5	1	1 *	1	1	4*	*4	3
3	*5	1	1 *	1	1	3*	1	4*
4	*5	1	1 *	1	1	2*	3	4*
5	*5	1	2	3*	2	3*	*4	3
6	*5	2	*3	1	1	3*	*4	3
7	*5	3	2 *	2	*4	2	4	5*
8	*5	2	4 *	4	1 *	1	*3	1
9	*5	4	*4	2	2 *	2	*4	3
10	*5	3	4 *	4	2 *	2	*4	2
11	*5	2	3	4*	2	4*	*4	3
12	*5	2	1	2*	2	4*	*5	1
13	*5	3	*2	1	2 *	2	*5	1
14	*5	3	2 *	2	2 *	2	*5	1
15	*5	1	*4	2	1	2*	*5	1
16	*5	2	1	3*	*3	1	*5	3

	13m43A 16F 0M 0 FM		14f35H 3F 10M 3 FM		15f30H 3F 2M 11 FM		16f39A 15F 0M 1 FM	
	F	M	F	M	F	M	F	M
1	*5	1	1	2*	1 *	1	*4	1
2	*5	2	2 *	2	1 *	1	*5	1
3	*5	1	1	3*	1 *	1	*5	1
4	*5	1	1	1*	1 *	1	1 *	1
5	*5	1	1	3*	*5	3	*5	1
6	*5	1	1	2*	*5	3	*5	1
7	*5	3	1	2*	3	5*	*4	1
8	*5	1	3 *	3	1 *	1	*4	1
9	*5	1	1	2*	3 *	3	*5	1
10	*5	1	3	4*	3 *	3	*4	1
11	*5	3	3	4*	1	3*	*4	1
12	*5	1	*4	3	3 *	3	*5	1
13	*5	1	*3	1	*3	1	*4	1
14	*5	1	2 *	2	1 *	1	*4	1
15	*5	1	1	3*	1 *	1	*5	1
16	*5	1	*3	2	3 *	3	*4	1

Analysis of Subject Data, Sub-Group 1
Inpatient Alcohol Unit (n=16)

These subjects were administered the AA-VVIQ individually. Test instructions were read to the subjects and the tester recorded the responses.

Gender: 11 male
                                5 female

Mean Age: 33

Age range: 23-47

Ethnic background: 11 African-American
                                3 Hispanic
                                2 Caucasian

Handedness: 1 subject reported left-handedness

Hemispheric position of parents' images seen in the front space:
    9 FM (Father seen on the left)
    7 MF (Mother seen on the left)

Dimming
    12 dim more under father
    4 dim more under mother
    Dimming under father vs. Dimming under mother: 300% (12:4)

Of the 4 subjects reporting dimmer images more often under mother, 2 were female and 2 were male. One of these males was left-handed.

Table 2

AA-VVIQ Scores for Subjects 17-47 (Sub-Group 2) in Inpatient Substance Abuse Unit (n=31)

	17f39A		18m59A		19m23A		20m27C	
	9F	2M	0F	0M	0F	0M	0F	0M
	5		16		16		16	
	FM		—		MF		MF	
	F	M	F	M	F	M	F	M
1	1 *	1	5 *	5	1 *	1	1 *	1
2	2 *	2	5 *	5	1 *	1	1 *	1
3	1	3*	5 *	5	1 *	1	2 *	2
4	1	4*	5 *	5	1 *	1	1 *	1
5	*3	1	5 *	5	1 *	1	1 *	1
6	1 *	1	5 *	5	1 *	1	1 *	1
7	*3	1	5 *	5	1 *	1	1 *	1
8	*3	1	5 *	5	1 *	1	1 *	1
9	*3	1	5 *	5	1 *	1	1 *	1
10	*2	1	5 *	5	1 *	1	1 *	1
11	*4	1	5 *	5	1 *	1	1 *	1
12	*5	1	5 *	5	1 *	1	1 *	1
13	*3	2	5 *	5	1 *	1	1 *	1
14	*3	2	5 *	5	1 *	1	1 *	1
15	3 *	3	5 *	5	1 *	1	1 *	1
16	2 *	2	5 *	5	1 *	1	1 *	1

	21m27H		22m29A		23m35A		24m37C	
	0F	0M	2F	0M	3F	0M	1F	2M
	16		14		13		13	
	FM		—		MF		MF	
	F	M	F	M	F	M	F	M
1	1 *	1	1 *	1	1 *	1	1 *	1
2	1 *	1	1 *	1	1 *	1	2 *	2
3	1 *	1	1 *	1	1 *	1	3 *	3
4	1 *	1	2 *	2	1 *	1	1 *	1
5	1 *	1	1 *	1	5 *	5	4	5*
6	1 *	1	1 *	1	1 *	1	*3	1
7	1 *	1	1 *	1	2 *	2	3 *	3
8	1 *	1	1 *	1	1 *	1	3 *	3
9	1 *	1	1 *	1	5 *	5	5 *	5
10	1 *	1	1 *	1	*3	2	5 *	5
11	1 *	1	*3	2	*4	2	5 *	5
12	1 *	1	*4	1	*3	1	5 *	5
13	1 *	1	1 *	1	1 *	1	4 *	4
14	1 *	1	2 *	2	1 *	1	1	4*
15	1 *	1	2 *	2	1 *	1	4 *	4
16	1 *	1	4 *	4	1 *	1	4 *	4

Table 2 (continued)

	25m40A F		M	26m42A F		M	27f34A F		M	28m54A F		M
	5F		11M	1F		1M	1F		4M	14F		0M
		0			14			11			2	
		MF			MF			MF			FM	
1	*5		2	1	*	1	1		2*	*2		1
2	2		4*	1	*	1	1		2*	4	*	4
3	2		5*	2	*	2	1		2*	*5		4
4	4		5*	1	*	1	*5		1	*5		1
5	1		5*	1	*	1	1	*	1	*5		1
6	3		5*	*2		1	1	*	1	4	*	4
7	*3		2	1	*	1	2	*	2	*5		3
8	4		5*	1	*	1	2	*	2	*5		4
9	3		5*	1	*	1	2	*	2	*5		3
10	2		4*	1	*	1	1		2*	*5		3
11	*5		1	1	*	1	1	*	1	*5		4
12	3		5*	1	*	1	1	*	1	*5		4
13	*3		2	2	*	2	2	*	2	*4		1
14	4		5*	1		2*	1	*	1	*5		2
15	2		5*	1	*	1	1	*	1	*5		2
16	*5		1	1	*	1	1	*	1	*5		3

	29m27H F		M	30m37C F		M	31m42H F		M	32m30A F		M
	5F		1M	8F		0M	8F		2M	10F		4M
		10			8			6			2	
		FM			FM			FM			FM	
1	*3		2	*4		1	*2		1	*3		1
2	4	*	4	*5		3	2	*	2	*3		1
3	5	*	5	1	*	1	*3		1	*5		1
4	5	*	5	*5		1	*3		2	*3		1
5	*3		1	5	*	5	*3		2	*3		2
6	*3		2	*5		3	*3		2	*4		1
7	4	*	4	*5		4	2	*	2	*4		2
8	1	*	1	4	*	4	2	*	2	*3		1
9	5	*	5	*5		3	*2		1	*4		1
10	5	*	5	*5		3	1		2*	*3		2
11	*3		2	4	*	4	*2		1	1		4*
12	1	*	1	*4		3	2	*	2	2		3*
13	2	*	2	1	*	1	2	*	2	2		4*
14	*3		2	1	*	1	1		2*	5	*	5
15	4	*	4	1	*	1	*2		1	2		5*
16	2		4*	1	*	1	2	*	2	5	*	5

Table 2 (continued)

	33m32— 2F 0M 14 FM		34f29H 16F 0M 0 FM		35m39A 1F 0M 15 FM		36m56A 15F 0M 1 FM	
	F	M	F	M	F	M	F	M
1	1 * 1		*4	1	1 * 1		*5	1
2	4 * 4		*4	1	1 * 1		*5	1
3	*5	1	*5	1	*2	1	*5	1
4	*4	1	*5	1	3 * 3		*5	1
5	5 * 5		*5	1	1 * 1		*5	1
6	5 * 5		*5	1	1 * 1		*5	4
7	5 * 5		*5	3	2 * 2		5 * 5	
8	5 * 5		*5	1	1 * 1		*5	4
9	1 * 1		*4	1	2 * 2		*5	1
10	4 * 4		*5	1	3 * 3		*5	4
11	4 * 4		*5	2	1 * 1		*5	1
12	5 * 5		*4	2	1 * 1		*5	1
13	4 * 4		*4	1	1 * 1		*5	4
14	5 * 5		*5	1	1 * 1		*5	1
15	5 * 5		*5	1	1 * 1		*5	1
16	5 * 5		*5	2	2 * 2		*5	1

	37f30A 14F 2M 0 FM		38m24H 5F 8M 3 FM		39m32C 0F 16M 0 MF		40m47C 4F 1M 11 FM	
	F	M	F	M	F	M	F	M
1	*5	2	1 * 1		2	4*	2	3*
2	*5	2	1 * 1		3	5*	4 * 4	
3	*5	2	1	3*	1	5*	4 * 4	
4	*5	2	1	2*	1	5*	*4	3
5	*4	3	*2	1	4	5*	*4	3
6	1	3*	1	2*	3	5*	4 * 4	
7	*5	1	2	5*	2	5*	3 * 3	
8	1	2*	*2	1	4	5*	4 * 4	
9	*5	1	3	5*	1	5*	3 * 3	
10	*5	1	2	3*	3	5*	*5	3
11	*5	1	1 * 1		2	5*	3 * 3	
12	*5	1	*2	1	1	5*	*5	3
13	*5	1	1	2*	4	5*	2 * 2	
14	*5	1	*3	1	4	5*	2 * 2	
15	*5	1	*2	1	4	5*	2 * 2	
16	*5	1	2	3*	4	5*	2 * 2	

Table 2 (continued)

	41m48— 6F 0M 10 MF		42m46C 1F 0M 15 MF		43m43H 11F 2M 3 MF		44m27H 2F 0M 14 —	
	F	M	F	M	F	M	F	M
1	1 *	1	1 *	1	*2	1	*2	1
2	1 *	1	1 *	1	*5	1	1 *	1
3	*2	1	1 *	1	*5	1	1 *	1
4	*2	1	2 *	2	*4	1	3 *	3
5	*3	2	1 *	1	1 *	1	2 *	2
6	1 *	1	1 *	1	*2	1	1 *	1
7	1 *	1	2 *	2	1	5*	*2	1
8	*2	1	1 *	1	*2	1	1 *	1
9	1 *	1	*2	1	*5	1	1 *	1
10	1 *	1	1 *	1	*3	1	3 *	3
11	1 *	1	1 *	1	*5	1	1 *	1
12	*2	1	1 *	1	*5	1	1 *	1
13	1 *	1	1 *	1	*3	2	1 *	1
14	*2	1	1 *	1	1 *	1	1 *	1
15	1 *	1	1 *	1	1 *	1	1 *	1
16	2 *	2	1 *	1	2	4*	1 *	1

	45m31C 2F 12M 2 FM		46m45H 1F 2M 13 —		47m34C(L) 4F 3M 9 FM	
	F	M	F	M	F	M
1	1	4*	5 *	5	1 *	1
2	1	5*	5 *	5	2 *	2
3	2	4*	5 *	5	5 *	5
4	1 *	1	5 *	5	1 *	1
5	2	4*	*4	1	5 *	5
6	2	3*	2	3*	2 *	2
7	2	4*	4 *	4	1	3*
8	2	3*	4 *	4	*5	1
9	1	4*	1 *	1	5 *	5
10	2	4*	2 *	2	*4	1
11	1	3*	4 *	4	*4	1
12	1	2*	3 *	3	*4	1
13	*3	2	1 *	2*	1	5*
14	1	3*	4 *	4	1 *	1
15	1 *	1	5 *	5	1 *	1
16	*2	1	3 *	3	1	2*

*Analysis of Subject Data, Sub-Group 2
Inpatient Substance Abuse Unit (n=31)*

These subjects were administered the AA-VVIQ in a group setting. They were read the test instructions by the tester and then asked to complete the test on their own. The tester and staff were available to answer a subject's questions.

Gender:	27 male 4 female
Mean Age:	37
Age range:	23-59
Ethnic background:	13 African-American 8 Hispanic 8 Caucasian 2 did not respond to question
Handedness:	1 of the 4 females reported left-handedness

Hemispheric position of parents' images seen in the front space:
   16 FM (Father seen on the left)
   11 MF (Mother seen on the left)

Dimming
   19 dim more under father
   7 dim more under mother
   Dimming under father vs. Dimming under mother: 271% (19:7)

Of the 7 subjects who reported seeing dimmer images more often under mother, 2 were African-American, 3 Caucasian, and 2 Hispanic.

Of the 19 who reported seeing dimmer images more often under father, 8 were African-American, 4 Caucasian, and 5 Hispanic. Two did not indicate ethnic background.

Table 3

AA-VVIQ Scores for Outpatient Alcohol and/or Substance Abuse Subjects 48-58 (Sub-Group 3) (n=11)

	48f39C 0F 1M 15 MF		49f32C 3F 7M 6 FM		50f38C 1F 9M 6 MF		51m47C(L) 3F 2M 11 MF	
	F	M	F	M	F	M	F	M
1	3 *	3	*4	1	1 *	1	1 *	1
2	2 *	2	*5	2	1	3*	*2	1
3	1 *	1	2	5*	1	4*	1 *	1
4	3 *	3	4 *	4	1	4*	1 *	1
5	1 *	1	4 *	4	1	5*	1 *	1
6	1 *	1	3	4*	1	5*	1	2*
7	2 *	2	*5	4	4	5*	1	2*
8	1 *	1	4 *	4	5 *	5	*3	1
9	2	3*	2	4*	2 *	2	2 *	2
10	1 *	1	2	4*	3 *	3	1 *	1
11	1 *	1	2	4*	1	2*	2 *	2
12	1 *	1	2	4*	2 *	2	1 *	1
13	1 *	1	3	4*	2 *	2	1 *	1
14	1 *	1	4 *	4	3	5*	2 *	2
15	1 *	1	4 *	4	*3	2	*3	2
16	1 *	1	5 *	5	2	4*	2 *	2

	52f43C(A) 2F 6M 8 MF		53f44C(A) 2F 14M 0 MF		54m35C 0F 8M 8 MF		55f36C 1F 2M 13 MF	
	F	M	F	M	F	M	F	M
1	*2	1	2	4*	2	4*	4 *	4
2	1	2*	1	4*	1	2*	2	4*
3	2	3*	1	3*	2 *	2	2	4*
4	1	2*	1	3*	5 *	5	4 *	4
5	1 *	1	1	4*	3	4*	4 *	4
6	1 *	1	1	4*	3	5*	4 *	4
7	1 *	1	1	2*	2 *	2	4 *	4
8	1 *	1	1	4*	3 *	3	4 *	4
9	1	2*	*4	1	2	3*	4 *	4
10	*2	1	1	2*	3	4*	5 *	5
11	1 *	1	*2	1	4 *	4	4 *	4
12	1 *	1	2	4*	2	4*	4 *	4
13	1 *	1	1	4*	4 *	4	4 *	4
14	1	2*	1	4*	4 *	4	*5	4
15	2	3*	1	4*	3	4*	5 *	5
16	1 *	1	1	4*	4 *	4	4 *	4

Table 3 (continued)

	56m33C		57f43C		58f34C	
	0F	10M	1F	1M	15F	0M
	6		14		1	
	FM		MF		MF	
	F	M	F	M	F	M
1	2 *	2	1 *	1	*3	2
2	2 *	2	1 *	1	*3	2
3	2	3*	1 *	1	3 *	3
4	2 *	2	1 *	1	*3	2
5	1 *	1	1 *	1	*4	1
6	2 *	2	1 *	1	*4	1
7	2	3*	1 *	1	*4	1
8	1 *	1	1 *	1	*4	3
9	2	4*	*5	3	*3	2
10	2	4*	2 *	2	*3	2
11	2	4*	5 *	5	*3	2
12	2	4*	1	5*	*3	2
13	1	2*	2 *	2	*3	2
14	1	2*	2 *	2	*4	2
15	1	2*	2 *	2	*4	2
16	1	2*	2 *	2	*4	2

Analysis of Subject Data, Sub-Group 3
Outpatient Alcohol and/or Substance Abuse Subjects (n=11)

Gender:	3 male
	8 female

Mean Age:	39

Age range:	32-47

Ethnic background:	Caucasian

Handedness:	1 subject reported left-handedness
	2 subjects reported being ambidextrous

Hemispheric position of parents' images seen in the front space:
    2 FM (Father seen on the left)
    9 MF (Mother seen on the left)

Dimming
    8 dim more under father
    2 dim more under mother
    Dimming under father vs. Dimming under mother: 400% (8:2)

Of the 8 subjects reporting dimmer images more often under mother, 6 were female and 2 were male. Of the 2 reporting dimmer images more often under father, 1 was female, 1 male.

Group Statistics Comparisons

Outpatients

Females	Males
n = 8	n = 3
6 dim more under mother	2 dim more under mother
1 dims more under father	1 dims more under father
1 same, no difference in dimming	
6 MF	2MF
2FM	1FM
2 ambidextrous	1 left-handed

Significance

Outpatients showed significant dimming under mother (400% as much dimming under mother as under father).

MF (Inversion) was reported by a highly significant number of subjects (8 of the 11, or 73%). Since the position of parents' images in front for general populations happens to be FM for 67% and MF for 33%, the reverse position of MF is considered to indicate a movement away from the norm. A significant inversion rate, coupled with a significant dimming rate under mother, indicates low processing ability under mother, as far as imagery operations are concerned.

Inpatients

Females	Male
n = 9	n = 38
3 dim more under mother	8 dim more under mother
6 dim more under father	25 dim more under father
	5 same, no difference in dimming
3MF	15 MF
6 FM	19 FM
	2 left-handed

Significance

Inpatients showed significant dimming under father (282% as much dimming under father as under mother).

MF (Inversion) among the inpatients (38%) is slightly higher than among the general population (33%). MF in the inpatient population is, however, not coupled with dimming under the mother, which distinguishes it from the outpatient population.

Caucasians

n = 21 (10 inpatient, 11 outpatient)
12 dim more under mother
7 dim more under father
15 of the 21 reported MF hemispheric position

Inpatient	*Outpatient*
n = 10	n = 11
4 dim more under mother	8 dim more under mother
5 dim more under father	2 dim more under father
6 MF	9 MF
4 FM	2 FM

Significance

White outpatients showed more of a problem of dimness under mother than under father, and it is significant to note that 82% of the white outpatients reported inversions (MF). 71% of the white inpatients and outpatients reported inversions (MF).

African-Americans and Hispanics

n = 35
7 dim more under mother
25 dim more under father
11 MF
20 FM

Significance

Dimming under father (25) was 357% as much as dimming under mother (7), a much higher percentage than found in the general population (201%) calculated from the Bent Hall Group (Ahsen, 1990b) and the Pakistani Women Group (Ahsen, 1991), and much closer to that of Sussman's (1993) African-American population from Erie Community College where dimming under father compared to under mother was 386% (female subjects). 173% (male subjects), and 279% overall.

ADDITIONAL DATA: SUB-GROUP 4
Yonkers General Hospital, Inpatient Unit (n = 12)

This group of inpatients were initially omitted from the database because of incomplete information in response to the items. However, when the items that were not responded to are rated 5, representing the inability to see any image at all, the 12 subjects' response take on a more statistically useful quality. There were no reports of an inability to see imagery among outpatients, and those inpatient subjects included in the database were, in most cases, able to see some images but occasionally failed to respond to an item, which was therefore rated 5. Thus, this inpatient group represents subjects with the greatest degree of inhibition in mental operations of all of those tested. Interestingly, dimming under the father was still in keeping with other inpatients as opposed to the outpatients, who dimmed under mother. None of the 12 subjects included in this group dimmed more under mother than under father.

Gender:

    8 male
    2 female
    2 no information given

Ethnic background:

    5 African-American
    2 Hispanic
    1 Caucasian
    1 Native American
    3 no information given

Handedness:

    2 left-handed
    1 ambidextrous
    2 had left-handed mother

Hemispheric position of the parents' images seen in the front space:
    4 FM (Father seen on the left)
    4 MF (Mother seen on the left)
    1 MM (Mother seen on both right and left)
    3 no information

Dimming:
    7 dim more under father
    1 dims more under mother
    4 same, rated 5 or no image

Three Alcohol Inpatients

Subject 59m34A (male, age 34, African-American, left-handed), reported that he could not see any of the images. He stated that both parents had died in 1991 and that his father had told him, "When we die, just go on with your life." The patient then said, "So I did." All of the items have been scored 5.

Subject 60m34A responded to 7 of the items, at which point he stated that he was too nervous to continue. The 7 responses reported included only responses with mother in mind; he could not see 6 of 7 images while keeping father in mind. "No image" was then rated as 5.

Subject 61m34A reported writing with the left hand, although he uses the right. He said that the images were too foggy for him to continue with the test after responding to 6 of the items. He did, however, report the hemispheric position of the parents as FM. The rated scores are listed and items not responded to are rated 5.

Table 4
AA-VVIQ Scores for Subjects 59-61 (Alcohol Inpatients in Sub-Group 4)

	59m34A		60m34A		61m34A	
	0F 0M		6F 0M		3F 2M	
	16		10		10	
	—		—		FM	
	F	M	F	M	F	M
1	5 *	5	*5	1	1	4*
2	5 *	5	*5	1	1 *	1
3	5 *	5	5 *	5	*3	1
4	5 *	5	*5	1	*2	1
5	5 *	5	*5	1	*5	3
6	5 *	5	*5	1	3	4*
7	5 *	5	*5	3	5 *	5
8	5 *	5	5 *	5	5 *	5
9	5 *	5	5 *	5	5 *	5
10	5 *	5	5 *	5	5 *	5
11	5 *	5	5 *	5	5 *	5
12	5 *	5	5 *	5	5 *	5
13	5 *	5	5 *	5	5 *	5
14	5 *	5	5 *	5	5 *	5
15	5 *	5	5 *	5	5 *	5
16	5 *	5	5 *	5	5 *	5

Nine Substance Abuse Inpatients

Subject 62f30H reported not being able to see any images while keeping the father figure in mind. She responded only to items with mother in mind.

Four Subject 63—44— (did not indicate gender or ethnic background) some items were left blank, indicating no images. These items have been rated 5. Subject did report the hemispheric position of the parents to be MF.

Subject 54—41— (did not indicate gender or ethnic background) only responded to one item under father; the rest of the items were blank and have been subsequently reported as 5.

Subject 65m39A responded to the first four items by rating each under only the mother or father; the other spaces remained blank and are now rated 5. The hemispheric position of both parents was rated, with mother seen in the left hemispheric space, father in the right.

Subject 66m25C rated the first eight items either under mother or father, leaving the other parental filter figure blank (now rated 5). For the last eight items there were no scores, and these are also now rated 5.

Subject 67m25N reported ethnic background as Native American, the only one reported as such in the total population tested.

Subject 68m39A responded to just four of the items by rating them as 5. The remaining items which were left blank have been rated 5. Mother was indicated in the left hemispheric space; the right hemispheric space was blank and it is assumed that this space was occupied by an image of father that the subject could not see or did not report.

Subject 69m30H responded only to the first item by rating it as 5; the subsequent items remained blank and have all now been rated 5. He reported the hemispheric position of the parents as FM.

Subject 70f32— (no ethnic background indicated) reported seeing images when mother was kept in mind but not when father was kept in mind. These items have been rated 5 for the under-father condition. She reported mother occupying both the left and right hemispheric spaces, symbolized as MM.

Table 5
AA-VVIQ Scores for Subjects 62-70 (Substance Abuse Inpatients in Subgroup 4)

	62f30H 16F 0M 0 MF	63—44— 6F 3M 7 MF	64—41— 0F 1M 15 —	65m39A 2F 2M 12 MF
	F M	F M	F M	F M
1	*5 1	*5 1	1 5*	*5 1
2	*5 3	2 * 2	5 * 5	2 5*
3	*5 1	*5 3	5 * 5	5 * 5
4	*5 1	5 * 5	5 * 5	5 * 5
5	*5 1	*5 2	5 * 5	1 5*
6	*5 2	*5 1	5 * 5	*5 2
7	*5 3	*5 3	5 * 5	5 * 5
8	*5 1	5 * 5	5 * 5	5 * 5
9	*5 1	2 5*	5 * 5	5 * 5
10	*5 2	4 5*	5 * 5	5 * 5
11	*5 2	*5 3	5 * 5	5 * 5
12	*5 2	5 * 5	5 * 5	5 * 5
13	*5 3	5 * 5	5 * 5	5 * 5
14	*5 1	5 * 5	5 * 5	5 * 5
15	*5 1	5 * 5	5 * 5	5 * 5
16	*5 1	1 4*	5 * 5	5 * 5

	66m25C 4F 0M 12 FM	67m25N 9F 3M 4 FM	68m39A 0F 0M 16 MF	69m30H 0F 0M 16 FM	70f32— 16F 0M 0 MM
	F M	F M	F M	F M	F M
1	*5 1	*5 1	5 * 5	5 * 5	*5 1
2	*5 2	*5 1	5 * 5	5 * 5	*5 1
3	*5 3	*5 1	5 * 5	5 * 5	*5 1
4	*5 1	1 5*	5 * 5	5 * 5	*5 1
5	5 * 5	*5 2	5 * 5	5 * 5	*5 2
6	5 * 5	2 5*	5 * 5	5 * 5	*5 2
7	5 * 5	*5 1	5 * 5	5 * 5	*5 1
8	5 * 5	*5 1	5 * 5	5 * 5	*5 1
9	5 * 5	5 * 5	5 * 5	5 * 5	*5 2
10	5 * 5	5 * 5	5 * 5	5 * 5	*5 2
11	5 * 5	5 * 5	5 * 5	5 * 5	*5 1
12	5 * 5	5 * 5	5 * 5	5 * 5	*5 1
13	5 * 5	*5 2	5 * 5	5 * 5	*5 2
14	5 * 5	*5 2	5 * 5	5 * 5	*5 1
15	5 * 5	*5 2	5 * 5	5 * 5	*5 1
16	5 * 5	2 5*	5 * 5	5 * 5	*5 3

Discussion

The AA-VVIQ has served several very useful functions over the last few years by providing a mechanism to elucidate important baseline information and transitional stages in the discovery process. It also serves to facilitate the integration of important new material from other sources of observation and can be utilized as a guide for social research and psychotherapy. For details of research theory and data, the interested reader is referred to Unvividness Paradox (Ahsen, 1993b). In brief, most of the evidence presented shows that subjects registered almost twice as much less ability to see images vividly when they kept father in mind as compared to when they kept mother in mind. These statistics held in general in research conducted across the world as well. Some different discriminating features regarding vividness and unvividness of images, however, were found among such specific populations as African-Americans and actors (see *Imagery Paradigm*; Ahsen, 1993a). In general, the AA-VVIQ research seems to indicate that the mere presence of the parental figures has a widespread relevance; consequently, their spontaneous presence in the space in front in left-right positions would also indicate a deep relevance. This ties the AA-VVIQ with hemispheric research (see Chapter 8, "Dynamics of Hemispheric Imagery: Vivid and Unvivid in Mental Functions;" in Ahsen, 1993a) and therapeutics.

Hemispherics

Recent literature indicates a correlation of handedness and addition: "A theoretical context for the association of alcoholism and cerebral lateralization asserts that anomalous dominance and left-handedness may be neurological-developmental phenomena related to fetal testosterone" (London, 1986, p.357). In another study, "several findings associated with being at high risk for alcoholism have also been associated with left-handedness or with left hemispheric dysfunction" (London, 1987, p.207). Also, it has been found that left-handed alcoholic men have a less favorable treatment outcome than right-handers. In physiology and behavior as well, neutral stimuli were processed faster in the left hemisphere, while negative stimuli were processed faster in the right. All these indications bring up several questions related to hemispheric lateralization, dominance and hemispheric processes, and suggest areas for future studies.

1. What is the relationship of hemispheric inversion (MF) to hemispheric lateralization and the dom-

inant versus non-dominant hemispheric processing?

2. There are reports which suggest that alcoholism results in subtle frontal lobe and right hemisphere dysfunction. Is the question more along the line, "Does hemispheric dysfunction result in alcoholism?" as this seems to be more the case vis-à-vis the results here.

3. When the hemispheric position of the parental figures is reinstated, that is, from MF to FM, can neurological and motoric effects be speculated about with regard to the reported hemispheric dysfunction and resultant effect on addiction?

The manipulation of parental images in front of the subject offers a variety of maneuvers and their associated effects through management, which has been discussed in Imagery Paradigm (Ahsen, 1993a). In brief, the conclusion seems to be that hemispheric tendencies can be reversed if they have been neurotically changed through negative effects from history, or they can be strengthened into their original power if the original hemispheric tendency has been weakened. The observations already found in the hemispheric research confirm the main direction of our project.

With regard to hemispheric asymmetries, the question arises: Do parental images themselves, due to their prolonged association with development, cause the medial hemispheric spaces to behave in an asymmetrical way? The evidence that the positive potential in these medial hemispheric spaces can be enhanced and changed, resulting in the change of parental imagery in the positive direction, is an interesting piece of evidence. That enhancement of neural potential through concentration changes the quality of negative images of the chronic type suggests a possible psychosomatic attribute embedded in hemispheric asymmetries (Ahsen, 1985b).

Research implies a right hemispheric dysfunction among male alcoholics. Among females, functioning appears to be less lateralized both in alcoholics and "normals." Drake, Hannay & Gam (1990) summarize that the right hemisphere of males is particularly vulnerable to the effects of chronic alcohol abuse. There appears to be no recovery of the right hemisphere function during the first 21 days of abstinence. Females do not appear to be vulnerable to the effects of chronic alcohol use. In females, as in males, there is some suggestion of a decrease of intellectual function, but in females, no alcohol-related changes were noted in hemispheric asymmetry of function.

What is the "protection" from chronicity that females seem to exhibit, as reported in the literature? Could this be related to the "underneath sense" reported by Ahsen (1990c) in his study of hyponoia? Does the innate quality of greater flexibility in consciousness, Ahsen's (1990B, 1991) other hypothesis concerning greater flexibility in maternal connection, and the capacity to tolerate complexity have neurological and immunological ramifications? How are these factors related to neurotransmitter substances so widely researched in the literature? Specifically, we need to research dopamine and serotonin uptakes in this respect.

Eidetic Process

Is there a change in hemispheric dominance and motoric preference as a result of eidetic process? When the correct neurological function is reinstated (MF changed to FM position of parents, called correction of inversion), are there neurological ramifications? For instance, does someone have neurological "symptoms" with the onset of alcoholic tendencies as a result of the change in eidetic structures? Is it enough to say that specific populations are consistently different from normals in a certain way depending on the findings from the filters and then interpret the results, or should other kinds of factors be included so that the data can be analyzed and interpreted more specifically; for instance, study the left-right position of parents to compare the findings on a variety of variables?

It is interesting to note also that similar findings to that of alcohol hemispheric damage is reported among aging males. Can it be theorized, therefore, that focusing over a long period of time results in over-focusing, which constricts the input from the periphery, resulting in generally narrowing down the total brain functioning? Here, again, it is interesting that, according to the research (Craft, Courovitch, Dowton, Swanson & Bonforte, 1992), females show no hemispheric asymmetry of function.

The eidetic process seems to be the most helpful medium for conducting not only the hemispheric maneuvers but also reducing the negative effects of over-focusing. The eidetic achieves this by enlarging the imagery potential in a more motoric way, and by reconnecting with the periphery, which over-focusing tends to cut off.

Sociology

Are the differences between males and females biological differences or can those differences be due to changing sociological conditions which demand that a certain sector of the population respond in a certain way? Imagery as a function responds to these challenges not only in content but also through the mode in which the function postures itself to the sociological challenge.

Being an authority figure, the father represents the ability to operationalize an already functioning culture. Since the culture is changing in the gender sense, and as more women are participating in a direct way in the culture's functioning mode, as in economics, the father may appear to interfere with women's operationalization of imagery, making it appear dimmer and more difficult to manage. This would mean that the father would be interfering in the reconstruction of reality in a futuristic way. Because things are changing and he does not know how to handle them, he just interferes with them. This may explain why the father's filter gives poor imagery results in both males and females. This may also suggest that if the imagery function is released from such a dysfunction and its stress, it may take away the underlying cause of alcoholism and drug addiction in many cases, because the expression has become available. The person can engage more with reality and not just cope with dysfunction.

Imagery

The data where the inpatient subjects failed to respond to most of the imagery items stand out. Almost a complete abolishing of imagery response was reported by this group. A therapeutic strategy specifically favoring imagery is clearly indicated here. If we can quickly and without delay reinstate the imagery function in the patients, this would help shorten their hospital stay. This approach would not only reduce the hospitalization expense but, after leaving the hospital, it would also help them return to their jobs earlier than they would otherwise. Reinstatement of the imagery function would also, no doubt, help increase the effectiveness of other therapeutic procedures which are being used because the patients would be more alert and more responsive.

It appears that carefully designed strategies involving all the above-mentioned levels may be useful in the treatment of alcoholism and drug addiction, especially when these strategies are employed with due care to the specifics which they address.

Appendix B

Eidetic Parents Test

Designed by Akhter Ahsen, the Eidetic Parents Test has been, over the decades, a part of mainstream testing for systematic psychotherapy. The following instructions and steps have been reproduced from Ahsen's book, *Psycheye: Self-Analytic Consciousness* (1977). The interested reader is also referred to Ahsen's *Eidetic Parents Test and Analysis* (1972) and *Eidetic Parents Test Desk Volume* (1989) for further information on test administration and analysis of the test responses.

Image: House

READ the instruction below slowly and allow the image to be formed.

> *EP1: Picture your parents in the house where you lived most of the time with them, the house which gives you the feeling of a home. Where do you see them? What are they doing? How do you feel when you see the images? Are there any memories connected with this picture?*

PICTURE: Write here what is seen in the mind.

STEPS: Concentrate on the above picture in the following stepwise manner and write the experience in each blank space in detail.

1. Picture your parents in the house. Where do you see them?

2. Does the house give you the feeling of a home? Describe it.

3. See your father. What is he doing in the picture?

4. Do you experience positive or negative feelings when you see him?

5. Relax and recall memories about the place where father appears.

6. Now, see your mother. What is she doing in the picture?

7. Do you experience positive or negative feelings when you see her?

8. Relax and recall memories about the place where mother appears.

9. Where are your siblings? What are they doing?

10. Now, see yourself in the picture. What are you doing?

Image: Left-Right Position of Parents

READ the instruction below slowly and allow the image to be formed.

> EP2: *Now, set aside this picture of the house and see your parents standing directly in front of you. Tell me, as you look at them, who is standing on your left and who is standing on your right? Now, try to switch their positions. Do you experience any difficulty or discomfort when you do this? Try to switch their positions again. Do you again feel any difficulty? Do you feel that these images are independent of your control?*

PICTURE: Write here what is seen in the mind.

STEPS: Concentrate on the above picture in the following stepwise manner and write the experience in each blank space in detail.

1. Picture your parents standing directly in front of you.

2. As you see them, who is on the left and who is on the right?

3. Now, try to switch their positions. Are you able to switch them?

4. Describe any difficulty you experience when you switch them.

5. Now, see your parents standing in front of you again.

6. Who is standing on the left and who is on the right now?

7. Switch your parents' positions again.

8. Do you again experience a problem when you switch them?

9. Notice the two different feelings: spontaneous and forced.

10. Notice that you have no control over parents' spontaneous images.

Image: Parents Separated or United

READ the instruction below slowly and allow the image to be formed.

> *EP3: As you see your parents standing in front of you, do they appear separated or united as a couple? Describe the character of the space each occupies. Do the spaces differ in temperature and illumination?*

PICTURE: Write here what is seen in the mind.

STEPS: Concentrate on the above picture in the following stepwise manner and write the experience in each blank space in detail.

1. Picture your parents standing in front of you.

2. Do they appear separated or united as a couple?

3. Describe your father as he appears alongside your mother.

4. Describe your mother as she appears alongside your father.

5. Describe your father's space with regard to warmth and light.

6. Describe your mother's space with regard to warmth and light.

7. Do the father's and mother's spaces appear friendly or clashing?

8. Which space appears stronger, mother's or father's?

9. Does friendliness between parents' spaces create security in you?

10. Does conflict between parents' spaces create conflict in you?

Image: Active-Passive Parents

READ the instruction below slowly and allow the image to be formed.

> EP4: *As you see them standing in front of you, which parent seems to be more active and aggressive in the picture? Is he/she extremely active, very active, or just active? How is the other parent in comparison? Is he/she extremely passive, very passive, or just passive?*

PICTURE: Write here what is seen in the mind.

STEPS: Concentrate on the above picture in the following stepwise manner and write the experience in each blank space in detail.

1. Picture your parents standing in front of you again.

2. Which parent seems to be more active in the picture?

3. How is the other parent in comparison?

4. Is this active-passive relationship pleasant or unpleasant to you?

5. Does the more active parent appear to have proper attitudes?

6. Does the less active parent appear to have proper attitudes?

7. Who is more of a controlling type, mother or father?

8. How do you generally relate in life to an active person?

9. How do you generally relate in life to a passive person?

10. How do you generally relate in life to a controlling person?

Image: Running Faster

READ the instruction below slowly and allow the image to be formed.

> *EP5: Now set aside this image and picture your parents running in an open countryside. Are they both running? Who seems to be running faster? Is he/she running extremely fast, very fast, or just fast? How is the other parent running: extremely slow, very slow or just slow?*

PICTURE: Write here what is seen in the mind.

STEPS: Concentrate on the above picture in the following stepwise manner and write the experience in each blank space in detail.

1. Picture your parents running in an open countryside.

2. Describe the countryside in which they are running.

3. See both parents running. Who is running faster?

4. How is the other parent running?

5. Does the parent who is ahead help the other parent?

6. Does the parent who is behind desire help?

7. If the leading parent does not extend help, what is the problem?

8. If the leading parent does extend help, what is the problem?

9. What do you understand about father from this picture?

10. What do you understand about mother from this picture?

Image: Pattern of Running

READ the instruction below slowly and allow the image to be formed.

> EP6: *Continue watching your parents running in the open countryside. Now pay attention to the way in which they run. Describe how each parent is running, the style and pattern of his running. What seems to be the purpose of their running? Why are they running?*

PICTURE: Write here what is seen in the mind.

STEPS: Concentrate on the above picture in the following stepwise manner and write the experience in each blank space in detail.

1. Picture your parents running in the open countryside.

2. Pay attention to their running.

3. Concentrate on the pattern of your father's running. Describe it.

4. What seems to be the purpose in his running?

5. Concentrate on the pattern of your mother's running. Describe it.

6. What seems to be the purpose in her running?

7. Does the pattern of your father's running remind you of anything?

8. Does the pattern of your mother's running remind you of anything?

9. Do you want any change in father's pattern of running?

10. Do you want any change in mother's pattern of running?

Image: Freedom of Limbs

READ the instruction below slowly and allow the image to be formed.

> *EP7: As you see your parents running, do their limbs appear stiff or relaxed? Whose limbs appear more stiff and whose limbs appear more relaxed?*

PICTURE: Write here what is seen in the mind.

STEPS: Concentrate on the above picture in the following stepwise manner and write the experience in each blank space in detail.

1. Picture your parents running in the open countryside.

2. As you see them running, concentrate on their bodies.

3. Now, see the father running. Do his limbs appear stiff or relaxed?

4. Now, see the mother running. Do her limbs appear stiff or relaxed?

5. Concentrate on the parent whose limbs appear more relaxed.

6. Describe your feelings concerning the relaxation in this parent.

7. Look at the parent whose limbs appear more stiff.

8. Describe your feelings concerning the stiffness in this parent.

9. Describe the mental states of the relaxed parent.

10. Describe the mental states of the stiff parent.

Image: Brilliance of Parents' Eyes

READ the instruction below slowly and allow the image to be formed.

> *EP8: Now set aside this picture and see your parents standing directly in front of you again. Look at their eyes. (Do not recollect their real eyes). Whose eyes are more brilliant? Are they extremely brilliant, very brilliant, or just brilliant? How do the other parent's eyes appear?*

PICTURE: Write here what is seen in the mind.

STEPS: Concentrate on the above picture in the following stepwise manner and write the experience in each blank space in detail.

1. Picture your parents standing in front of you again.

2. Look at their eyes in the picture.

3. Whose eyes appear more brilliant?

4. How are the eyes of the other parent in comparison?

5. What kind of brilliance or dullness do the father's eyes have?

6. What kind of brilliance or dullness do the mother's eyes have?

7. Look at the parent with brilliant eyes. How do the eyes affect you?

8. Look at the parent who has dull eyes. How do the eyes affect you?

9. Relax and recall memories as you look at father's eyes.

10. Relax and recall memories as you look at mother's eyes.

Image: Object Orientation

READ the instruction below slowly and allow the image to be formed.

> *EP9: Now set aside this image and look at me. As I look at objects, my eyes focus on one object and then another. Now I am staring into space and my eyes focus on nothing. Now see your parents' eyes in the image again. Whose eyes focus on objects more easily? Are the eyes extremely object-oriented, very object-oriented, or just object-oriented? How are the other parent's eyes?"*

PICTURE: Write here what is seen in the mind.

STEPS: Concentrate on the above picture in the following stepwise manner and write the experience in each blank space in detail.

1. Picture your parents' eyes focusing on objects.

2. Whose eyes focus on objects more easily, mother's or father's?

3. How do the eyes of the other parent focus in comparison?

4. Now, concentrate on your father focusing on objects.

5. Does his focusing on objects feel pleasant or unpleasant to you?

6. Relax and recall memories as you see father's eyes focusing.

7. Now, concentrate on your mother focusing on objects.

8. Does her focusing on objects feel pleasant or unpleasant to you?

9. Relax and recall memories as you see mother's eyes focusing.

10. Do you focus on objects more like your father or your mother?

Image: Story in the Eyes

READ the instruction below slowly and allow the image to be formed.

> *EP10: Continue concentrating on your parents' eyes in the picture. Do they give you any feeling or tell you any story?*

PICTURE: Write here what is seen in the mind.

STEPS: Concentrate on the above picture in the following stepwise manner and write the experience in each blank space in detail.

1. Picture your parents' eyes again.

2. Concentrate on your father's eyes in the picture.

3. Do his eyes give you any feeling or tell you any story?

4. Concentrate on the story in father's eyes.

5. Do you experience pleasant or unpleasant feelings?

6. Now, concentrate on your mother's eyes in the picture.

7. Do her eyes give you any feeling or tell you any story?

8. Concentrate on the story in mother's eyes.

9. Do you experience pleasant or unpleasant feelings?

10. Which story do you feel is more true?

Image: Loudness of Parents' Voices

READ the instruction below slowly and allow the image to be formed.

> *EP11: Now set aside this picture and see that you are hearing your parents' voices. Whose voice sounds louder to you? It is extremely loud, very loud, or just loud? How does the other parent's voice sound to you?*

PICTURE: Write here what is seen in the mind.

STEPS: Concentrate on the above picture in the following stepwise manner and write the experience in each blank space in detail.

1. Picture your parents and hear their voices.

2. Whose voice sounds louder to you? Describe the voice.

3. How is the voice of the other parent in comparison?

4. Concentrate on father's voice. Is the sound pleasant or unpleasant?

5. Relax and recall memories as you continue to hear his voice.

6. Concentrate on mother's voice. Is the sound pleasant or unpleasant?

7. Relax and recall memories as you continue to hear her voice.

8. Whose voice do you pay attention to less, mother's or father's?

9. What is this voice you attend less saying to you?

10. Why do you pay less attention to this voice?

NEW TREATMENT OF ALCOHOL AND DRUG ABUSE

Image: Meaningfulness of Voices

> *EP12: Now hear your parents' voices again. Do the voices seem meaningful, or are they merely patterns of sound in the air? Whose voice carries more meaning? It is extremely meaningful, very meaningful, or just meaningful? How does the other parent's voice sound to you?*

PICTURE: Write here what is seen in the mind.

STEPS: Concentrate on the above picture in the following stepwise manner and write the experience in each blank space in detail.

1.   Picture your parents and hear their voices.

2.   Are the voices meaningful, or merely patterns of sound?

3.   Whose voice carries more meaning, mother's or father's?

4.   Concentrate on your father's voice.

5.   What message does your father's voice carry for your mother?

6.   Concentrate on your mother's voice.

7.   What message does your mother's voice carry for your father?

8.   Concentrate on the voice that you hear more. How do you react?

9.   Concentrate on the voice that you hear less. How do you react?

10. Which ear do you use more, your right or your left?

Image: Story in the Voices

READ the instruction below slowly and allow the image to be formed.

> EP13: *Continue listening to your parents' voices. Do they give you any feeling or tell you any story?*

PICTURE: Write here what is seen in the mind.

STEPS: Concentrate on the above picture in the following stepwise manner and write the experience in each blank space in detail.

1. Picture your parents and hear their voices again.

2. Concentrate on your father's voice in the picture.

3. Does his voice give you any feeling or tell you any story?

4. Concentrate and hear the story in your father's voice.

5. Do you experience pleasant or unpleasant feelings?

6. Now, concentrate on your mother's voice in the picture.

7. Does her voice give you any feeling or tell you any story?

8. Concentrate and hear the story in your mother's voice.

9. Do you experience pleasant or unpleasant feelings?

10. What do you understand from these two stories?

Image: Hearing by Parents' Ears

READ the instruction below slowly and allow the image to be formed.

> *EP14: Now see yourself talking to both your parents. Who seems to hear you better or has good ears for you? Does he/she hear you extremely well, very well, or just well? Describe how the other parent hears you.*

PICTURE: Write here what is seen in the mind.

STEPS: Concentrate on the above picture in the following stepwise manner and write the experience in each blank space in detail.

1. Picture yourself talking to both your parents.

2. Who seems to hear you better?

3. How does the other parent hear you in comparison?

4. Concentrate on how your father hears you in the picture.

5. When he hears you, do you feel secure or insecure?

6. Concentrate on how your mother hears you in the picture.

7. When she hears you, do you feel secure or insecure?

8. Concentrate on the parent whose hearing creates security in you.

9. Concentrate on the parent whose hearing creates insecurity in you.

10. Which parent do you approach more, for listening to you?

Image: Understanding by Ears

READ the instruction below slowly and allow the image to be formed.

> *EP15: As you talk to your parents in the image, do they seem to understand you? Who seems to understand you better? Does he/she understand you extremely well, very well, or just well? Describe how much the other parent understands you.*

PICTURE: Write here what is seen in the mind.

STEPS: Concentrate on the above picture in the following stepwise manner and write the experience in each blank space in detail.

1. Picture yourself talking to both your parents again.

2. Who seems to understand you better, mother or father?

3. Concentrate on how your father understands you in the picture.

4. Do you feel understood?

5. Concentrate on how your mother understands you in the picture.

6. Do you feel understood?

7. See father. What kind of ideas would you like to exchange with him?

8. See mother. What kind of ideas would you like to exchange with her?

9. Which parent exchanges ideas with you more?

10. Which parent do you feel should exchange ideas with you more?

Image: Parents Sniffing

READ the instruction below slowly and allow the image to be formed.

> *EP16: Now set aside this image and look at me. I am sniffing the air here in this room, and you can tell by my facial expression whether I like the air or not. Now see the parents sniffing the air in the house in the same way. Do they appear to like or dislike the house atmosphere?*

PICTURE: Write here what is seen in the mind.

STEPS: Concentrate on the above picture in the following stepwise manner and write the experience in each blank space in detail.

1. Picture you parents sniffing the air in the house.

2. Who appears to like the house air more, mother or father?

3. How does the other parent respond to the house air?

4. Concentrate on father sniffing. What are his thoughts?

5. Concentrate on mother sniffing. What are her thoughts?

6. Is the parent who approves of the house air active or passive?

7. Is the parent who disapproves of the house air active or passive?

8. How does the father reconcile his conflict about the house?

9. How does the mother reconcile her conflict about the house?

10. How do you respond to the conflict in the house?

Image: Warmth of Parents' Bodies

READ the instruction below slowly and allow the image to be formed.

> *EP17: Now see your parents standing directly in front of you again. Do you get a feeling of personal warmth from their bodies? Whose body gives you a better feeling of personal warmth? What kind of feeling does other parent's body give?*

PICTURE: Write here what is seen in the mind.

STEPS: Concentrate on the above picture in the following stepwise manner and write the experience in each blank space in detail.

1. Picture your parents standing directly in front of you.

2. Which parent's body has more personal warmth?

3. How is the other parent's body in comparison?

4. Concentrate on your feelings concerning father's body.

5. Describe how you feel as you see his body.

6. Relax and recall memories as you concentrate on your father's body.

7. Concentrate on your feelings concerning mother's body.

8. Describe how you feel as you see her body.

9. Relax and recall memories as you concentrate on your mother's body.

10. Which parent's body do you wish to know more? Why?

Image: Body Acceptance

READ the instruction below slowly and allow the image to be formed.

> *EP18: Now look at your parents' skin and concentrate on it for a while. Does it seem to accept you or reject you? Describe how you feel when you look at their skin.*

PICTURE: Write here what is seen in the mind.

STEPS: Concentrate on the above picture in the following stepwise manner and write the experience in each blank space in detail.

1. Picture your parents standing in front of you again.

2. Concentrate on their skin.

3. Whose skin gives you the feeling of acceptance? To what degree?

4. Whose skin gives you the feeling of rejection? To what degree?

5. Concentrate on your feelings concerning father's skin.

6. Describe how you feel as you experience father's skin.

7. Concentrate on your feelings concerning mother's skin.

8. Describe how you feel as you experience mother's skin.

9. Which parent usually touches you more?

10. Which parent do you usually touch more?

Image: Health of Skin

READ the instruction below slowly and allow the image to be formed.

> *EP19: Continue looking at your parents skin. Does it appear healthy or unhealthy? Whose skin appears healthier?*

PICTURE: Write here what is seen in the mind.

STEPS: Concentrate on the above picture in the following stepwise manner and write the experience in each blank space in detail.

1. Picture your parents and concentrate on their skin.

2. Whose skin appears healthier?

3. How does the other parent's skin appear?

4. Experience feelings as you concentrate on the healthier skin.

5. Experience feelings as you concentrate on the less healthy skin.

6. What does blemish in father's skin mean to you?

7. What does health in father's skin mean to you?

8. What does blemish in mother's skin mean to you?

9. What does health in mother's skin mean to you?

10. Which parent's skin do you want to see improved in your mind?

Image: Arms Giving

READ the instruction below slowly and allow the image to be formed.

> *EP20: Now picture your parents giving you something. Which parent extends the hand more completely for giving? Show me how your mother extends her arms when she gives. How does your father extend his arms when he gives?*

PICTURE: Write here what is seen in the mind.

STEPS: Concentrate on the above picture in the following stepwise manner and write the experience in each blank space in detail.

1. Picture your parents giving you something.

2. Which parent extends the hand more completely to give?

3. How does the other parent extend the hand?

4. Concentrate on your father giving to you.

5. As he gives, do you experience pleasant or unpleasant feelings?

6. Concentrate on your mother giving to you.

7. As she gives, do you experience pleasant or unpleasant feelings?

8. What does the parent who does not extend the hand have in the hand?

9. What does the parent who extends the hand have in the hand?

10. Which gift feels more precious to you?

Image: Arms Receiving

READ the instruction below slowly and allow the image to be formed.

> *EP21: Now picture yourself taking something from your parents.*
> *To whom do you extend your arms completely?*

PICTURE: Write here what is seen in the mind.

STEPS: Concentrate on the above picture in the following stepwise manner and write the experience in each blank space in detail.

1. Picture yourself taking something from your parents.

2. To which parent do you extend you hands completely for receiving?

3. How do you extend your hands to the other parent?

4. Relax and recall memories as you extend your hands toward parents.

5. Concentrate on how you take something from your father.

6. Describe what you see.

7. Concentrate on how you take something from your mother.

8. Describe what you see.

9. Wish something from the parent toward whom you do not feel free.

10. Wish something from the parent toward whom you do feel free.

Image: Strength of Grasp

READ the instruction below slowly and allow the image to be formed.

> *EP22: Now see that your parents are holding something in their hands. Tell me, which parent grasps more firmly? How is the grasp of the other parent?*

PICTURE: Write here what is seen in the mind.

STEPS: Concentrate on the above picture in the following stepwise manner and write the experience in each blank space in detail.

1. Picture your parents holding something in their hands.

2. Which parent grasps more firmly? How does the other parent grasp?

3. Concentrate on your father's grasp.

4. Do you experience pleasant or unpleasant feelings?

5. Concentrate on your mother's grasp.

6. Do you experience pleasant or unpleasant feelings?

7. See that the parent who grasps firmly is holding your hand lightly.

8. Concentrate on the picture. How do you feel?

9. See that the parent who grasps lightly is holding your hand firmly.

10. Concentrate on the picture. How do you feel?

Image: Swallowing Food

READ the instruction below slowly and allow the image to be formed.

> EP23: *Now see your parents eating. Do they swallow easily?*
> *Who swallows with more ease?*

PICTURE: Write here what is seen in the mind.

STEPS: Concentrate on the above picture in the following stepwise manner and write the experience in each blank space in detail.

1. Picture your parents eating.

2. Which parent swallows with more ease?

3. How does the other parent swallow?

4. Is the image of your father swallowing pleasant or unpleasant?

5. What is your father's attitude toward food in the picture?

6. Relax and recall memories as you concentrate on father swallowing.

7. Is the image of your mother swallowing pleasant or unpleasant?

8. What is your mother's attitude toward food in the picture?

9. Relax and recall memories as you concentrate on mother swallowing.

10. As they swallow, which parent attracts your attention more? Why?

Image: Drinking Fluid

READ the instruction below slowly and allow the image to be formed.

EP24: Now see your parents drinking fluid. Who drinks faster?

PICTURE: Write here what is seen in the mind.

STEPS: Concentrate on the above picture in the following stepwise manner and write the experience in each blank space in detail.

1. Picture your parents drinking fluid.

2. Which parent drinks faster?

3. How does the other parent drink in comparison?

4. Is the image of your father drinking pleasant or unpleasant?

5. What is your father's attitude toward the drink in the picture?

6. What is your father drinking? Look at it closely.

7. Is the image of your mother drinking pleasant or unpleasant?

8. What is your mother's attitude toward the drink in the picture?

9. What is your mother drinking? Look at it closely.

10. As they drink, which parent attracts your attention more? Why?

Image: Jaw Pressure

READ the instruction below slowly and allow the image to be formed.

> *EP25: Now see your parents chewing something. Describe how they chew. Do they chew with pressure? Who chews with more pressure?*

PICTURE: Write here what is seen in the mind.

STEPS: Concentrate on the above picture in the following stepwise manner and write the experience in each blank space in detail.

1. Picture your parents chewing something.

2. Which parent chews with more pressure?

3. How does the other parent chew in comparison?

4. Is the image of your father chewing pleasant or unpleasant?

5. What is your father's attitude toward what he is chewing?

6. What is your father chewing in the picture?

7. Is the image of your mother chewing pleasant or unpleasant?

8. What is your mother's attitude toward what she is chewing?

9. What is your mother chewing in the picture?

10. As they chew, which parent attracts your attention more? Why?

Image: Parents' Brains

READ the instruction below slowly and allow the image to be formed.

> *EP26: Now look at me. Imagine that my upper skull has been sur-*
> *gically removed and that you can see my brain. You can touch my*
> *visible brain with your finger and feel the temperature there. Now*
> *picture your parents in a similar way. Touch their brains alter-*
> *nately with your finger. You will similarly get a feeling of tem-*
> *perature there. Describe the temperature of each parent's brain, is*
> *it cold, warm, or hot?*

PICTURE: Write here what is seen in the mind.

STEPS: Concentrate on the above picture in the following stepwise manner and write the experience in each blank space in detail.

1. Picture your parents' visible brains.

2. Touch each parent's brain and feel the temperature there.

3. Now, touch your father's brain. Describe the temperature.

4. Is touching your father's brain pleasant or unpleasant?

5. Now, touch your mother's brain. Describe the temperature.

6. Is touching your mother's brain pleasant or unpleasant?

7. What does hot temperature of a brain mean to you?

8. What does cold temperature of a brain mean to you?

9. What does neutral temperature of a brain mean to you?

10. Which parent's brain do you tend to avoid touching?

Image: Brain Efficiency

READ the instruction below slowly and allow the image to be formed.

> EP27: *Look at your parents' exposed brains again. Imagine them as thinking machines, and describe how they look. How do you feel about their efficiency as thinking machines? Whose brain looks more efficient?*

PICTURE: Write here what is seen in the mind.

STEPS: Concentrate on the above picture in the following stepwise manner and write the experience in each blank space in detail.

1. Picture your parents' exposed brains again.

2. Imagine their brains as thinking machines.

3. Which parent's brain appears more efficient?

4. How is the other parent's brain in comparison?

5. Concentrate on how your father's brain looks.

6. Describe what your father's brain signifies to you.

7. Concentrate on how your mother's brain looks.

8. Describe what your mother's brain signifies to you.

9. Picture a defect or blemish in a brain. What does it look like?

10. Picture a perfect brain. What does it look like?

Image: Parents' Heartbeats

READ the instruction below slowly and allow the image to be formed.

> EP28: *Now see your parents' complete images standing in front of you again. Imagine that a window has been carved in each chest and that you can see their hearts beating there. See the hearts beating, and describe how each parent's heart beats. Is there any sign of anxiety in the heartbeats?*

PICTURE: Write here what is seen in the mind.

STEPS: Concentrate on the above picture in the following stepwise manner and write the experience in each blank space in detail.

1. Picture your parents' complete images standing in front of you.

2. Imagine a window in each parent's chest and see the hearts beating.

3. See father's heart beating. Describe its beat and its appearance.

4. Is there any sign of anxiety in father's heartbeats?

5. Imagine a picture of someone in father's heart. Who do you see?

6. See mother's heart beating. Describe its beat and its appearance.

7. Is there any sign of anxiety in mother's heartbeats?

8. Imagine a picture of someone in mother's heart. Who do you see?

9. In what way do you wish your father's heart to appear different?

10. In what way do you wish your mother's heart to appear different?

Image: Parents' Intestines

READ the instruction below slowly and allow the image to be formed.

> EP29: *Now look at your parents' intestines. Do they appear healthy or unhealthy? Whose intestines appear healthier?*

PICTURE: Write here what is seen in the mind.

STEPS: Concentrate on the above picture in the following stepwise manner and write the experience in each blank space in detail.

1. Picture your parents' intestines.

2. Which parent's intestines appear healthier?

3. How do the other parent's intestines appear?

4. Is the image of your father's intestines pleasant or unpleasant?

5. Does concentration on father's intestines remind you of anything?

6. Is the image of your mother's intestines pleasant or unpleasant?

7. Does concentration on mother's intestines remind you of anything?

8. In your view, what causes healthy intestines?

9. In your view, what causes unhealthy intestines?

10. Picture perfectly healthy intestines. What do they look like?

Image: Parents' Genitals

READ the instruction below slowly and allow the image to be formed.

> *EP30: Now see your parents' genitals. Touch the genitals of each parent and describe the feelings of temperature there. Describe how each parent reacts to the touch and any feelings you have while seeing this image. Are there any memories associated with this image?*

PICTURE: Write here what is seen in the mind.

STEPS: Concentrate on the above picture in the following stepwise manner and write the experience in each blank space in detail.

1. Picture your parents' genitals.

2. Touch each parent's genitals and feel the temperature there.

3. Describe the temperature and appearance of father's genitals.

4. How does your father react to you touching his genitals?

5. Does touching his genitals remind you of anything?

6. Now, describe the temperature and appearance of mother's genitals.

7. How does your mother react to you touching her genitals?

8. Does touching her genitals remind you of anything?

9. In your opinion, how did your mother influence your sexual life?

10. In your opinion, how did your father influence your sexual life?

Bibliography

ADAMHA News Supplement. (1990, Jan/Feb). *XVI*(1).

Ahsen, A. (1965). *Eidetic psychotherapy: A short introduction.* New York: Brandon House.

Ahsen, A. (1968). *Basic concepts in eidetic psychotherapy.* New York: Brandon House.

Ahsen, A. (1972). *Eidetic Parents Test and analysis.* New York: Brandon House.

Ahsen, A. (1977a). *Psycheye: Self-analytic consciousness.* New York: Brandon House.

Ahsen, A. (1977b). Eidetics: An overview. *Journal of Mental Imagery, 1*(1), 5-38.

Ahsen, A. (1978) Eidetics: Neural experiential growth potential for the treatment of accident traumas, debilitating stress conditions, and chronic emotional blocking. *Journal of Mental Imagery, 2,* 1-22.

Ahsen, A. (1979). Image for effective psychotherapy: An essay on consciousness, anticipation, and imagery. In A.A. Sheikh & J.T. Shaffer (Eds.), *The potential of fantasy and imagination* (pp.11-26). New York: Brandon House.

Ahsen, A., (1984a) Imagery, drama and transformation. *Journal of Mental Imagery, 8*(1) 53-78.

Ahsen, A. (1984b). ISM: The Triple Code Model for imagery and psychophysiology. *Journal of Mental Imagery, 8*(4), 15-42.

Ahsen, A. (1985a). Unvividness Paradox. *Journal of Mental Imagery, 9*(3), 1-18.

Ahsen, A. (1985b). Medial hemispheric imbalance: Experiments on a clinically related imagery function. *Journal of Mental Imagery, 9*(1), 1-8.

Ahsen, A. (1986a). Prologue to Unvividness Paradox. *Journal of Mental Imagery, 10*(1), 1-8.

Ahsen, A. (1986b). *The New Structuralism: Images in dramatic interlock.* New York: Brandon House.

Ahsen, A. (1987). *Image Psychology and the empirical method.* With open peer commentary and response. New York: Brandon House. (Target article originally published 1985, *Journal of Mental Imagery, 9*(2), 1-40.)

Ahsen, A. (1988a). Hypnagogic and hypnopompic imagery transformations. *Journal of Mental Imagery*, 12(2), 1-50.

Ahsen, A. (1988b). *Age Projection Test: Short-term imagery treatment of hysterias, phobias and other themes*. New York: Brandon House.

Ahsen, A. (1989a). Hyponoia, hypnosis, and the eidetic: The underneath sense of images, impulses and thoughts. *Journal of Mental Imagery* 13(2), 1-82.

Ahsen, A. (1989b). *Eidetic Parents Test desk volume*. New York: Brandon House.

Ahsen, A. (1990a). AA-VVIQ and imagery paradigm: Vividness and unvividness issues in VVIQ research programs. *Journal of Mental Imagery*, 14(3 & 4), 1-58.

Ahsen, A. (1990b). *Behaviorists' misconduct in science: The untold story of the image in cognitive psychology*. New York: Brandon House.

Ahsen, A. (1990c). *Hyponoia: The underneath sense of being*. New York: Brandon House.

Ahsen, A. (1991). A second report on AA-VVIQ: Role of vivid and unvivid images in consciousness research. *Journal of Mental Imagery*, 15(3 & 4), 1-32.

Ahsen, A. (1992). *Prolucid dreaming*. New York: Brandon House.

Ahsen, A. (1993a). Imagery treatment of alcoholism and drug abuse: A new methodology for treatment and research. *Journal of Mental Imagery*, 17(3 & 4), 1-60.

Ahsen, A. (1993b). *Imagery paradigm: Imaginative consciousness in the experimental and clinical setting*. New York: Brandon House.

Ahsen, A. (1997). Visual imagery and performance in multisensory experience, synaesthesia and phosphenes. *Journal of Mental Imagery*, 21(3&4), 1-40.

Ahsen, A., & Lazarus, A.A. (1972). Eidetics: An internal behavior approach. In A.A. Lazarus (Ed.), *Clinical behavior therapy*. New York: Brunner/Mazel.

Alcohol Alert Supplement. (1991, July). NIAAA, No. 13, PH297

Alexi, T., & Azmitia, E.C. (1991, March 29). Ethanol Stimulates (3H) 5HT high affinity uptake in rat forebrain synaptosomes: Role of 5HT receptors and voltage channel blockers. *Brain Research*, 544(2), 243-247.

Annis, H.M., & Davis, C.S. (1988). Assessment of expectancies. In D.M. Donovan, & A.G. Marlatt (Eds.), *Assessment of Addictive Behaviors* (pp. 84-111). New York: Guilford Press.

Baekeland, F., Lundwall, L., & Kissen, B. (1975). Method for treatment of chronic alcoholism: A critical appraisal. In R.J. Gibbons, Y. Israel, H. Kalant, R.E. Popham, W. Schmidt, & R.J. Smart (Eds.), *Research advances in alcohol and drug problems*, Vol. 2. New York: Wiley.

Bandura, A. (1969). *Principles of behavior modification*. New York: Holt, Reinhart and Winston.

Bandura, A. (1975). The ethics and social purposes of behavior modification. In C.M. Franks, & G.T. Wilson, (Eds.), *Annual review of behavior therapy, Theory and practice*, Vol. 3, New York: Brunner-Mazel.

Beaubrum, M.H. (1967). Treatment of alcoholism in Trinidad and Tobago, 1956-1965. *British Journal of Psychiatry*, 113, 643-658.

Bent, N., (1995). *Beyond MS: It's all in the image*. New York, Brandon House.

Brecher, E.M. (1972). *Licit and illicit drugs*. Consumers Union, 71.

Brown, S., Goldman, M.S., Inn, A., & Anderson, L.R. (1980). The expectation of reinforcement from alcohol: Their domain and relation to drinking patterns. *Journal of Consulting and Clinical Psychology*, 48(4), 419-426.

Califano, J.A., Jr. (1982). *The 1982 report of drug abuse and alcoholism*. Warner Books.

Carboni, E., Acquas, E., Fraw, R., & Dichiara, G. (1989, May 30). Differential inhibitory effects of a 5HT3 antagonist on drug-induced stimulation of dopamine release. *European Journal of Pharmacology, 164*(3), 515-519.

Christiansen, B.A., Goldman, M.S., & Inn,A. (1982). Development of alcohol-related expectancies in adolescents: Separating pharmacological for social learning influences. *Journal of Consulting and Clinical Psychology, 50*(3), 336-344.

Conners, G.J., Maisto, S.A., & Watson, D.W. (1988). Racial factors influencing college students' ratings of alcohols' usefulness. *Drug and Alcohol Dependence, 21*, 247-252.

Cooper, M.L., Russell, M., Skinner, J.B., Frone, M.R. & Mudar., P. (1992). Stress and alcohol use: Moderating effects of gender, coping, and alcohol expectancies. *Journal of Abnormal Psychology, 101*(1), 139-152.

Cooper, M.L., Russell, M., & Frone, M.R. (1990, September). Work stress and alcohol effects: A test of stress-induced drinking. *Journal of Health and Social Behavior, 31*, 260-276.

Craft, S., Gourovitch, M.L., Dowton, S.B., Swanson, J.M., & Bonforte, S. (1992, April). Lateralized deficits in visual attention in males with developmental dopamine depletion. *Neuropsychologia, 30*(4), 341-351.

Curtis, Q.F. (1937, September). The experimental neurosis in the pig. Read before the American Psychological Association.

Daoust, C., Campagnon, P., Legrand, E., & Boucly, P. (1991). Ethanol intake and 3H serotonin uptake I: A study in Fawn Hooded rats. *Life Science, 48*(20), 1969-76.

DATA (Digest of Addiction Theory and Application). (1991, June). Brown University, *10*(5).

Diagnostic and statistical manual of mental disorders. (1994). (4th ed.) Washington, DC: The American Psychiatric Association.

Dolan, A. T. (1972). Introduction. In A. Ahsen, *Eidetic Parents Test and analysis: A practical guide to systematic & comprehensive analysis.* New York, Brandon House.

Dolan, A.T. (1977a). Introduction. In A. Ahsen, *Psycheye: Self-analytic consciousness.* New York: Brandon House.

Dolan, A.T. (1977b). Eidetic and general imagery theory of primary image objects and identification processes. *Journal of Mental Imagery,, 1*, 217-228.

Dolan, A. T. (1997). *Imagery treatment of phobias, anxiety states and other symptom complexes in Akhter Ahsen's Image Psychology.* New York, Brandon House.

Dolan, A.T., & Sheikh, A. (1976). Eidetics: A visual approach to psychotherapy. *Psychologia: An International Journal of Psychology in the Orient, XIX*(4)

Donovan, D.M., & Marlatt, A.G. (1980). Assessment of expectancies and behaviors associated with alcohol consumption: A cognitive behavioral approach. *Journal of Studies on Alcohol, 41*(11), 1153-1184).

Drake, A.I., Hannay, H.J., & Gam, J. (1990). Effects of chronic alcoholism on hemispheric functioning: An examination of gender differences for cognitive and dichotic listening, *Journal of Clinical and Experimental Neuropsychology, 12*(5), 781-797.

Emrich, C.D. (1975). A review of psychologically oriented treatment of alcoholism. II. The relative effectiveness of different treatment approaches and the effectiveness of treatment versus no treatment. *Journal of Studies on Alcohol, 36*(1), 88-108.

Eysenck, H.J., & Beech, H.R. (1971). Counter conditioning and related methods. In A.E. Bergin, & S.L. Garfield (Eds.), *Handbook of psychotherapy and behavior change; An empirical analysis* (pp. 543-611). New York: Wiley.

Eysenck, H.J., & Rachman, S. (1965). *Causes and cures of neurosis.* San Diego: Knopf.

Evans, D.M., & Dunn, N.J. (1995, March). Alcohol expectancies, coping responses and self-efficacy judgments: A replication and extension of Cooper et al.'s 1988 study in a college sample. *Journal of Studies on Alcohol, 56*(2), 186-193.

Faber, D.S., & Klee, M.R. (1977). Actions of ethanol on neuronal membrane properties and synaptic transmission (pp. 41-63). In K. Blum, D.L. Bard, & M.G. Hamilton (Eds.), *Alcohol and opiates: Neurochemistry and behavior mechanisms.* New York: Academic Press.

Feigenbaum, J.J., Fishman, R.H., & Yanai, J. (1982). Mechanisms of dopamine antagonism by morphine in rodents. *Substance-Alcohol Actions Misuse, 3*(6), 307-324.

Fingarette, H. (1991). Alcoholism: The mythical disease. In D.J. Pittman, & H.R. White (Eds.), *Society, culture and drinking patterns re-examined.* New Brunswick, NJ: Rutgers Center of Alcohol Studies.

Frank, J.D. (1961). *Persuasion and healing: A comparative study of psychotherapy.* Baltimore, Johns Hopkins University Press.

Franks, C.M. (1967). Reflections upon the treatment of sexual disorders by the behavioral clinician: A historical comparison with the treatment of the Alcoholic. *Journal of Sex Research 3*, 212-222.

Gerard, D.L. Saenger, G., & Wile, R. (1962). The abstinent alcoholic. *Archives of General Psychiatry, 6*, 83-95.

Gero, A. (1985). Desensitization and coupled receptors: A model of drug dependence. *Journal of Theoretical Biology, 115*(4), 603-617.

Goldman, M.S., Brown, S.A., Christiansen, B.A., & Smith, G.T. (1991). Alcoholism and memory: Broadening the scope of alcohol-expectancy research. *Psychological Bulletin, 110*(1), 137-146.

Gordis, E. (1976). Editorial: What is alcoholism research? *Annals of Internal Medicine, 85*, 821-823.

Goldstein, D. (1979, November). The biological perspective. *Journal on Studies in Alcohol, Supplement #8.*

Gustafson, R. (1988). Self-reported expected effects of a moderate dose of alcohol by college women. *Alcohol and Alcoholism, 23*(5), 409-414.

Harvard Mental Health Letter. (1996, August). Treatment of alcoholism - Part I. *13*(2).

Harvard Mental Health Letter. (1996, September). Treatment of alcoholism - Part II. *13*(3).

Hebb, D.O. (1968). Concerning imagery. *Psychological Review, 75*(6), 466-477.

Henderson, M.L., Goldman, M.S., Coovert, M.D., & Carnevalla, N. (1994, May). Covariance structure models of expectancy. *Journal of Studies on Alcohol. 55*(3), 315-326.

Hilgard, E.R. (1973). A neodissociation interpretation of pain reduction in hypnosis. *Psychological Review, 80*(5), 396-411

Hilgard, E.R. (1977). *Divided consciousness: Multiple controls in human thought and action.* New York: Wiley Interscience.

Hochman, J. (1994). Ahsen's Image Psychology. *Journal of Mental Imagery, 18*(3&4), 1-118.

Holden, C. (1987). Is alcoholism treatment effective? *Science, 236*, 20-22.

Hore, B. (1991). The disease concept of alcoholism. In D.J. Pittman, & H.R. White (Eds.), *Society, culture and drinking patterns re-examined.* New Brunswick, NJ: Rutgers Center of Alcohol Studies.

Hull, J.G., & Bond, C.F., Jr. (1986). Social and behavioral consequences of alcohol consumption and expectancy: A meta analysis. *Psychological bulletin, 99*(3), 347-360.

Keller, M, (1960). Definition of alcoholism. *Quarterly Journal of Studies on Alcohol, 21*(1), 125-134.

Keehn, J.D., Bloomfield, F.F., & Hug, M.A. (1970). The use of the reinforcement survey. *Quarterly Journal for Studies in Alcohol, 31*, 602-615.

Kissen, B. (1979, November). Biological investigations in alcohol research. *Journal of Studies in Alcohol, Supplement #8.*

LaBerg, J.C. (1986). Alcohol and expectancy: Subjective, psychophysiological and behavioral responses to alcohol stimuli in severely, moderately and non-dependent drinkers. *British Journal of Addiction, 81,* 797-808.

Lapp, W.M., Collins, L., & Izzo, C.V. (1994, Summer). On the enhancement of creativity by alcohol: Pharmacology or expectation? *American Journal of Psychology, 10(.2),* 173-206.

Lazarus, A.A. (1965). Towards the understanding and effective treatment of alcoholism. *South African Medical Journal, 39,* 736-741.

Leigh, B.C., & Stacy, A.W. (1991). On the scope of alcohol expectancy research: Remaining issues of measurement and meaning. *Psychological Bulletin, 110*(1), 147-154.

London, W.P. (1986, June). Handedness and alcoholism: A family history of left-handedness. *Alcoholism: Clinical and Experimental-Research, 10*(3), 357.

London, W.P. (1987, May-June). Cerebral laterality and the study of alcoholism. *Alcohol,* 4(3), 207-208.

Longabaugh, R., Wirtz, P.W., DiClemente, C.C., & Litt, M. (1994, December). Issues in the development of client-treatment matching hypotheses. *Journal of Studies on Alcohol, Supplement No.12,* 46-58.

Maisto, S.A., Conners, G.J., & Sachs, P. (1981). Expectation as a mediator in alcohol intoxication: A reference level model. *Cognitive Therapy and Research, 5,* 1-18.

Marks, D.F. (1973). Visual imagery differences in the recall of pictures. *British Journal of Psychology, 64,* 17-24.

Marks, D.F. (1987). Resolving the Unvividness Paradox. *Journal of Mental Imagery, 11*(1), 3-9.

Marlin, E. (1986). *Hope.* New York: Random House.

Marlatt, A.G., & Rohsenow, D.J. (1980). Cognitive processes in alcohol use: Expectancy and the balanced placebo design. *Advances in Substance Abuse, 1,* 159-199.

Merck manual of diagnosis and therapy. (1992). (16th ed.). R. Berkow (Ed.). Rahway, NJ: Merck, Sharp, and Dohme Research Laboratories, division of Merck and Co.

McCord, W., & McCord, J. (1960). *Origins of alcoholism.* Stanford: Stanford University Press.

Miller, P.M., & Eisler, R.M. (1975). Alcohol and drug abuse. In W.E. Craighead, A.E. Kazdin, & M.J. Mahoney (Eds.), *Behavior modification: Principles, issues and applications.* Boston: Houghton Mifflin.

Miller, P.M., Smith, G.T. & Goldman, M.S. (1990). Emergence of alcohol expectancies in childhood: A possible critical period. *Journal of Studies on Alcohol, 51*(4), 343-349.

Miller, W.R., & Hester, R.K. (1986). Inpatient alcoholism treatment: Who benefits? *American Psychologist, 41,* 794-805.

Milner, P.M. (1970). *Physiological psychology.* New York: Holt, Rinehart & Winston.

Mowrer, O.H. (1938). Preparatory set (expectancy)—a determinant in motivation and learning, *Psychological Review, 45,* 61-91.

Mowrer, O.H. (1977). Mental imagery: An indispensable psychological concept. *Journal of Mental Imagery, 1,* 303-326.

Naranjo, C.A., & Sellers, E.M. (1989). Serotonin uptake inhibitors attenuate ethanol intake in problem drinkers. *Recent Developments in Alcohol, 7,* 255-266.

Nathan, P.E. (1978a). Behavioral theory and behavioral theories of alcoholism. In G.A. Marlatt & P.E. Nathan (Eds.), *Behavioral approaches to alcoholism* (pp. 3-6). New Brunswick, NJ: Publications Division, Rutgers Center of Alcohol Studies.

Nathan, P.E. (1978b). Overview of behavioral treatment approaches. In G.A. Marlatt & P.E. Nathan (Eds.), *Behavioral approaches to alcoholism* (pp. 77-89). New Brunswick, NJ: Publications Division, Rutgers Center of Alcohol Studies.

Neiss, R. (1993). The role of psychobiological states in chemical dependency: Who becomes addicted? *Addiction, 88*, 745-756.

Neisser, U. (1967). *Cognitive psychology.* New York: Appleton-Century-Crofts.

Newsweek (1996, August 26). Heroin alert: Rockers, models and the new drug crisis. Are teens at risk?

Noble, E.P. (1996, March/April). The gene that rewards alcoholism. *Scientific American Science and Medicine*, 52-61.

Oei, T.P.S., & Baldwin, A.R. (1994, September). Expectancy theory: A two-process model of alcohol use and abuse. *Journal of Studies on Alcohol, 55*(5), 525-534.

Ogborne, A.C, & Glaser F.B. (1985). Evaluating Alcoholics Anonymous. In T.E. Bratter & G.G. Forrest (Eds.), *Alcoholism & substance abuse: Strategies for clinical intervention* (pp. 176-188). New York: The Free Press.

Olden, S.B., Ritchie, T., & Noble, E.P. (1989). Ethanol exposure alters K+ – but not bradykinin induced dopamine release in PC 12 cells. *Alcohol, 24*(1), 43-54

Orford, J., & Edwards, G. (1977). *Alcoholism.* New York: Oxford University Press.

Pattison, E.M., Headley, G.C., Gles, E.R., & Gottschalk, L.A. (1968). Abstinence and normal drinking: An assessment of change in drinking patterns in alcoholics after treatment. *Quarterly Journal on Studies in Alcohol, 29*, 610-633.

Pavlov, I.P (1941). *Conditioned reflexes and psychiatry.* E. Horsley Gantt (Trans. and Ed.) New York: International Publishing Co.

Peele, S. (1989). *Diseasing of America: Addiction treatment out of control.* Lexington, MA: Lexington Books, D.C. Heath & Co.

Penfield, W. (1952). Memory mechanisms. *AMA Archives of Neurology and Psychiatry, 67*, 178-191.

Penfield, W., (1959). The interpretive cortex. *Science 129*, 1719.

Pribram, K. (1971). *Languages of the brain.* New York: Brandon House.

Pribram, K. (1965). Proposal for a structural pragmatism: Some neuropsychological considerations of problems in philosophy. In B.B. Wolman (Ed.), *Scientific psychology.* New York: Basic Books.

Pribram, K. (1958). Comparative neurology and the evolution of behavior, In A. Roe, & G.G. Simpson (Eds.), *Behavior and evolution* (pp. 141-164). New Haven: Yale University Press.

Prince, M. (1906). *The dissociation of a personality.* London: Longmans.

Project MATCH Research Group. (1993, November/December). Project MATCH: Rationale and methods for a multisite clinical trial matching patients to alcoholism treatment. *Alcoholism: Clinical and Experimental Research, 17*(6), 1130-1145.

Pylyshyn, Z.W. (1973). What the mind's eye tells the mind's brain: A critique of mental imagery. *Psychological Bulletin, 80*, 1-24.

Rathman, R.B. (1990). High affinity dopamine reuptake inhibitors as potential cocaine antagonists: a strategy for drug development. *Life Science, 46*(20), 17-21.

Rather, B.C., Goldman, M.S., Roehrich, L., & Brannick, M. (1992). Empirical modelling of an alcohol expectancy memory network using multidimensional scaling. *Journal of Abnormal Psychology. 101*(1), 174-183.

Robinson, T.E., & Berridge, K.C. (1993). The neural basis of drug craving: An incentive-sensitization theory of addiction. *Brain Research Reviews, 18*, 247-291.

Rothman, R.B. (1990). High affinity dopamine reuptake inhibitors as potential cocaine antagonists: A strategy for drug development. *Life Science, 46*(20), 17-21.

Rotter, J.B. (1966). Generalized expectancies for internal vs. external control of reinforcement. *Psychological Monograph, 80*, 1-28.

Senter, R.J., Heintzelman, M., Dorfmueller, M, & Hinkle, H. (1979). A comparative look at ratings of the subjective effects of beverage alcohol. *Psychological Record, 29*, 49-56.

Schlosberg, H. (1934). Conditioned responses in the white rat. *Journal of Genetic Psychology, 45*, 303-335.

Sher, K.J. (1985). Subjective effects of alcohol: The influence of setting and individual differences in alcohol expectancies. *Journal of Studies on Alcohol, 46*(2).

Sherrington, C.S. (1906) *The interactive action of the nervous system.* London, Cambridge University Press.

Seilicovich, A., Rubio, M., Duvilanski, B., Munoz Maines, V., & Rettori, V. (1985). Inhibition by naloxone of the rise of hypothalamic dopamine and serum prolactin induced by ethanol. *Psychopharmacology* (Berlin), 461-463.

Sobell, L.C. (1979). Critique of alcoholism treatment evaluation. In G.A. Marlatt & P.E. Nathan (Eds.), *Behavioral approaches to alcoholism* (pp. 3-6). New Brunswick, NJ: Publications Division, Rutgers Center of Alcohol Studies.

Sokolov, E.N. (1960). Neuronal models and the orienting reflex. In M.A.B. Brazier (Ed.), *The central nervous system and behavior.* New York: Josiah Macy Jr. Foundation.

Southwick, L., Steele, C., Marlatt, A., & Lindell, M. (1981). Alcohol-related expectancies: Defined by phase of intoxication and drinking experience. *Journal of Consulting and Clinical Psychology, 49*(5), 713-721.

Steele, C.M., & Josephs, R.A. (1990, August). Alcohol myopia: Its prized and dangerous effects. *American Psychologist, 45*(8), 921-933.

Sun, A.Y., Seaman, R.N., & Middleton, C.C. (1977). Effects of acute and chronic alcohol administration in brain membrane transport systems. In M.M. Gross (Ed.), *Alcohol intoxication and withdrawal IIIa, biological aspects of ethanol* (pp. 123-138). *Advanced Experimental Medical Biology, 85A.* New York: Plenum.

Sussman, J.L. (1993). Imagery: A feminist perspective. *Journal of Mental Imagery, 17*(1&2), 319-336.

Szara, S. (1982). Opiate receptors and endogenous opiates: Panorama of opiate research. *Neuropsychopharmacology and Biological Psychiatry, 6*(1), 3-15.

Tan, A.T., Dulvar, R., & Innes, I.R. (1981). Alcohol feeding alters 3H dopamine uptake into rat cortical and brain stem synaptosomes. *Progress in Biochemical Pharmacology, 18*, 224-230.

Tournier, R.E. (1979). Alcoholics Anonymous as treatment and as ideology. *Journal of Studies on Alcohol, 40*, 230-239.

Trachtenberg, M.D., & Blum, K. (1987). Alcohol and opioid peptides: Neuropharmacological rationale for physical craving of alcohol. *American Journal of Drug and Alcohol Abuse, 13*, 365-372.

Upton, M. (1929). The auditory sensitivity of guinea pigs. *Journal of Psychology 41*, 412-421.

Vaillant, G.E. (1983). *The natural history of alcoholism: Causes, patterns and paths to recovery.* Cambridge, MA: Harvard University Press.

Vaillant, G.E. (1995). *The natural history of alcoholism, revisited.* Cambridge MA: Harvard University Press.

Weil, A. (1972). *The natural mind*. Boston: Houghton Mifflin.

Wever, E.G. (1930). The upper limit of learning in the cat. *Journal of Comparative Psychology (10)* 221-233.

White, H.R., Bates, M.E., & Johnson, V. (1991). Learning to drink: Familial, peer & media influences. In D.J. Pittman & H.R. White (Eds.), *Society, culture and drinking patterns re-examined* (pp. 177-197). New Brunswick, NJ: Rutgers Center of Alcohol Studies.

Wilnick, C. (1972). Maturing out of narcotic addiction. *Social Problems, 14*, 1-7.

Wilson, G.T., & Tracey, D.H. (1976). An experimental analysis of aversive imagery vs. electrical aversive conditioning in the treatment of chronic alcoholics. *Behavior Research Therapy, Oxford, 24*, 41-51.

Wilson, G.T. (1978). Alcoholism and aversion therapy: Issues, ethics and evidence. In G.A. Marlatt & P.E. Nathan (Eds.), *Behavioral approaches to alcoholism* (pp. 90-113). New Brunswick, NJ: Publications Division, Rutgers Center of Alcohol Studies.

Wolpe, J. (1969). *The practice of behavior therapy*. New York: Pergamon Press.

Woodward, J.J., & Gonzales, R.A. (1990, February). Ethanol inhibition of N-methyl-D-aspartate-stimulated endogenous dopamine release from rat striatal slices: Reversal by glycine. *Journal of Neurochemistry, 54*(2), 712-715.

Young, R.McD., Oei, T.P.S., & Knight, R.G. (1990). The tension reduction hypothesis revisited: an alcohol expectancy perspective. *British Journal of Addiction, 85*, 31-40.

Young, R.McD., & Oei, T.P.S. (1993). Grape expectations: The role of alcohol expectancies in the understanding and treatment of problem drinking. *International Journal of Psychology, 28*(3), 337-364.

Index